WITHDRAWN

HARVARD LIBRARY

WITHDRAWN

THE TRINITARIAN AXIOM OF KARL RAHNER

THE TRINITARIAN AXIOM OF KARL RAHNER
The Economic Trinity is the Immanent Trinity and Vice Versa

Dennis W. Jowers

The Edwin Mellen Press
Lewiston•Queenston•Lampeter

Library of Congress Cataloging-in-Publication Data

Jowers, Dennis W.
　The Trinitarian axiom of Karl Rahner : the economic Trinity is the immanent Trinity and vice versa / Dennis W. Jowers.
　　p. cm.
　"Works by Karl Rahner"--P.
　Includes bibliographical references (p.　) and index.
　ISBN-13: 978-0-7734-5584-9
　ISBN-10: 0-7734-5584-1
　1. Rahner, Karl, 1904-1984. 2. Trinity. I. Title.

BX4705.R287J69 2006
231'.044092--dc22

2006046984

hors série.

A CIP catalog record for this book is available from the British Library.

Copyright　©　2006　Dennis W. Jowers

All rights reserved. For information contact

　　　　The Edwin Mellen Press　　　　The Edwin Mellen Press
　　　　Box 450　　　　　　　　　　　　Box 67
　　　　Lewiston, New York　　　　　　Queenston, Ontario
　　　　USA 14092-0450　　　　　　　　CANADA L0S 1L0

　　　　　　The Edwin Mellen Press, Ltd.
　　　　　　Lampeter, Ceredigion, Wales
　　　　　　UNITED KINGDOM SA48 8LT

　　　　　Printed in the United States of America

This book is dedicated to my loving and supportive parents, Charles M. and Jane T. Jowers, and to my beautiful wife, Judy, without whose encouragement and assistance this book would never have been written.

TABLE OF CONTENTS

FOREWORD by David Fergusson i
PREFACE iii
ACKNOWLEDGMENTS vii
CHAPTER 1 1
I. THE RELEVANCE OF RAHNER'S PHILOSOPHY TO HIS THEOLOGY 1
  1. The competing positions 2
  2. Formal vs. material distinctions 3
    a. Absence of material distinctions 3
    b. Formally philosophical premises 4
    c. Conclusion 5
  3. Discontinuities in Rahner's thought 6
    a. The supernatural existential 7
      i. Introduction 7
      ii. Rahner's motive 8
      iii. Rahner's proposal 8
      iv. Conclusion 10
    b. Transcendental revelation 11
    c. Reservations 13
    d. Formally philosophical presuppositions 15
    e. Conclusion 16
  4. Gnoseological concupiscence 16
    a. What is gnoseological concupiscence? 17
    b. Contradictions between secular knowledge and faith 18
    c. Inability to survey the range of philosophies and theologies 19
    d. Kilby's response 22
    e. Conclusion 25
  5. Moderate nonfoundationalism 26
    a. The *Vorgriff auf esse* as theological hypothesis 27
    b. Evaluation 29
    c. Philosophy and theology 30
    d. Conclusion 33
  6. Recapitulation 34
II. RAHNER'S PHILOSOPHY ITSELF 34
  1. Methodology 35
  2. Rahner's metaphysics of knowledge 35
    a. Vindicating the point of departure 35
      i. Why these conditions? 36
      ii. Does Rahner's point of departure satisfy these conditions? 37

  b. Elaborating the point of departure 38
   i. The *Woher*... 38
   ii. The unity of knowledge.. 39
   iii. The knowability of being... 41
   iv. The identity of being and knowing 42
   v. The analogy of being 42
   vi. Matter... 44
  c. Transcendental reduction 45
   i. Materiality... 46
   ii. The sensible species.. 47
   iii. Substantial forms and their determinations 49
   iv. The objectivity of knowledge 51
   v. Abstraction.. 52
   vi. The agent intellect.. 54
   vii. The *Woraufhin* of the *Vorgriff*... 56
  d. Transcendental deduction 58
   i. The expanse of the *Woraufhin* 58
   ii. The knowability of God.. 62
 3. Criticisms 63
 4. Conclusion 65
 III. OUTLOOK 65
CHAPTER 2 67
 I. REVELATION AS SUCH 67
 1. Transcendental experience... 67
 2. The universal history of revelation 71
 3. Particular histories of revelation 73
 4. The absolute savior 76
 5. Scripture... 77
 II. THE REVELATION OF THE TRINITY 85
 1. Introduction... 85
 2. Rahner's *Grundaxiom*.. 87
  a. Four misconstruals 87
   i. Trivially obvious identity.. 87
   ii. Absolute identity.. 88
   iii. Copy theory 88
   iv. Merely *de facto* identity 89
  b. Rahner's actual meaning.. 89
  c. Rahner's arguments for the *Grundaxiom* 90
   i. The argument from divine self-communication 91
   ii. The methodological rationale 95
  d. Conclusion 96
 3. The Trinitarian structure of the revelatory event 97
  a. Rahner's objective.. 97
  b. Dual modalities of divine self-communication........................... 97

- c. Rahner's dyads 99
  - i. Introduction 99
  - ii. Origin—future 99
  - iii. History—transcendence 101
  - iv. Offer—acceptance 102
  - v. Knowledge—love 103
    - α. The problematic 103
    - β. Truth 103
    - γ. Love 107
    - δ. Criticism 108
  - vi. Evaluation 110
- d. Results 110
- III. CONCLUSION 111
- CHAPTER 3 113
- I. INTRODUCTION 113
- II. DIVINE TRANSCENDENCE AND SELF-COMMUNICATION 114
  - 1. Introduction 114
  - 2. Rahner's acknowledgement of divine transcendence 114
    - a. Simplicity 115
    - b. Immutability 115
    - c. Atemporality 115
    - d. Impassibility 115
    - e. No real relations to the world 116
    - f. Distinctness from the world 116
  - 3. Absolute self-communication 117
    - a. "God becomes world." 117
    - b. Real relations to the world 118
    - c. Temporality 119
    - d. Passibility 119
    - e. Mutability 119
  - 4. Conclusion 120
- III. BERT VAN DER HEIJDEN 120
  - 1. Introduction 120
  - 2. Van der Heijden's argument 120
    - a. *Selbstmitteilung vs. Seinsmitteilung* 120
    - b. *Der Kampf gegen Tritheismus* 121
    - c. *Der Kampf gegen Monophysitismus* 122
    - d. *Sein = Beisichsein* 124
    - e. Rahner's immutability formula 125
  - 3. Response 127
    - a. *Selbstmitteilung vs. Seinsmitteilung* 127
    - b. Persons and essence 128
    - c. Autonomy of Christ's humanity 130
    - d. Unity and distinction in God 130

4. Conclusion 132
IV. CONCILIAR AUTHORITY AND THE CONSISTENCY OF RAHNER'S
VIEWS 132
  1. Introduction 132
  2. Sanctifying grace 133
    a. Introduction 134
    b. Rahner's arguments 134
      i. Uncreated grace as presupposition of the beatific vision 135
        α. Introduction 135
        β. Being and knowing 136
        γ. God as impressed species 137
        δ. Conclusion 139
      ii. The priority of uncreated over created grace 139
        α. Introduction 139
        β. The "scholastic" view of uncreated grace 140
        γ. Rahner's alternative 141
        δ. Conclusion 142
    c. Response 143
      i. Introduction 143
      ii. Uncreated grace as ontological presupposition of the beatific vision
.... 143
        α. Introduction 144
        β. Being and knowing 145
        γ. God as impressed species 146
        δ. Conclusion 147
      iii. The priority of uncreated over created grace 147
        α. The scholastic views 148
        β. Rahner's position 150
        γ. Criticisms 153
    d. Conclusion 155
  3. The Incarnation 156
    a. Introduction 156
    b. Rahner's theory of the "uniting unity" in the Incarnation 157
    c. Advantages of Rahner's theory 159
      i. Reconciling Christ's divinity with his full humanity 160
      ii. Correlating intra-divine processions and divine acts *ad extra* 160
      iii. Adjusting to a contemporary worldview 161
    d. Difficulties for Rahner's theory 162
      i. Unification through differentiation 163
      ii. The singularity of the hypostatic union 165
        α. The extent of the problem 166
        β. The absoluteness of the divine nature 167
        γ. The oscillating hypostasis 167

  e. Assessment.. 171
 4. Christ's absolute saviorhood... 172
  a. Introduction... 172
  b. Rahner's argument.. 172
  c. Criticisms 174
   i. Introduction... 174
   ii. The mysteries of Jesus' life. 174
    α. The mysteries' significance for Rahner's Christology............ 174
    β. Implications for the concept of absolute savior...................... 176
   iii. The *Heilsbedeutsamkeit* of all categorical experience 177
   iv. Assessment.. 177
  d. Excursus on the views of Bruce Marshall....................................... 178
   i. Introduction... 178
   ii. Difficulties for Marshall's position 179
    α. Introduction 179
    β. Textual evidence against Marshall's thesis 179
    γ. Evidence for Marshall's thesis?.. 180
    δ. Evaluation 182
   iii. Conclusion.. 182
  e. Summary 183
 5. Results... 183
 V. CONCLUSION.. 184
CHAPTER 4 187
I. INTRODUCTION 187
II. THE IMPOSSIBILITY OF A NON-VERBAL, NON-CONCEPTUAL
REVELATION OF THE DOCTRINE OF THE TRINITY OTHER THAN
THE BEATIFIC VISION. 188
 1. Introduction... 188
 2. Rahner's case against the minor premise of syllogism 1 190
  a. What does Rahner actually believe?.. 190
  b. Difficulties for Rahner's position 192
  c. Rahner's response 197
   i. *Mystici Corporis* 197
   ii. Three alleged counterexamples 200
    α. Introduction 200
    β. The Incarnation... 201
    γ. The indwelling of the Holy Spirit... 207
    δ. The beatific vision.. 209
    ε. Conclusion.. 210
 3. Rahner's case against the major premise of syllogism 4 211
 4. Conclusion 211
III. CHRIST"S ANOINTING WITH THE HOLY SPIRIT AS A TEST CASE
FOR THE *GRUNDAXIOM* 212
 1. Introduction... 212

2. Methodological considerations 213
   a. Does Rahner consider Scripture a legitimate measure of the truth or
   falsehood of theological statements? 213
   b. Is Scripture an appropriate norm for the *Grundaxiom* of Rahner's
   theology of the Trinity? 217
      i. The relevance of the Bible to the theology of the Trinity 218
      ii. The hermeneutical character of the *Grundaxiom* 219
   c. Is Christ's anointing with the Holy Spirit an appropriate matrix within
   which to test Rahner's *Grundaxiom*? 220
      i. The supernaturalism of the anointing narratives 221
      ii. The relevance of the anointing accounts 222
3. Reconciling the anointing accounts, when interpreted in accordance with
the *Grundaxiom*, with Rahner's filioquism. 223
   a. Involvement of the Spirit in the begetting of the Son 224
      i. Patristic precedents 225
      ii. Difficulties 226
   b. The anointing accounts manifest a prior occurrence in which the
   missions and the processions correspond 227
      i. Mühlen's dogmatic understanding of the anointing 228
      ii. Grace and the person 229
      iii. Patristic precedents 231
      iv. Difficulties 232
   c. The Spirit as intra-Trinitarian gift of the Father to the Son 233
      i. The identity of active spiration and active filiation 234
      ii. The Holy Spirit as *medius nexus* of the Father and the Son 235
      iii. Difficulties 236
      iv. Responses 237
      v. The order of circumincession and human knowledge of the Trinity
      239
   d. Conclusion 240
IV. CONCLUSION 241
BIBLIOGRAPHY 245
   Works by Karl Rahner 245
   Works by Other Authors 252
INDEX 261

FOREWORD

The renaissance of the doctrine of the trinity in recent theology has often been noted. In large measure, this dates from Karl Barth's positioning of the doctrine at the outset of the *Church Dogmatics*, a hermeneutical decision of enormous significance. For Barth and other writers, the coordination of the immanent with the economic trinity is vital. It serves at least two major functions. The unity of immanent and economic ensures that there is no God behind God, an unknowable and inscrutable deity who may be wholly other than the God given to us in faith and revelation. This might be understood as an expression of the classical Nicene assumption that in Jesus Christ we are given nothing less than the true God. Hence, the divine act and being cannot be separated in any properly Christian doctrine of God. At the same time, the distinction between immanent and economic enables one to maintain the transcendence and freedom of God even in the act of revelation. The divine being is neither exhausted nor constituted by the economy of creation and salvation. While distinguished, therefore, the immanent and the economic must also be thought together and never apart. One might liken this to a Chalcedonian unity in distinction.

Yet whether such unity in distinction is altogether stable and unproblematic is a matter of intense debate that continues through the interpretation of key figures, including Barth. Does excessive stress on the immanent trinity lead to a disengagement of the divine being from the work of creation and redemption? Alternatively, does an over-concentration on the economic trinity produce a Hegelian trajectory in which God cannot be God without the world or does it lead simply to an implicit agnosticism about the divine self? These tensions may lurk in the famous *Grundaxiom* of Karl Rahner that proclaims the identity and equivalence of the immanent and economic trinity. In this study, the nature of that *Grundaxiom* is explored with particular attention to its epistemological justification. To what extent is this a necessary presupposition of the Christian doctrine of God, a reflexive movement of faith, and an article grounded in Scripture and tradition? These important questions are explored by Dennis Jowers in a searching and provocative treatment of Rahner's work.

David Fergusson
Professor of Divinity
Head of the School of Divinity
New College, Edinburgh

PREFACE

According to John O'Donnell, the *Grundaxiom* of Karl Rahner's theology of the Trinity, "The economic Trinity *is* the immanent Trinity and vice versa," is "accepted by practically all contemporary theologians."[1] This statement, as O'Donnell himself surely recognizes, might seem to gloss over a tremendous amount of disagreement. Paul Molnar, for instance, criticizes Rahner's axiom on the grounds that it compromises divine freedom vis-à-vis creation.[2] Yves Congar and others pointedly reject the second half of the axiom, the vice versa, because it appears to restrict God's freedom to express Godself in a variety of ways and to reduce the mystery of God's inner being to its economic self-expression.[3] Hans Urs von Balthasar argues that "Trinitarian inversions," sc. reversals of the intra-Trinitarian τάξις in the economy of salvation, warrant severe qualifications of the axiom;[4] and Catherine LaCugna rejects the axiom on the grounds that human beings know nothing of God that transcends the divine οἰκονομία.[5]

O'Donnell's statement, nevertheless, is fundamentally correct insofar as all of the aforementioned theologians embrace the methodological assumption to which Rahner's *Grundaxiom* gives voice: viz. that God's action in salvation history, the threefold form in which God communicates Godself to humanity, constitutes the sole foundation of human knowledge about the Trinity. The *Grundaxiom* expresses the correspondence that must obtain in order for one validly to infer

---

[1] "Trinité. II. Développement dans la tradition. 5. La Trinité économique est la Trinité immanente," *DSAM* xv, 1311.
[2] Cf. Molnar's *Divine Freedom and the Doctrine of the Immanent Trinity: In Dialogue with Karl Barth and Contemporary Theology* (London and New York: T & T Clark, 2002), esp. 83–124.
[3] Cf. Congar's *I Believe in the Holy Spirit 3: The River of Life Flows in the East and in the West* (David Smith, tr.; New York: Seabury, 1983), 13–18.
[4] Cf. e.g. Balthasar's *Theologik 3: Der Geist der Wahrheit* (Basel: Johannes Verlag), esp. 166–8, 192.
[5] Cf. LaCugna's *God for Us: The Trinity and Christian Life* (San Francisco: HarperSanFrancisco, 1991), esp. 222–4.

conclusions about God's inner being from the form of God's economic self-expression. Notwithstanding their disagreements about the precise character of this correspondence, therefore, all of the figures mentioned above implicitly assent to some qualified version of the *Grundaxiom* simply by taking God's self-revelation in deed as the point of departure for their Trinitarian theologies.

The critique of Rahner's axiom contained in this work differs radically from the criticisms proposed by these authors in that we reject the propriety of making the economy of salvation Trinitarian theology's exclusive starting point. We propose, specifically, to demonstrate that Rahner's own core assumptions about the doctrine of the Trinity conflict with any version of the *Grundaxiom* sufficiently robust to warrant inferences from God's economic self-manifestation to God's inner triunity. This does not imply, naturally, that the doctrine of the Trinity is either false or groundless. It implies, rather, that one must found the theology of the Trinity on some basis other than, or at least some basis supplementary to, the divine acts that make up the economy of salvation.

The most plausible alternative source of information about God's inner being, it seems, is Scripture and/or tradition (*traditiones*) conceived of as a body of statements revealed by God. If one accepts our conclusions, then, consistency dictates that one either abandon any recognizably orthodox doctrine of the Trinity or acknowledge the existence, in written and/or oral form, of inspired testimony: testimony that supplies information as to the character of God's eternal being otherwise inaccessible to non-beatified human beings. Ultimately, therefore, our critique of Rahner's *Grundaxiom* constitutes an indirect argument for a high and relatively supernaturalistic conception of divine revelation.

The case by which we hope to falsify Rahner's *Grundaxiom*, at least in the sense in which he himself accepts it, consists fundamentally in the following four criticisms. First, if God is simple, as Rahner admits, and incapable of communicating Godself without undergoing some metamorphosis, as Rahner insists, then the economic Trinity cannot correspond precisely to the immanent

Trinity in any respect. Since every aspect of a simple God is absolutely, albeit not necessarily relatively, identical with every other, a simple God cannot change in any respect without also changing in every respect. If, then, the immanent Trinity, i.e. God *in se* prescinding from any self-communication, must mutate in some way in order to become the economic Trinity, i.e. God communicating Godself to God's creation, then the tripersonal structure of the economic Trinity can coincide with that of the immanent Trinity in no respect whatsoever. In such a case, it seems, one could not justifiably attribute the triune form God exhibits in the economy of salvation to God as God would have existed irrespective of any self-communication.

Second, even if a simple God could somehow exempt the inner, relational structure of the divine being from the comprehensive metamorphosis entailed by self-communication as Rahner conceives of it, human beings could never, it seems, discern which aspects of God communicated actually correspond to the hypothetical, uncommunicated God and which do not unless God either: a) endowed them with the beatific vision; or b) simply told them through a verbal, or at least a conceptual, revelation. Even if the first criticism were invalid, then, a communication of the doctrine of the immanent Trinity to human beings would still require a verbal/conceptual revelation, the possibility of which Rahner does not countenance. To the extent, then, that he constructs his account of the Trinity's self-revelation precisely in order to prove that human beings can attain to warranted, true belief in the doctrine of the Trinity without a verbal/conceptual revelation, Rahner's account fails to achieve its purpose.

Third, if, as Rahner admits: a) the Trinitarian persons possess as peculiar to themselves only their relations of opposition to each other; and b) "in God the relation is real only through its identity with the real divine essence"[6] ; then God can influence creation only through the one, undifferentiated divine omnipotence:

---

[6] *The Trinity* (Joseph Donceel, tr.; New York: Herder, 1970), 71; "Der dreifaltige Gott als transzendenter Urgrund der Heilsgeschichte" in *MS* ii, 317-401 at 363.

and not through any powers peculiar to the persons. In this case, it seems, one could not infer God's intrinsic triunity from the triune character of the causality God excercises in divine self-communication, because every divine influence would proceed from a strictly unitary principle. Rahner's own presuppositions, therefore, imply that a non-verbal, non-conceptual revelation other than the beatific vision cannot convey to human beings the doctrine of the immanent Trinity.

Fourth and finally, the biblical accounts of Christ's anointing with the Holy Spirit (Matt 3:16, 17; Mark 1:10, 11; Luke 3:22; and John 1:32), when interpreted in accordance with the *Grundaxiom* of Rahner's theology of the Trinity, "The economic Trinity *is* the immanent Trinity and vice versa," entail conclusions incompatible with Rahner's orthodox, Latin Trinitarianism. One can, we shall argue, so expand one's concept of what qualifies as correspondence between economy and theology as to allow for a projection of the pattern of relations displayed in the anointing into the immanent Trinity, which would not undermine Latin Trinitarianism. Yet one can do so, as we hope to prove, only at the expense of depriving the *Grundaxiom* of its power to warrant inferences from the triune structure(s) manifested in the economy of salvation to the doctrine of the immanent Trinity.

Through these four criticisms, we intend to challenge the notion that one can, with the aid of Rahner's *Grundaxiom*, derive the doctrine of the immanent Trinity merely from God's self-revelation in act. It seems both more plausible and more orthodox to trace human knowledge of the Trinity ultimately to a cognitive and at least mediately verbal revelation of God.

ACKNOWLEDGMENTS

I have incurred numerous debts in the process of writing this work. I should like, first, to thank my parents, Charles M. and Jane T. Jowers, without whose love, guidance, encouragement, and financial support, I could never have written this work. Second, I should like to thank my wife, who has assisted me by photocopying reams of articles and books for this project and unfailingly loving and encouraging me.

I am doubly indebted to David Fergusson, who both agreed to author the foreword of this work and served as the internal examiner of my doctoral dissertation, which I completed at the University of Edinburgh in 2004. I am grateful also to Francesca Murphy, my external examiner; to Michael Purcell, my *Doktorvater*; and especially to John McDowell, my Assistant Supervisor, mentor, and friend. I should also like to thank Katie O'Brien-Weintraub, Stephen Meredith, and Peter Miller, all faculty at the University of Chicago, for their assistance at an earlier stage in my studies. I owe enormous gratitude, likewise, to John A. Battle, Jr., President of Western Reformed Seminary, who offered me my first academic job; and Michael Adams, President of Faith Evangelical Seminary, who has contributed extraordinarily to the advancement of my academic career.

I am indebted, in addition, to the publishers and individuals who have granted me permission to quote others' works. Crossroad Publishers has generously granted me permission to quote from Karl Rahner's *The Trinity* (Joseph Donceel, tr.; New York: Herder, 1970; repr., Crossroad, 1997) as well as Rahner's *Foundations of Christian Faith: An Introduction to the Idea of Christianity* (William V. Dych, tr.; New York: Crossroad, 1978); *Theological Investigations 1: God, Christ, Mary, and Grace* (Cornelius Ernst, tr.; London and Baltimore: DLT and Helicon, 1961); *Theological Investigations 4: More Recent Writings* (Kevin

Smyth, tr.; London and Baltimore: DLT and Helicon, 1966); and *Theological Investigations 9: Writings of 1965–1967 1* (Graham Harrison, tr.; London and New York: DLT and Herder, 1972). Johannes Verlag (Einsiedeln) has kindly permitted me to quote from Bert van der Heijden's *Karl Rahner: Darstellung und Kritik seiner Grundpositionen* (Einsiedeln: Johannes Verlag, 1973); and Simon Gaine has graciously allowed me to quote from his *Indwelling Spirit and a New Creation: The Relationship between Uncreated Grace and Created Grace in Neo-Scholastic Catholic Theology* (Oxford: D.Phil. Diss., 1994).

CHAPTER 1

In this introductory chapter, we should like to describe and, to some extent, evaluate certain elements of Rahner's philosophy that bear on the theological issues to be addressed later in the book. Drawing on the early Rahner's principal philosophical works, viz. *Geist in Welt*,[7] *Hörer des Wortes*,[8] and "Die Wahrheit bei Thomas von Aquin,"[9] accordingly, we intend to consider in some detail the early Rahner's ontological gnoseology. Before so doing, however, we should like to vindicate the relevance of a philosophical introduction to our inquiry by responding to a recent attack on the view that philosophical considerations play an appreciable role in the construction of Rahner's theology.

I. THE RELEVANCE OF RAHNER'S PHILOSOPHY TO HIS THEOLOGY

Numerous theologians, in Karen Kilby's view, employ objections to Karl Rahner's philosophy as pretexts for ignoring Rahner's apparently philosophy-laden theology. In order to rehabilitate Rahner's theology, therefore, Kilby attempts in her *Karl Rahner: Theology and Philosophy*[10] to disentangle Rahner's theology from its putative philosophical moorings. In accomplishing this task, however, she seems to exaggerate the independence of Rahner's theology from his philosophy. We intend in the following, therefore, to answer some of the criticisms Kilby levels at what she calls the "semi-foundationalist" interpretation

---

[7] *SW* ii, 5–300; ET = *Spirit in the World* (Johannes Baptist Metz, ed.; William V. Dych, tr.; New York: Herder & Herder, 1968).

[8] *SW* iv, 2–278; ET = *Hearer of the Word* (Andrew Tallon, ed.; Joseph Donceel, tr.; New York: Continuum, 1994).

[9] *SW* ii, 303–16; ET = "Thomas Aquinas on Truth," *TI* xiii, 13–31.

[10] London & New York: Routledge, 2004.

of Rahner's thought: the interpretation, that is to say, according to which philosophy plays an integral role in the construction of Rahner's theology.

1. The competing positions. Those who adopt the "semi-foundationalist" perspective on Rahner's thought, explains Kilby, hold that "what Rahner first does as relatively pure philosophy in *Spirit in the World* and *Hearer of the Word* he subsequently takes up to become an element in his theology...[so that] the theology...contains, and requires, as one of its elements, specifically philosophical arguments."[11] Kilby designates this interpretation "semi-foundationalist" rather than simply "foundationalist," because its advocates do not regard Rahner's theology as a mere philosophy in disguise. "No serious reader," as Kilby correctly observes, "could suppose Rahner to be a rationalist who thinks that Christianity as a whole can be philosophically demonstrated."[12] Advocates of the semi-foundationalist interpretation, rather, hold that Rahner's distinctive philosophy constitutes one of the many elements that together comprise Rahner's mature theology.

Those who adopt what Kilby describes as the "nonfoundationalist" perspective, by contrast, view the seemingly philosophical aspects of Rahner's theology as defensible on exclusively theological grounds. "The same claims," writes Kilby, probably the foremost exponent of the nonfoundationalist interpretation, "may function differently in different parts of Rahner's corpus: what is at one point presented as the conclusion of a philosophical argument may elsewhere function as a theological hypothesis."[13]

"What must be denied, for the nonfoundationalist," Kilby continues:

is that Rahner's theology is dependent on a philosophy *formally* distinct from it, [i.e.] on an independently argued philosophy that makes no appeal to revelation. But in a *material* sense, insofar as philosophy is defined not by its method but by its subject matter, it is clearly the case

---

[11] Ibid. 75.
[12] Ibid.
[13] Ibid. 76.

that philosophy is an inner moment of theology: theology, to speak of grace and revelation, must include philosophy in the sense of a reflection on human nature. On the nonfoundationalist reading, significant elements of Rahner's own philosophical works do indeed become an inner moment of his theology, but in so doing they remain philosophy only in...a material sense.[14]

At least three considerations seem to favor a nonfoundationalist construal of the relation between philosophy and theology in Rahner's thought. First, Kilby's formal/material distinction renders the employment of at least materially philosophical terminology and concepts in Rahner's theology considerably less problematic for the nonfoundationalist perspective. Second, significant discontinuities do exist between Rahner's mature theology and his early, philosophical thought. Third, and finally, the later Rahner does hold that the immense "gnoseological concupiscence" characteristic of contemporary society renders present-day Christians incapable: a) of adequately synthesizing the knowledge that they derive from secular sources with the truths of the Christian faith; and b) of evaluating objectively the range of at least seemingly incompatible philosophies and theologies. In the following, however, we shall attempt to show that none of these considerations suffices to discredit the semi-foundationalist interpretation.

2. Formal vs. material distinctions. Kilby's first contention in particular, viz. that the philosophical premises employed in the later Rahner's arguments differ from their theological counterparts materially rather than formally, in that they concern nature instead of grace, seems to run contrary to the later Rahner's understanding of the relation between the supernatural and the natural orders.

a. Absence of material distinctions. For, as Kilby observes, the later Rahner believes that human beings, in the present economy, cannot distinguish between: a) those aspects of their constitution that exist purely because of human beings' ordination to grace; and b) those other aspects of their constitution that would

---

[14] Ibid.

belong to them even if God had chosen to create them in a purely natural state.[15] Kilby concludes, accordingly, that, at least within the categories of Rahner's thought, "the distinctive nature of philosophy...is undermined....One can still conceive of a philosophy in the formal sense—a philosophy which makes no appeal to revelation—but this is no longer materially distinct from theology, because the philosopher too lives in and reflects upon a world transformed by grace."[16]

Kilby grants, in other words, that the later Rahner's emphasis on nature as borne and suffused by grace renders a concrete, material distinction between philosophy and theology impossible. Now, if this is the case, her claim that Rahner, in his theological arguments, appeals to no arguments of any philosophy that is formally distinct from theology[17] appears to imply a counterintuitive conclusion: that Rahner the theologian appeals to no distinctively philosophical arguments at all.

b. Formally philosophical premises. This conclusion, as Kilby would readily admit, is manifestly false. For Rahner the theologian frequently makes remarks like the following: "the same conclusion which we have been able to demonstrate on the basis of a direct dogmatic datum can also be arrived at by approaching the question rather from the standpoint of the philosophy of transcendentality."[18] In defending a modified version of the psychological analogy of the Trinity, likewise, Rahner appeals to the datum that "an authentic metaphysics of the spirit tells us that there are two (and only two!) basic activities of the spirit: knowledge

---

[15] Ibid. 64–7, 73–4.

[16] Ibid. 74.

[17] The claim that Rahner refrains from formally philosophical reasoning in his theology seems to be at least implicit in Kilby's contention (ibid. 76) that although "significant elements of Rahner's own philosophical works do indeed become an inner moment of his theology,...in so doing they remain philosophy only in...a material sense." We recognize that Kilby frequently has recourse to a more moderate position, however, and we discuss this position in detail later in this chapter.

[18] "Reflections on Methodology in Theology," *TI* xi, 68–114 at 104; "Überlegungen zur Methode der Theologie," *ST* ix, 79–126 at 116.

and love."[19] Similarly, the later Rahner once employs as a premise of a theological argument the following statement: "contemporary philosophy only recognises humanity's spiritual life in so far as it is also and at the same time material in any given case."[20] Rahner introduces one of his later essays, in fact, as "a study which unashamedly refuses to observe with too much exactitude the difference between philosophy and theology, but which, on the contrary, freely employs the methods and basic principles of both disciplines."[21] One cannot credibly deny, therefore, that Rahner at least occasionally inserts arguments that he considers formally philosophical into discussions of a broadly theological nature.

c. Conclusion. To recapitulate, then, our argument for the inconclusiveness of Kilby's first reason: Rahner does employ formally philosophical reasoning in constructing his theology. As we have seen, moreover, the all-encompassing character of the supernatural in Rahner's later theology implies that one cannot distinguish, at least in the concrete, between the subject matter of philosophy and that of theology. If this is the case, however, then no material distinction between philosophy and theology, as Rahner conceives of them, exists; and to say that the later Rahner's philosophical reasoning is only materially distinct from its theological counterpart is tantamount to saying that the two are not distinct at all. Kilby's opposition of a merely material distinction between philosophy and theology to a more robust, formal distinction, therefore, does not suffice to render

---

[19] *The Trinity* (Joseph Donceel, tr.; New York: Herder & Herder, 1970), 116; "Der dreifaltige Gott als transzendenter Urgrund der Heilsgeschichte," *MS* ii, 317–401 at 394.

[20] "The Intermediate State," *TI* xvii, 114–24 at 120; Über den "Zwischenzustand," *ST* xii, 455–66 at 462. We have emended translations of Rahner's writings so as to remove gender–exclusive language.

[21] "Immanent and Transcendent Consummation of the World," *TI* x, 273–89 at 273; Immanente und transzendente Vollendung der Welt," *SW* xv, 544–66 at 544.

the philosophical aspects of the later Rahner's theology innocuous for the nonfoundationalist perspective.[22]

3. Discontinuities in Rahner's thought. The second item adduced above as evidence for the nonfoundationalist construal of the later Rahner's thought, viz. the existence of significant discontinuities between Rahner's early philosophical presuppositions and his mature theology, seems to buttress the nonfoundationalist perspective rather more than the previous consideration.[23] The existence of such discontinuities, however, seems insufficient to falsify the central, semi-foundationalist contention that Rahner's "theology...contains, and requires, as one of its elements, specifically philosophical arguments."[24]

Prescinding from the subject of "gnoseological concupiscence," to be addressed in the next section, the relevant discontinuities include: a) that between the early Rahner's understanding of concrete, human nature as roughly equivalent

---

[22] Kilby's material–formal distinction may, however, suffice to vindicate Rahner of Hans–Jürgen Verweyen's charge that Rahner's understanding of the relation between the natural and the supernatural orders, which implies, as we have seen, the impracticability of a precise material distinction between philosophy and theology, also "implies the impossibility of a methodologically autonomous philosophy" ("Wie wird ein Existential übernatürlich? Zu einem Grundproblem der Anthropologie Karl Rahners," *TTZ* 95 [1986], 115–31 at 129). For, if the formal–material distinction is legitimate, then it seems that one can conceive of a formally, sc. methodologically, autonomous philosophy regardless of whether this philosophy can isolate a purely natural subject matter that is materially distinct from that of theology. Cf. the comprehensive examination of Verweyen's criticisms in Thomas Peter Fössel's "Warum ein Existential *übernatürlich* ist: Anmerkungen zur kontroversen Diskussion um Karl Rahners Theologoumenon vom 'übernatürlichen Existential,'" *ThPh* 80 (2005), 389–411.

[23] For the purposes of this book, the later phase of Rahner's career begins with Rahner's introduction of the theory of the supernatural existential in Rahner's "Antwort." *Orientierung* 14 (1950), 141–5, which was later published in augmented form as "Über das Verhältnis von Natur und Gnade," *ST* i, 323–45 (ET = "Concerning the Relationship Between Nature and Grace," *TI* i, 297–317). For an English translation of Émile Delaye's "Ein Weg zur Bestimmung des Verhältnisses von Natur und Gnade," *Orientierung* 14 (1950), 138–41, the article to which Rahner responds in this essay, and a rationale for identifying the latter article's author, who identifies himself only as "D," with Delaye, cf. David Coffey, "Some Resources for Students of *La nouvelle théologie*" *Philosophy & Theology* 11 (1999), 367–402.

[24] Kilby, *Karl Rahner*, 75.

to "pure nature" [25] and the later Rahner's theory of the "supernatural existential"; and b) that between the early Rahner's conception of revelation as categorical and spatio-temporally localized and the later Rahner's doctrine of "transcendental revelation."

a. The supernatural existential.

i. Introduction. First, the later Rahner, in contrast to the early Rahner, believes that "pure nature," i.e. human nature as it would have existed if God had not called human beings to the beatific vision, does not exist in isolation from the supernatural. In the later Rahner's view, rather, pure nature always exists in combination with the "supernatural existential": sc. a universal,[26] unconditional,[27] unexacted,[28] and inescapable[29] "burning longing for God...in the immediacy of God's own threefold life."[30]

---

[25] That the Rahner of *Hörer des Wortes* (1941) considers humanity as it presently exists a sufficiently close approximation of "pure nature" for him to investigate it on an exclusively philosophical plane appears from two considerations. First, the young Rahner sharply distinguishes the obediential potency for the reception of revelation, which forms the principal object of his inquiry in *Hörer des Wortes*, from "the obediential potency for *supernatural* life" (*Hearer*, 16; *Hörer*, *SW* iv: 38; cf. n. 5 below). Second the Rahner of *Hörer des Wortes* repeatedly ascribes to God the freedom not to reveal himself to the human nature that he is investigating: a freedom which, the later Rahner holds, God does possess vis-à-vis human beings in a state of "pure nature," but does not possess vis-à-vis human beings endowed with the supernatural existential (cf. Kilby, *Karl Rahner*, 67–9).

[26] *Foundations of Christian Faith: An Introduction to the Idea of Christianity* (trans. William V. Dych; New York: Crossroad, 1978), 127; *Grundkurs des Glaubens: Einführung in den Begriff des Christentums*, *SW* xxvi, 3–442 at 127.

[27] "Relationship," *TI* i, 312, n. 1; "Verhältnis," *ST* i, 338, n. 1.

[28] Ibid. 312–13; ebd. 339.

[29] Ibid. 311; ebd. 338.

[30] Ibid. 312; ebd. 338. Cf. the diametrically opposed views expressed by the young Rahner in "The Meaning of Frequent Confession of Devotion," *TI* iii, 177–89 at 184; "Vom Sinn der häufigen Andachtsbeichte," *SW* xi, 401–11 at 407 (written in 1934) and "The Ignatian Mysticism of Joy in the World," *TI* iii, 277–93 at 285–6; "Die ignatianische Mystik der Weltfreudigkeit," *ST* iii, 329–48 at 339–40 (written in 1937).

ii. Rahner's motive. The later Rahner posits the existence of this existential, at least in part, in order to counteract typically neoscholastic understandings of human nature.

In neoscholastic theology, writes Rahner:

> it has been usual to presuppose a sharply circumscribed human 'nature' with the help of a concept of nature one-sidedly orientated to the nature of less than human things. It has been felt that one knows quite clearly what *precisely* this human nature is and how far precisely it extends....It is tacitly or explicitly presupposed [moreover] that whatever human beings come to know by themselves...about themselves or in themselves belongs to their nature..., and that so a sharply circumscribed concept of human nature can be produced out of the anthropology of everyday experience and of metaphysics. Thus it is presupposed that the concretely experienced (contingently factual) quiddity of the human being squarely coincides with human 'nature' as the concept opposed by theology to the supernatural.[31]

This neoscholastic equation of humanity's concrete, contingently factual nature with "pure nature," i.e. human nature minus the supernatural, engenders, in Rahner's view, an acute difficulty. According to the neoscholastic conception, one must deny that concrete, human nature possesses an unconditional orientation to the beatific vision if one wishes to vindicate that vision's gratuity.[32] Yet, in Rahner's view, one cannot deny the existence of such an unconditional orientation without portraying both the beatific vision and the grace that is its prelude as irrelevant to the needs and desires of concrete, human beings. The neoscholastic view thus forces one to choose between loyalty to the doctrine of the vision's absolute gratuity and a pastoral concern for demonstrating Christianity's relevance to everyday life.

iii. Rahner's proposal. Rahner proposes to resolve this dilemma by introducing a distinction, which, although alien to neoscholastic thought, nonetheless respects the neoscholastics' legitimate concern for upholding the gratuity of divine grace and the beatific vision. Specifically, Rahner proposes

---

[31] "Relationship," *TI* i, 298–9; "Verhältnis," *ST* i, 324–5.
[32] Cf. e.g. Adolphe Tanquerey, *Synopsis theologiae dogmaticae ad usum seminariorum ad mentem S. Thomae et S. Alphonsi hodiernis moribus accomodatae: tomus III* (Paris: Desclée 1950²⁷), §206, p. 154.

sharply to distinguish between: a) pure nature, i.e. that which must characterize human beings in order for them to be human and which would characterize them even if God had not called humanity to a supernatural end; and b) concrete nature, which includes pure nature as a moment within itself, but which, in the present order of salvation, includes additional elements that derive from human beings' ordination to supernatural grace.

That human beings actually possess such supernatural elements in their concrete nature follows inevitably, in Rahner's view, from God's universal, salvific will. "If God gives creation and the human person above all a supernatural end and this end is first 'in intentione',"[33] writes Rahner, "then the human person (and the world) *is* by that very fact always and everywhere inwardly other in structure than she would be if she did not have this end, and hence other as well before she has reached this end partially (the grace which justifies) or wholly (the beatific vision)."[34] In other words, Rahner reasons, one can plausibly infer from God's antecedent will to bestow the beatific vision on all human beings that God created human beings in such a way that they would constitute apt receptacles for supernatural grace: something God would not have done, or at least would not have done to the same extent, if God had called humanity to a merely natural end.

In Rahner's view, accordingly, human beings universally and inexorably exemplify certain properties that do not belong to their nature, in the theological sense of the term. This conclusion, Rahner reasons, implies that pure nature, in the world as it actually is, never occurs in isolation; if one can know of it at all, therefore, one can know of it only by abstracting from the supernatural elements that characterize humanity as it exists and then examining what remains. In Rahner's words:

---

[33] Rahner invokes in this sentence, explains David Coffey, "the Scholastic principle that the end is first *in intentione*, meaning that the end determines everything else about the being under consideration" ("The Whole Rahner on the Supernatural Existential," *TS* 65 [2004], 95–118 at 100).

[34] "Relationship," *TI* i, 302–3; "Verhältnis," *ST* i, 328–9.

'Nature' in the theological sense (as opposed to nature as the substantial content of an entity always to be encountered in contingent fact), i.e. as the concept contraposed to the supernatural, is consequently a remainder concept (*Restbegriff*). By that is meant that starting as we have done, a reality must be postulated in humanity which remains over when the supernatural existential as unexacted is subtracted.[35]

The theologoumenon of the supernatural existential thus warrants a sharp distinction between pure nature and contingently factual nature. The idea that the natural and the supernatural exist in an integrated fashion in the concrete, human being, moreover, implies that one cannot determine the contents of human nature as such, i.e. pure nature, simply by inspecting actual, human persons. One must, rather, have recourse to revelation to distinguish the natural from the supernatural constituents of concretely existing humanity; and even then, Rahner cautions, one cannot reasonably expect one's data to yield a precise description of pure nature. Again, in Rahner's words:

This 'pure' nature is not...an unambiguous delimitable, de-finable quantity; no neat horizontal (to use Philipp Dessauer's way of putting it) allows of being drawn between this nature and the supernatural (both existential and grace). We never have this postulated pure nature for itself alone, so as in all cases to be able to say exactly what in our existential experience is to be reckoned to its account, what to the account of the supernatural.[36]

Rahner asserts, then, that although human beings inevitably possess the supernatural existential, it does not pertain to pure nature, i.e. human nature in the strictest sense of the term. The supernatural existential and pure nature, rather, constitute imprecisely distinguishable components of the internally differentiated human being; and pure nature constitutes an only ambiguously definable entity the possibility of whose existence in isolation one must posit in order to safeguard the gratuity of supernatural grace.

iv. Conclusion. The mature Rahner, therefore, seems implicitly to repudiate his earlier attempt in *Hörer des Wortes* to construct an ontology of the human

---

[35] Ibid. 313–14; ebd. 340.
[36] Ibid. 314; ebd. 340–1.

being's natural potency[37] for hearing a possible revelation as: a) overambitious; and b) perhaps even extrinsicist insofar as, in *Hörer des Wortes*, Rahner does not ascribe to concrete, human beings an unconditional ordination to the beatific vision.[38] At least "the overarching framework of *Hearer of the Word*, and presumably also *Spirit in the World*," then, is, as Kilby correctly observes, "inconsistent with a central theme of Rahner's theology."[39]

b. Transcendental revelation. Second, the later Rahner, unlike the early Rahner, believes that God's supernatural self-revelation consists primarily not in historical events, but in God's gracious bestowal on all human beings of a "supernatural formal object": i.e. a transcendental horizon of knowing and willing that is objectively identical with God.[40] This supernatural elevation of humanity's transcendence constitutes a revelation, Rahner asserts:

in the sense of a change of consciousness..., which originates from a free personal self-communication of God in grace. It is therefore absolutely legitimate to call it already a revelation, especially since it already communicates or offers in an ontologically real sense as 'grace'

---

[37] "We may speak of that part of fundamental theology that concerns us here as the ontology of our obediential potency for the free revelation of God. In connection with this formula, we must note at once that we are not speaking of the obediential potency for *supernatural* life" (*Hearer*, 16; *Hörer*, *SW* iv, 38). For the Rahner of *Hörer des Wortes*, writes Max Seckler, "the term *potentia oboedientialis* describes...[a] capacity...that comes with the *natural structure* of the spirit. From this point of view, the outlook of *Hörer des Wortes* is based on the idea of *natura pura*" ("La dimensione fondamentale della teologia di Karl Rahner" *L'eredità teologica di Karl Rahner* [Ignazio Sanna, ed.; Rome: LUP, 2005], 49–67 at 59.

[38] The later Rahner condemns as extrinsicist all views of the nature/grace relation that attribute a merely conditional desire for the beatific vision to human beings ("Relationship," *TI* i, 303; "Verhältnis," *ST* i, 329).

[39] Kilby, *Karl Rahner*, 69.

[40] "A formal object," writes Rahner, "is the *a priori* horizon given in consciousness, under which, in grasping the individual *a posteriori* object, everything is known which is grasped as an object strictly speaking" ("Nature and Grace," *TI* iv, 165–88 at 178; "Natur und Gnade," *ST* iv, 209–36 at 225). As to the identity of the human intellect's supernatural, formal object with God, Rahner writes: "The formal *a priori* of faith, in contrast to the natural transcendence of the spirit and its *a priori* relationship,...is none other than the triune God...in God's real self–communication" ("Considerations on the Development of Dogma ," *TI* iv, 3–35 at 25–6; "Überlegungen zur Dogmenentwicklung," *SW* ix, 442–71 at 462).

something which also ultimately constitutes the whole content of divine revelation contained in...propositions and human concepts, viz. God and God's eternal life itself.[41]

Rahner, in fact, identifies this transcendental mode of revelation as "the mode on which all other revelation is based."[42] "One can without hesitation," Rahner writes, "view the material contents of historical revelation as verbalized objectifications of the 'revelation' which is already present in the gratuitous radicalizing of human transcendentality in God's self-communication."[43]

Now, these remarks and the whole idea of "transcendental revelation"[44] seem thoroughly incompatible with the sentiments of the young Rahner as expressed in *Hörer des Wortes*. "It is inadmissible," writes the young Rahner:

that we should be permanently and miraculously raised above our natural way of thinking and of acting by God's revelation. This would ultimately reduce God's free revelation...to be but an essential element of humanity itself, since we would no longer come to know it as the unexpected, as the act of God's freedom with regard to us as already constituted in our essence. Therefore, at least within the existence of the individual human being, the free revelation can occur only at a definite point.[45]

Once more, accordingly, a central aspect of Rahner's theology stands in stark contradiction to an equally central aspect of his philosophy: a circumstance Kilby correctly regards as evidence against the view that Rahner's early philosophy constitutes a foundation for his later, theological synthesis.

---

[41] "History of the World and Salvation-History," *TI* v, 97–114 at 104; "Weltgeschichte und Heilsgeschichte," *SW* x, 590–604 at 596.

[42] *Foundations*, 150; *Grundkurs*, *SW* xxvi, 148.

[43] "The Act of Faith and the Content of Faith," *TI* xxi, 151–61 at 158; "Glaubensakt und Glaubensinhalt," *ST* xv, 152–62 at 158.

[44] Cf. *Foundations*, 172–4; *Grundkurs*, *SW* xxvi, 169–70. For a more thorough discussion of transcendental revelation's nature and meaning, cf. Roman Siebenrock's "'Transzendentale Offenbarung': Bedeutungsanalyse eines Begriffs in Spätwerk Rahners als Beispiel methodisch geleiteter Rahnerforschung," *ZKT* 126 (2004), 33–46 and our treatment of the subject in the following chapter.

[45] *Hearer*, 135; *Hörer*, SW iv, 240, 242. Cf. the early Rahner's similar remarks in "Confession of Devotion," *TI* iii, 184–5; "Andachtsbeichte," *ST* iii, 219–20 (written in 1934) and "Priestly Existence," *TI* iii, 239–62 at 242; Priesterliche Existenz, *ST* iii, 285–312 at 288–9 (written in 1942).

c. Reservations. Admittedly, certain passages within the early Rahner's corpus suggest that even in the late 1930s and early 1940s he recognized the existence of supernatural elements in the constitution of concrete, human beings and advocated an incipient version of the idea of transcendental revelation. In 1942,[46] for instance, Rahner writes:

> This depth of a person's being of which she becomes conscious in faith...is established by Christ alone even before a single word of our preaching reaches human beings. Therefore the preaching of the word in point of fact reaches a person who by her ontological status...already inhabits that order of reality which is announced by the message. Only because the means of grace ('Church') already belong to her existence is she a potential hearer of the Christian message of faith. This latter is accordingly really an awakening, albeit an absolutely necessary one, of that Christian self-consciousness which has already been in principle established in us with the 'anointing' which is in us.[47]

Here as elsewhere the young Rahner states, more or less unambiguously, that the human beings to whom the gospel is addressed possess an "ontological status" that transcends pure nature and that endows them with an inchoate consciousness of their ordination to grace. Such statements might seem to invalidate Kilby's claim that the later Rahner's views on human nature and revelation diverge radically from those he had earlier maintained.

That this is not the case, however, appears from the following considerations. The early Rahner believes that human beings are ontologically other than they would have been in a state of pure nature not because they possess a supernatural existential as a constituent of their being, but because through his Incarnation Christ has become an aspect of the corporate reality of humanity in the world. "Every human being," he writes:

> lives necessarily in an order of existence which includes the reality of Christ. The order of human history to which Christ belongs is already 'Church'; not yet indeed in the sense of a visible society... but certainly in the sense that the historical order of the human being's existential

---

[46] 1942 is the date of the publication of the essay in which the quoted remarks appear. Paul Rulands, however, calls attention to a hectographed version of this essay (Rahn I, A 25) dated June, 1939 in the Karl–Rahner–Archiv in Innsbruck (*Menschsein unter dem An–Spruch der Gnade: Das übernatürliche Existential und der Begriff der natura pura bei Karl Rahner* [ITS 55; Innsbruck: Tyrolia, 2000], 128, n. 341).

[47] "Priestly Existence," *TI* iii, 252; "Priesterliche Existenz," *ST* iii, 299–300.

decision has become, before any visible organization of the Church, through the Incarnation and the Cross, already quite different from one in which Christ did not exist.[48]

For the early Rahner, in other words, human beings are elevated beyond pure nature not by an inescapable, burning desire for the beatific vision, but by membership in the same species as God Incarnate.[49] The young Rahner regards the Incarnation itself as an implicit call to supernatural life addressed to all human beings and reasons that since this appeal constitutes "a factual determination of the human race as a whole," it also constitutes "a real ontological determination of the nature of each human being."[50]

In this case, the young Rahner concludes, human beings are, by virtue of the Incarnation, members of a "Church" or "people of God" in a loose acceptation of those terms, and this membership constitutes an aspect of their nature:[51] an aspect, that is to say, of "everything which, as a condition for its possibility, precedes...[the] free activity of the human being as a person and...which sets bounds to the autonomous sovereignty of her person."[52]

A determination of one's nature that springs solely from participation in a species whose historical context has been altered by the acts of one human being, it seems, cannot fail to be less radical and less intimate than the determination the later Rahner describes as the "supernatural existential." A determination of the

---

[48] Ibid. 247–8; ebd. 294–5.

[49] It seems misleading, therefore, both: a) to claim, with Cornelius Keppeler ("Begnadung als berechtigte Forderung? Gedanken zur Bedeutung des übernatürlichen Existentials in der Gnadenlehre Karl Rahners," *ZKTh* 126 [2004], 65–82 at 75–7), that Rahner advocates a rough equivalent of his mature theory of the supernatural existential already in 1939; and b) to claim, with Paul Rulands (*Menschsein*, 131–6), that Rahner ascribes an ontological ordination to grace to no one but the baptized before he composes "Die Gliedschaft in der Kirche nach der Lehre der Enzyklika Pius' XII. 'Mystici Corporis Christi'," which was published in 1947. Rahner appears, rather, to attribute some elevation above pure nature to all human beings already in 1939 when he wrote the two preceding bloc quotes; and yet not to envision a radical transformation of all human beings by grace before 1950.

[50] "Membership of the Church According to the Teaching of Pius XII's Encyclical 'Mystici Corporis Christi,'" *TI* ii, 1–88 at 81; "Die Gliedschaft in der Kirche nach der Lehre der Enzyklika Pius' XII. 'Mystici Corporis Christi,'".*SW* x, 3–71 at 67.

[51] Ibid. 82–3; ebd. 67–8.

[52] Ibid. 80; ebd. 65.

former sort, for instance, would seem to constitute actual grace; whereas the supernatural existential constitutes habitual grace. Possession of the supernatural existential, likewise, would seem to imply an ordination to a supernatural formal object. An extrinsic determination, resulting from the influence of another, possibly quite remote, human being, by contrast, would seem to imply some alteration of consciousness, inasmuch as *ens et verum convertuntur*,[53] but nothing as radical as the addition of a supernatural, *a priori* horizon to the horizon of natural, human consciousness.

Superficial similarities aside, therefore, a wide chasm seems to separate: 1) the theological anthropology of the younger Rahner, according to whom the situation of pure nature is modified in the human race as a whole only by an extrinsic influence that does not imply the existence of a transcendental revelation; and 2) the theological anthropology of the mature Rahner who considers human beings intrinsically different from purely natural persons in that they possess an unconditional ordination to the beatific vision and constant access to an athematic, but nonetheless real and supernatural, divine revelation. To the extent that Rahner's early philosophical works presuppose his earlier, relatively extrinsicist understanding of human nature, accordingly, the philosophical synthesis Rahner articulates in these works can hardly serve as a foundation for his later theology.

d. Formally philosophical presuppositions. Kilby recognizes, nonetheless, that the elements of dissonance between Rahner's philosophy and his theology do "not rule out the possibility that Rahner might…continue to use *particular arguments* from these works to underpin this same theology."[54] Nor, we should like to add, do these elements of dissonance preclude the possibility of Rahner's drawing arguments and presuppositions from philosophies not uniquely his own.

---

[53] Cf. *Spirit*, 167, n. 12; *Geist*, 133, n. 98. In Rahner's parlance, this formula expresses the original unity of being and knowing.

[54] Kilby, *Karl Rahner*, 69.

It requires little diligence, in fact, to locate instances, in addition to those cited in the previous section, in which Rahner appeals, directly or indirectly, to formally philosophical conclusions in his theological arguments. In defense of the idea that the intellect could possess multiple, formal objects without explicitly distinguishing between them,[55] for instance, Rahner appeals to "considerations...taken from a metaphysics of the spirit."[56] Likewise, in discussing the relation between the body and the soul, Rahner writes, "in Thomist metaphysics, which are perfectly justifiable, one is bound to say...."[57] Even the later Rahner, furthermore, appeals frequently to "the axiom of the thomistic metaphysics of knowledge according to which...something which exists is present to itself, to the extent in which it has or is being."[58]

e. Conclusion. In spite of the discontinuities between Rahner's early philosophy and his late theology, then, the evidence of Rahner's writings disallows the conclusion that philosophy in the formal sense of the term plays no role in the molding of Rahner's later theology.

4. Gnoseological concupiscence. The third item adduced above as evidence for the nonfoundationalist interpretation of the later Rahner's theology, viz. the later Rahner's ascription of far-reaching effects to "gnoseological concupiscence" in contemporary culture, seems somewhat weightier than the previous two considerations. Nonetheless, as we shall attempt to show, it does not suffice to

---

[55] In the same context, incidentally, Rahner describes this view as a truth, which "for a metaphysics of knowledge, there is no great difficulty in recognizing" ("Nature and Grace," *TI* iv, 178; "Natur und Gnade," *ST* iv, 225).

[56] Ibid. 179; ebd. 225.

[57] "The Hermeneutics of Eschatological Assertions," *TI* iv, 323–46 at 340, n. 16; "Theologische Prinzipien der Hermeneutik eschatologischer Aussagen," *SW* xii, 489–510 at 505, Anm. 16.

[58] "Dogmatic Reflections on the Knowledge and Self-Consciousness of Christ," *TI* v, 193–215 at 205; "Dogmatische Erwägungen über das Wissen und Selbstbewußtsein Christi," *SW* xii, 335–52 at 343; cf. "Theology and Anthropology," *TI* ix, 28–45 at 34; "Theologie und Anthropologie," *ST* viii, 43–65 at 51.

establish that the later Rahner refuses to employ distinctively philosophical reasoning in constructing his theology.

a. What is gnoseological concupiscence? "By 'gnoseological concupiscence,'" Rahner writes, "I mean the fact that in human awareness there is a pluralism between the various branches of knowledge such that we can never achieve a full or comprehensive view of them all together, and that they can never be integrated into a unified system by human beings in a way which makes them fully controllable or comprehensible to them."[59] In Rahner's view, this "gnoseological concupiscence" constitutes a permanent existential of human beings no less than moral concupiscence.[60] "The human person is a pluralistic being," he writes, "who can never adequately synthesize the protean manifestations of her reality, her history and her experience—and today less than ever."[61] Again, in Rahner's words, gnoseological concupiscence "has been the lot of human beings from time immemorial, since people have always been burdened with errors which were incompatible with other true insights that they had."[62]

Rahner insists, however, that the explosion of human knowledge in the twentieth century has exacerbated the situation of gnoseological concupiscence

---

[59] "On the Relationship between Theology and the Contemporary Sciences," *TI* xiii, 94–102 at 95; "Zum Verhältnis zwischen Theologie und heutigen Wissenschaften," *SW* xv, 704–10 at 705.

[60] Rahner conceives of moral concupiscence, incidentally, not as a tendency to sin, but as an irresolvable pluralism between oneself as one is (one's "nature") and oneself as one wishes to be (one's "person"): a pluralism that inhibits sinful decisions as well as righteous ones (cf. "The Theological Concept of Concupiscentia," *TI* i, 347–82 at 360–6; "Zum theologischen Begriff der Konkupiszenz," *SW* viii, 3–32 at 14–19). By thus portraying concupiscence, Rahner seeks to prove that concupiscence is not intrinsically evil and so to vindicate the unexactedness of the gift of integrity from it (ibid. 357, 369–70; ebd. 11, 21–2). Likewise, Rahner regards gnoseological concupiscence as "innocent and unblameworthy" ("Theological Reflections on the Problem of Secularisation," *TI* x, 318–48 at 344; "Theologische Reflexionen zum Problem der Säkularisation," *ST* viii, 637–66 at 662) and condemns pretensions to having overcome it before the eschaton as sin (ibid. 346; ebd. 665).

[61] "Transformations in the Church and Secular Society," *TI* xvii, 167–80 at 170; "Kirchliche Wandlungen und Profangesellschaft," *ST* xii, 513–28 at 516.

[62] "Intellectual Patience with Ourselves," *TI* xxiii, 38–49 at 44; "Über die intellektuelle Geduld mit sich selbst," *ST* xv, 303–14 at 309.

tremendously. "However limited an individual's knowledge is when compared with the amount of knowledge available today," explains Rahner:

> it is, nonetheless, still enormous taken in itself and thus it is no longer possible for an individual to gain a full grasp of the mutual consistency of its individual elements. If an individual today should subject his or her knowledge to an honest and objective appraisal, he or she would have to say, "So much knowledge, so many opinions and views from every side have found their way into the storehouse of my consciousness that, try as I may, I really couldn't tell you anymore if and how it all fits together, and I couldn't even tell you how even in principle it could be synthesized into a consistent 'system.'"[63]

In Rahner's view, accordingly, the vast expansion of human knowledge in the twentieth century has engendered a level of gnoseological concupiscence so acute that reasonable and intelligent human beings cannot honestly claim to have integrated all of the data of their knowledge into a consistent system of ideas.[64]

b. Contradictions between secular knowledge and faith. As we have already seen, Rahner holds at least two beliefs about the consequences of these unprecedented degrees of gnoseological concupiscence that might seem to exclude the possibility of his consistently employing philosophically derived arguments in theological contexts. First, Rahner maintains, the Christian faith co-exists in the minds of contemporary Christians with existentially significant data that admit of no reconciliation, at least in the practical order, with Christianity. "Today's faith," in Rahner's view:

> co-exists with positively contradictory elements in some kind of mostly unconscious schizoid state. Even if we suppose that no objective contradictions exist among the particulars in an individual's consciousness (statements of faith included), these contents are incredibly complex and almost impossible to harmonize. It is practically impossible for individuals to harmonize all the data of consciousness with the contents of the faith, although it is a tenet of faith that such a harmonization is theoretically possible.[65]

---

[63] Ibid. 44; ebd. 308–9.

[64] "We cannot refrain," writes Rahner, "from considering others to be obtuse, naïve, and primitive if they are not aware of this fragmentation and fail in their utterances to realize the lack of clarity in their concepts and the inconsistency in their knowledge" (ibid. 44; ebd. 309).

[65] "What the Church Officially Teaches and What the People Actually Believe," *TI* xxii, 165–75 at 167; "Offizielle Glaubenslehre der Kirche und faktische Gläubigkeit des Volkes," *ST* xvi, 217–30 at 219.

Rahner maintains, in other words, that gnoseological concupiscence affects the individual Christian's consciousness in such a way as implicitly to place Christianity itself, and not merely some or all theological or philosophical systems, in question. Yet Rahner does not take this to mean that one cannot reasonably believe both in Christianity's general truthfulness and in the truthfulness of many, specific, doctrinal claims.

If the practical impossibility of reconciling the Christian faith with secular data in his consciousness does not lead Rahner to renounce Christianity, then; neither, *a fortiori*, should his skepticism about the possibility, practically speaking, of refuting all conceivable objections to particular, philosophical theses lead him to renounce them altogether. It would be inconsistent for the later Rahner to abandon formally philosophical reasoning simply because every philosophical system is inescapably disputable.

c. Inability to survey the range of philosophies and theologies. The second of Rahner's theses about gnoseological concupiscence that might seem to favor a nonfoundationalist construal of his thought, viz. Rahner's judgment that no individual can possibly survey the range of existing philosophies and theologies, seems much less consequential in the light of the preceding considerations. Admittedly, Rahner does affirm the impotence of individual theologians to comprehend the range of alternative theological and philosophical systems. Of theology, for instance, Rahner writes, "the substance of the theology and the theologies which are possible and actual today can no longer be contained even approximately by the mind of any one individual theologian, or assimilated in the time available to her."[66] Of philosophy, likewise, he remarks, "Every theologian, although she must philosophise in theology, knows less and less of 'Philosophy',

---

[66] "Pluralism in Theology and the Unity of the Creed in the Church," *TI* xi, 3–23 at 6; "Der Pluralismus in der Theologie und die Einheit des Bekenntnisses in der Kirche," *ST* ix 11–33 at 14.

since there are continually more and more philosophies, which no single person can assimilate."[67]

Such remarks, however, do not necessarily suggest skepticism on Rahner's part about the possibility of fruitfully employing philosophy, in the formal sense of the term, as a presupposition and internal component of theology. Obviously, Rahner rejects the view that one can reasonably expect all interested parties to understand and accept conclusions based on the presuppositions of one, particular philosophy. To that extent, moreover, the following remarks of Kilby seem abundantly justified.

> To maintain...that a religiously neutral, universally persuasive argument can be developed to demonstrate that everyone is aware of God whether they know it or not is anything but modest and is not very much in line with the affirmation of an inescapable pluralism of philosophies....To think that one could in this way philosophically demonstrate the existence of the *Vorgriff* would be to think that one had found an escape route from pluralism and from the historically conditioned nature of our understanding, that one was somehow able to wriggle one's way underneath it all and build something sturdy and unquestionable on an ahistorical and indubitable basis.[68]

Kilby is correct in holding that to affirm the possibility of establishing the existence of the *Vorgriff* or any other meta-empirical reality "in this way," i.e. in a way that would be intelligible and persuasive to all persons concerned, would be implicitly to deny the existence of an insurmountable pluralism of philosophies. It is by no means obvious, however, that one could not affirm the possibility of constructing a merely probable, and yet genuinely philosophical, argument for, say, the existence of the *Vorgriff* without implicitly denying the inescapability of pluralism.

It seems, in fact, that, without rejecting Kilby's insight as to the incompatibility of a robust affirmation of pluralism with pretensions to developing universally acceptable philosophical arguments, one can allow for the possibility that Rahner: a) employs a modest, disputable philosophy within his theological reflections; and yet b) does not attempt to transcend the irreducible

---

[67] "Philosophy and Philosophising in Theology," *TI* ix, 46–63 at 54; "Philosophie und Philosophieren in der Theologie," *ST* viii, 66–77 at 75.
[68] Kilby, *Karl Rahner*, 96–7.

pluralism of philosophies. That Rahner understands himself to employ a philosophy of this unassuming sort in his own theology seems to follow from comments Rahner made in 1965 about the necessity of "metaphysics" in theology.

> I am sometimes amazed that theologians are quick to declare that a metaphysics must be false or unsuitable for theology simply because it is a matter of dispute. How can they not see that their own theology too is itself a matter of dispute, and yet they do not straightway regard this as a criterion for saying that their own theology is false? The person who has not the courage to pursue a metaphysics (which is not the same thing as a closed system) cannot be a good theologian. Even when one is conscious of possessing a constantly inadequate metaphysics, it is still possible to rely on it, to use it in addressing the true God and in directing human beings towards the experience which they always have already from God. For it is the human being's inalienable blessing that her words say more and purer things than she herself knows and can enclose in her impure words, provided…that her pride does not make her keep silent…because, as soon as she begins to speak about God, her words immediately sound foolish.[69]

Rahner does not seem to believe, accordingly, that if he cannot survey all of the possible alternatives and objections to his philosophy and cannot hope to make his philosophy universally persuasive, he ought, therefore, to abstain from philosophizing altogether.[70] If the inexorable pluralism of philosophies does not imply that the enterprise of philosophy itself ought to be abandoned, however, Rahner's affirmation of this inexorable pluralism seems quite compatible with his own continued employment of formally philosophical arguments within his theology. In any event, Rahner considers contemporary theology as well as philosophy irreducibly pluralistic; yet the uncontrollable pluralism of theologies does not lead him to cease formulating distinctively theological arguments. Why, then, should he renounce the employment of formally philosophical reasoning on account of the insurmountable pluralism of philosophies?

These considerations, again, do not detract from the soundness of Kilby's demonstration that the later Rahner's views on pluralism imply the impossibility

---

[69] "Observations on the Doctrine of God in Catholic Dogmatics," *TI* ix, 127–44 at 138; "Bemerkungen zur Gotteslehre in der katholischen Dogmatik," *ST* viii, 165–86 at 178–9.

[70] It is not without significance, as Albert Raffelt observes, that Rahner juxtaposes his early philosophical essay, "Die Wahrheit bei Thomas von Aquin" (*SW* ii, 303–316), with essays in which he emphatically affirms the insuperable pluralism of philosophies in *ST* 10 ("Pluralismus—ein Plädoyer für Rahner und eine Bemerkung zur Sache" in *Hoffnung, die Gründe nennt: Zu Hansjürgen Verweyens Projekt einer erstphilosophischen Glaubensverantwortung* [Gerhard Larcher, Klaus Müller, and Thomas Pröpper, ed.; Regensburg: Pustet, 1996], 127–38 at 132–3).

of a universally intelligible and persuasive philosophy. They do, however, show that if one is willing to include merely probable arguments, whose conclusions do not derive from specifically Christian premises, within the compass of "philosophy in the formal sense of the term"; then Rahner's views on contemporary pluralism do not constitute evidence for the absence of formally philosophical reasoning in his later, theological works.

d. Kilby's response. To this line of reasoning, Kilby would presumably respond that an argument's lack of distinctively Christian premises need not imply that the argument is formally philosophical rather than formally theological. Kilby would claim, that is to say, that the datum that an argument:

> is not yet *specifically* Christian...means neither that it is not Christian nor that it is justified independently of Christian considerations. It does not follow that it is not Christian, first of all, from the fact that some claims fall into the intersection of Christianity and some other way of interpreting experience (tea is no less an English form of sustenance than crumpets even though the one is consumed elsewhere and the other is not). And second, because it is not a uniquely Christian claim it does not follow that Rahner is trying to justify it on purely general, a-Christian grounds.[71]

Now, Kilby seems correct in insisting that arguments that draw on premises that Christianity holds in common with various non- or pre-Christian philosophies can be formally theological. This insight, however, does not imply that the apparently philosophical arguments within Rahner's theological corpus actually are formally theological. In order to establish this more controversial conclusion, rather, Kilby must show that Rahner the theologian defends ideas like the *Vorgriff auf esse* and the equivalence of being, knowing, and willing with formally theological arguments alone.

Kilby admits, however, that Rahner explicitly and repeatedly states that a central element of his theology is demonstrable by purely philosophical means. "At some points," she writes, "Rahner is in fact quite clear that he thinks that something like the *Vorgriff* can be known independently of theology, and he

---

[71] Kilby, *Karl Rahner*, 82

23

makes explicit reference to the possibility of a philosophical justification."[72] She argues, nonetheless, that the brevity with which Rahner frequently alludes to philosophical arguments indicates that he regards them as a matter of indifference. "The semi-foundationalist," Kilby writes:

> will assume that when Rahner writes something like "but this philosophical argument for...will not be pursued any further in the present context," he is not wanting to interrupt his theology with long philosophical discussions, and that he does not need to precisely because he has done it before. But the nonfoundationalist can put a different construal on the situation: if Rahner neither offers a full demonstration, nor explicitly point[s] to where he has already set one out, this only underlines the fact that prior philosophical demonstration is not needed for theology—if Rahner assumes that a philosophical demonstration can be given, he also assumes that it is not important to do it because his theological position does not depend on it.[73]

Two characteristics of this argument seem particularly striking. First, it is of a purely defensive character. Kilby does not pretend positively to refute what she describes as "the strongest point in favor of a semi-foundationalist reading," but only to prove that "it is not absolutely decisive."[74] Second, and more importantly, Kilby seems to posit something of a false dichotomy. Either, she suggests: a) Rahner regards the philosophical arguments to which he alludes as unimportant; or b) he expects his readers to understand, without being told, that he is appealing to arguments advanced in his early, philosophical works. In the latter case, presumably, Rahner would expect his readers either to consult these works or to resign themselves to ignorance of the arguments in question.

Few persons, it seems, if confronted with these two alternatives, would find the second scenario, the only scenario Kilby presents that is compatible with the semi-foundationalist interpretation, remotely plausible. The prominence of the semi-foundationalist perspective in the secondary literature[75] on Rahner,

---

[72] Ibid. 84.

[73] Ibid.

[74] Ibid.

[75] In addition to the texts listed in Kilby, *Karl Rahner*, 131–3, n. 22, cf. esp. Harald Schöndorf, "Die Bedeutung der Philosophie bei Karl Rahner" in *Die philosophischen Quellen der Theologie Karl Rahners* (Schöndorf, ed.; Freiburg: Herder, 2005), 13–29; Nicholas Adams, "The Present Made Future: Karl Rahner's Eschatological Debt to Heidegger," *Faith and Philosophy* 17 (2000), 191–211; and Günter Kruck, "Christlicher Glaube und Moderne: Eine Analyse des Verhältnisses

therefore, strongly suggests that some third explanation of the brevity with which Rahner frequently alludes to points of philosophical interest may be conceivable. We should like, in particular, tentatively to propose the following rationale for this peculiarity in the later Rahner's argumentative style.

The intended audience for the majority of Rahner's theological essays consists in progressive, central European, Catholic theologians. Such persons, whether directly acquainted with *Geist in Welt* and *Hörer des Wortes* or not, would presumably be broadly familiar with philosophical ideas like the basic identity of being and knowing and the *Horizonthaftigkeit* of human knowledge. Such persons, moreover, would also presumably be familiar with the appropriation and translation into Thomistic terminology of these and similar ideas by Joseph Maréchal and other Maréchalian Thomists: a circle including, but not limited to, Johannes B. Lotz, Max Müller, Emerich Coreth, Bernhard Welte, and Rahner himself. When Rahner, therefore, alludes to typically "transcendental Thomistic" conceptions such as the basic identity of being and knowing, the limitless transcendence of the human spirit, the human being's necessary, albeit unthematic awareness of God, etc., he can reasonably assume that his readers are familiar with these themes. *Pace* Kilby, then, the brevity with which Rahner refers to philosophical arguments in his theological writings may reflect neither the unimportance of philosophical premises in Rahner's later work, nor a desire on his part for readers to consult *Geist in Welt* and *Hörer des Wortes*. Rahner's brevity may simply reflect his expectations of a readership educated in scholastic philosophy and theology and well-informed about Continental philosophy in the mid-twentieth century.

Rahner explicitly indicates that this is the case, in fact, in the most philosophically sophisticated of his later essays, "Zur Theologie des Symbols."[76]

---

von Anthropologie und Theologie in der Theologie Karl Rahners im Rekurs auf die Philosophie G. W. F. Hegels," *ThPh* 73 (1998), 225–46.

[76] Hugo Rahner ("Eucharisticon fraternitatis," *Gott in Welt: Festgabe für Karl Rahner zum 60. Geburtstag* 2 [Johannes Baptist Metz, Walter Kern, Adolf Darlap, and Herbert Vorgrimler, ed.;

"We choose here a method," he writes, "which will bring us to our goal as quickly and easily as possible, even though it simplifies matters by presupposing ontological and theological principles which would have to be demonstrated, not supposed, in a properly worked out ontology of the symbol. However, in view of the reader who is primarily envisaged here, these presuppositions may be made without misgiving."[77] One need not choose, therefore, between hypothesizing: a) that philosophy is unimportant to the later Rahner, and that he, therefore, sees little point in clarifying the philosophical arguments he mentions; or b) that Rahner continually refers his readers to *Geist in Welt* and *Hörer des Wortes*. It seems, rather that Rahner not unreasonably assumes that the progressive, German-speaking, Catholic theologians who constitute his primary audience are already aware of the basic theses of Maréchalian Thomism and the arguments for them. The brevity with which Rahner frequently refers to formally philosophical arguments within his theological works, then, does not appear to betray an attitude of indifference on the later Rahner's part to such arguments in theological contexts.

e. Conclusion. One can reasonably conclude, therefore, that Rahner's theology does contain philosophical elements, which he may and presumably does, at times, regard as of great importance. Gnoseological concupiscence, according to the later Rahner, does, admittedly, render it impossible for theologians: a) to reconcile all aspects of their knowledge with the Christian faith; and b) to survey the entire range of theologies and philosophies. Gnoseological concupiscence, however, does not, in Rahner's view, absolve the theologian from the responsibility to engage in philosophy, or metaphysics, in order responsibly to

---

Freiburg–im–Breisgau: Herder 1964], 895–9 at 897) famously describes the theology of the symbol as the "kernel" of his brother's theology.

[77] "The Theology of the Symbol," *TI* iv, 221–52 at 225–6, n. 4; "Zur Theologie des Symbols," *SW* xviii, 423–57 at 427, n. 4.

speak about God; "the person who has not the courage to pursue a metaphysics (which is not the same thing as a closed system) cannot be a good theologian."[78]

5. *Moderate nonfoundationalism.* This conclusion, it is important to note, does not suffice to substantiate the semi-foundationalist interpretation. For, as Kilby notes, the semi-foundationalist holds not merely that Rahner's theology contains formally philosophical components, but that it "requires, as one of its elements, specifically philosophical arguments."[79]

The mere existence of formally philosophical aspects of Rahner's theology, by the same token, does not necessarily entail the falsehood of Kilby's nonfoundationalist interpretation. For, although Kilby does assert that, according to the nonfoundationalist view, the later Rahner eschews philosophy in the formal sense of the term,[80] she does not portray this tenet as indispensable to the nonfoundationalist position. In Kilby's view, rather, "What must be denied, for the nonfoundationalist, is that Rahner's theology is dependent on a philosophy *formally* distinct from it."[81] Kilby indicates, that is to say, that a mitigated nonfoundationalist interpretation, according to which Rahner's theology contains but does not require philosophy in the formal sense of the term, may satisfy her principal concerns. In her words:

Even if one did take these passages [in which Rahner alludes to philosophical proofs] to involve an implicit reference back to Rahner's own early philosophical arguments, though this would count against a nonfoundationalist reading, it would not count *decisively* against it. This is because the real case for a nonfoundationalist reading does not rest on the construal of individual passages....The real case for the nonfoundationalist reading is that it makes possible the most plausible and most coherent reading of Rahner's theology taken as a whole. Even if, then, it turns out that at particular points Rahner makes appeal to his earlier philosophy, the nonfoundationalist

---

[78] "Observations," *TI* ix, 138; "Bemerkungen," *ST* viii, 179.

[79] Kilby, *Karl Rahner*, 75.

[80] "On the nonfoundationalist reading," she writes (ibid. 76), "significant elements of Rahner's own philosophical works do indeed become an inner moment of his theology, but in so doing they remain philosophy only in...a material sense."

[81] Ibid.

would argue that this represents merely a remnant of an earlier kind of thinking, one which is extraneous to the basic drift and at odds with the overall thrust of Rahner's theology.[82]

It seems, therefore, that although Kilby prefers a robustly nonfoundationalist construal of Rahner's mature theology, according to which it simply lacks formally philosophical components; she also allows that a mildly nonfoundationalist interpretation, according to which Rahner's theology contains superfluous, philosophical appendages, may suffice to establish the essentially nonfoundationalist character of the later Rahner's thought.

a. The Vorgriff auf esse as theological hypothesis. In order to corroborate this less ambitious version of the nonfoundationalist construal, Kilby attempts to show that a notoriously philosophical element of Rahner's anthropology, viz. his understanding of the *Vorgriff auf esse*, admits of justification through theological considerations alone. She attempts, specifically, to validate Rahner's claims about the *Vorgriff* by the following argument:

1) Human beings, on account of God's universal will to save, must possess a prethematic awareness of God.
2) All means of accounting for this awareness that do not involve a *Vorgriff* are inadmissible from Rahner's perspective for strictly theological reasons.
3) If Rahner's assumptions are correct, therefore, all human beings must, in their acts of knowing and willing, accomplish a *Vorgriff auf esse* of the sort described in *Geist in Welt* and *Hörer des Wortes*.

In defense of the first plank of her argument, Kilby writes:

God wills the salvation of all human beings, so justifying grace must be universally present, at least as offer. Furthermore, faith in God and in Christ is a necessary means of salvation, so it is necessary that the transformation of human beings brought about by justifying grace include a cognitive element. Since explicit belief in the church's proclamation is not in fact a possibility for

---

[82] Ibid. 84–5.

all human beings, this cognitive element must be at something other than an explicit level: it must be possible somehow to accept God and God's redemptive action in Christ in an unthematic way....Now in order that grace not be conceived as introducing something completely new into human consciousness, something that has no connection whatsoever to human nature, the human being must be thought of as already, by nature, standing in some sort of cognitive but unthematic relation to God.[83]

Hence, Kilby concludes, human beings must be unthematically aware of God by their very nature; "if there is going to be an unthematic supernatural faith there must also be an unthematic natural knowledge of God."[84] In the second plank of her argument, then, Kilby explains that Rahner finds unacceptable both: a) ontologism, according to which human beings naturally enjoy a direct intuition of God; and b) the typically neoscholastic view that human beings know God naturally only by virtue of their natural capacity to infer God's existence and attributes from human experience of the world. For the Catholic Church's teaching authority, as Kilby correctly notes, condemned ontologism in the late nineteenth century; and the latter view seems to exclude the possibility that human beings possess a simultaneously natural and non-thematic knowledge of God.

Likewise, Kilby reasons, the "'prospective *fides ex auditu*' theory,"[85] according to which God explicitly communicates the gospel to unevangelized persons in or after death, conflicts with fundamental tenets of Rahner's theology of death. Kilby observes, for instance, that in Rahner's view, "the moment of death is not...independent of or distinct from the life that precedes it."[86] Rahner conceives of the life of the dead, moreover, as a state of finality that precludes both temporal prolongation and the possibility of making new decisions such as a

---

[83] Ibid. 77

[84] Ibid. 77.

[85] Ibid. 78. This theory's chief exponent in contemporary theology is George Lindbeck (cf. e.g. Lindbeck's "Unbelievers and the '*Sola Christi*'" in his *The Church in a Postliberal Age* [Grand Rapids: Eerdmans, 2003], 77–87).

[86] Kilby, *Karl Rahner*, 78.

postmortem acceptance of the gospel.[87] The "'prospective *fides ex auditu*' theory," like ontologism and exclusively inferential understandings of human knowledge of God, thus seems ill-suited to the task of accounting for athematic, human awareness of the divine within the framework of Rahner's assumptions.

Having rejected the prospective *fides ex auditu* theory, exclusively inferential understandings of human knowledge of God, and ontologism, then, Kilby finds herself in possession of no plausible explanation of humanity's unthematic knowledge of God other than Rahner's theory of the *Vorgriff auf esse*. As a result, she concludes, Rahner's theory of the *Vorgriff* merits acceptance, because it alone, among the available alternatives, explains how persons can possess the awareness that Rahner's theology ascribes to all human beings.

b. Evaluation. This argument for the *Vorgriff*, admittedly, constitutes something of a *tour de force*; Kilby successfully transforms one of Rahner's most rarefied philosophical theses into a genuinely theological hypothesis defensible on exclusively theological grounds. This is no mean achievement. At least two objections, however, suggest that Kilby's argument does not suffice, of itself, to render the nonfoundationalist position plausible. First, as Kilby herself observes, one could challenge her argument from the inadequacy of alternative accounts of human beings' unthematic awareness of God to the existence of the *Vorgriff* with the following counterargument: 1) no human being can survey all of the hypotheses that might be proposed to account for humanity's athematic awareness of God; 2) yet Kilby could know that the *Vorgriff* is the sole, viable hypothesis for this purpose only if she could survey the entire range of possibilities; therefore 3)

---

[87] Cf. e.g. Rahner *Foundations*, 436–7; *Grundkurs*, *SW* xxvi, 411–12; "The Life of the Dead," *TI* iv, 347–54 at 347–9; "Das Leben der Toten," *SW* xii, 540–46 at 540–41; "Ideas for a Theology of Death," *TI* xiii, 169–86 at 174–5; "Zu einer Theologie des Todes," *ST* x, 181–99 at 186–7.

Kilby does not succeed in establishing that the idea of the *Vorgriff* constitutes the sole, viable explanation of humanity's unthematic knowledge of God.[88]

Kilby demurs at this criticism, however, noting that the "uniqueness claim"[89] the critic ascribes to her is by no means essential to her argument. For, Kilby asserts, she seeks not so much to prove the *Vorgriff* hypothesis correct as to show that it "can reasonably be viewed as *one* way of working out the compatibility of God's universal salvific will with the insistence that there can be no salvation apart from faith in Christ."[90] Kilby reasons, that is to say, that since she does not seek to establish that Rahner's position is apodictically certain, one cannot justly reproach her for failing to reach this goal.

By similar reasoning, it seems, one could perhaps vindicate the entirety of Kilby's moderately nonfoundationalist interpretation. In her work's opening pages, after all, she characterizes the book's principal burden as "an argument for the possibility of a particular kind of interpretation of Rahner":[91] a relatively unambitious project that could succeed even if Kilby neglected fully to warrant her position. A remark several pages later, admittedly, calls into question this modest interpretation of Kilby's intention. "I will not claim," she writes, "that this is the *only* way Rahner can be read, but only that this is the *best* way he can be read."[92] In the following section, however, we shall attempt to show that either view, i.e. that the nonfoundationalist construal is merely plausible or that it is demonstrably superior to semi-foundationalist alternatives, founders on two aspects of the later Rahner's thought.

c. Philosophy and theology. First, the later Rahner seems to reject any methodological separation of philosophy and theology on specifically theological

---

[88] This counterargument mirrors Kilby's own critique (*Karl Rahner*, 43–7) of the transcendental arguments employed by Rahner in his early philosophical works.
[89] Ibid. 79.
[90] Ibid. 79.
[91] Ibid. 2.
[92] Ibid. 10.

grounds. The character of the Christian faith, as the late Rahner understands it, renders efforts to isolate theology from the intellectual climate of its time both impracticable and counterproductive. "Faith itself," explains Rahner:

(as *fides qua* and *quae*) is the ultimate, comprehensive interpretation of human existence, involving its real concreteness in which the whole salvation of existence is to be effected....It is precisely expressions of faith (and thus theology)...[therefore] which must by their very nature involve themselves above all in the human being's historical situation. This means dialogue with and within this situation...; it also means [the] courage to become involved with the unreflected situation, accepting and speaking from within it in the Christian hope that the truth of God...will not...be substantially corrupted (either objectively or subjectively) by being expressed from within the particular historical situation.... It is obvious from this point of view that a complete, self-enclosed theological system is an absurdity. Seen in this way theology is and has always been eclectic theology. A truly living theology is free from the fear of not being sufficiently pure and systematic; the fear that it must not draw concepts, complexes of problems and perspectives from simply any quarters.[93]

Here Rahner seems to declare "a complete, self-enclosed theological system" not only undesirable, but impossible on account of the comprehensive character of faith: an ultimate commitment that impinges on every aspect of human existence. Admittedly, Rahner does not at this juncture state expressly that formally philosophical ideas must necessarily form a part of any theology. His sweeping affirmation of the mutual relevance of faith and all other aspects of human consciousness, however, suggest that no theology can free itself entirely from influence by, and therefore dependence upon, philosophy and every other science in the formal sense of the term.

In this context, certain explicit statements by Rahner concerning the relationship of philosophy to theology appear highly relevant. "Philosophy," Rahner affirms, "is not merely an instrument for the practice of theology,...[but] an intrinsic element in theology itself."[94] Likewise, Rahner explains, "It is...true that theology is necessarily and of its innermost nature in the truest sense also philosophical theology. For otherwise it would compose faith and creed indeed, but no longer theology as such. Indeed it would no longer comprise faith and

---

[93] "The Historicity of Theology," *TI* ix, 64–82 at 72–3; "Zur Geschichtlichkeit der Theologie," *ST* viii, 88–110 at 98–9.

[94] "Methodology," *TI* xi, 85; "Methodologie," *ST* ix, 96.

creed in any real sense unless it also included this philosophical element."[95] Again, in Rahner's words, "'Natural', 'philosophical' theology is first and last not one sphere of study side by side with revealed theology, as if both could be pursued quite independently of each other, but an internal factor in revealed theology itself."[96]

One cannot plausibly account for such statements by claiming that Rahner refers to philosophy in its material rather than in its formal sense; for Rahner's views concerning the ubiquity of divine self-communication render material distinctions between the two disciplines otiose.[97] The just-quoted statements, along with their parallels throughout Rahner's corpus, thus seem to warrant the conclusion that Rahner does consider philosophy, in the formal sense of the term, indispensable to the work of the theologian.

Second, the later Rahner seems to think that philosophy, in the formal sense of the term, inevitably constitutes an interior moment of theology because of the nature of human understanding. "An individual truth," Rahner explains:

exists only within a totality of truths, in a wider perspective of understanding. This may not always be clear in each case because this totality of meaning, the perspective of understanding, the intellectual system of co-ordinates and references within which and by means of which any particular statement can alone be understood, may be felt as utterly self-evident and hence inaccessible to reflection. But all the same it is so. What is apparently a quantitative additional growth to a previous totality of knowledge in fact changes the totality, introduces new perspectives and puts new questions to previous insights.[98]

Now, philosophy and theology, in the formal sense of those terms, exist side by side in the consciousness of the individual theologian. Rahner's views on the mutual relations of data within the human psyche, therefore, seem to imply that even if a theologian attempts systematically to exclude philosophical

---

[95] Ibid. 90; ebd. 101.
[96] "Theology and Anthropology," *TI* ix, 34; "Theologie und Anthropologie," *ST* viii, 51.
[97] Cf. Kilby, *Karl Rahner*, 74 and section I.2.
[98] "Historicity," *TI* ix, 67; "Geschichtlichkeit," *ST* viii, 92. Cf. Rahner's similar remarks in "Natural Science and Reasonable Faith ," *TI* xxi, 16–55 at 20; "Naturwissenschaft und vernünftiger Glaube," *ST* xv, 24–62 at 28.

considerations from her theology, philosophy in the formal sense of the term will, nonetheless, exert at least an anonymous influence on her theology as a whole.[99]

Complete independence of philosophy in the formal sense of the term, therefore, appears, at least by Rahner's standards, to constitute an unrealizable goal for theology. Since the late Rahner's model of theological understanding, then, implies that his theology, like all theologies, depends on a philosophy formally distinct from it, it seems that one cannot construct a putatively nonfoundationalist version of Rahner's theology without falling into self-contradiction. Even if one derives Rahner's conclusions from strictly theological premises, that is to say, Rahner's conclusions themselves: a) imply that they depend on philosophy in the formal sense of the term; and b) thereby at least tacitly conflict with nonfoundationalism.

d. Conclusion. Nonfoundationalist interpretations of the sort that Kilby proposes thus seem ill-suited to the later Rahner's theology as a whole. Moderate nonfoundationalism does, admittedly, weather criticisms fatal to more radically nonfoundationalist perspectives. Its concession to the semi-foundationalist position that Rahner's theology may contain peripheral elements of a formally philosophical character, however, does not suffice to immunize it from semi-foundationalist critique. For Rahner believes, as we have seen, that "in the unity of the one subject, every bit of knowledge is also the function of every other part of knowledge possessed by this subject";[100] and this conviction implies that as long as a theologian is aware of philosophy in the formal sense of the term, this philosophy must exert some influence on all other aspects of her knowledge.

---

[99] Likewise, the later Rahner affirms that one cannot so much as hear Scripture understandingly without engaging in theology, because one necessarily confronts the data of Scripture with the totality of other elements in one's consciousness (cf. e.g. "Theology in the New Testament," *TI* v, 23–41 at 28; "Theologie im Neuen Testament," *SW* xii, 193–208 at 197; "What is a Dogmatic Statement," *TI* v, 42–66 at 48; "Was ist eine dogmatische Aussage?" *SW* xii, 150–70 at 155; "Philosophy and Theology," *TI* vi, 71–81 at 73; "Philosophie und Theologie," *SW* xii, 216–33 at 218).

[100] "Philosophy and Theology," *TI* vi, 74; "Philosophie und Theologie," *SW* xii, 218.

6. Recapitulation. In *Karl Rahner: Philosophy and Theology*, then, Karen Kilby seeks to vindicate Rahner's theology from the charge of dependence on a philosophy widely considered implausible in the English-speaking world. In order to accomplish this end, she proposes two nonfoundationalist interpretations of Rahner's theology. The first, and more radical of the two, consists in the claim that Rahner's theology contains no philosophy in the formal sense of the term. The second, by contrast, asserts merely that formally philosophical theses are dispensable to Rahner's theology as a whole.

While each of these construals of Rahner's theology seems ultimately wanting, Kilby nonetheless succeeds in justifying a number of controversial claims about the character of Rahner's thought: e.g. that his early philosophy and his late theology are, in certain respects at least, radically discontinuous and that one can substantiate Rahner's views on the *Vorgriff auf esse* without appealing to philosophy in the formal sense of the term. The latter discovery in particular seems to open the way towards a constructive retrieval of certain of Rahner's hypotheses by self-consciously nonfoundationalist theologians.

Such findings, however, do not imply that Rahner's theology as a whole admits of translation into a Lindbeckian idiom. Philosophy in the formal sense of the term, rather, remains sufficiently central even to the late Rahner's conception of theology's nature to exclude any bracketing of philosophy from an accurate representation of the late Rahner's theology.

II. RAHNER'S PHILOSOPHY ITSELF

It is quite appropriate, therefore, to preface our consideration of Rahner's theology of the Trinity with an overview of those aspects of his philosophy that pertain to it. In the following, accordingly, we shall briefly outline and comment on, first, Rahner's philosophical methodology, and, second, his metaphysics of knowledge.

1. Methodology. Besides remarks as to the necessity of transcendental analysis in philosophy and the centrality of the metaphysics of knowledge to metaphysics as a whole, Rahner comments little on the methodology he employs in his early philosophical corpus. In his two, principal, philosophical works, *Geist in Welt* and *Hörer des Wortes*, however, Rahner's actual manner of proceeding seems to reflect a four-stage approach to philosophical inquiry: 1) vindication of the point of departure; 2) elaboration of the point of departure; 3) transcendental reduction to the *a priori* conditions within the knowing and willing subject; and 4) transcendental deduction to the character of the objects intended in the subject's acts of knowing and willing.[101] That Rahner's procedure in these works actually reflects this methodology will appear from our exposition of their contents.

2. Rahner's metaphysics of knowledge.

a. Vindicating the point of departure. Rahner's practice indicates that, in his view, an adequate point of departure for metaphysics must satisfy at least three conditions: necessity, universality, and irreducibility. In this section, we should like, first, to show why Rahner considers these conditions indispensable in a starting point for metaphysics; and, second, to sketch Rahner's arguments to the

---

[101] We depart from Peter Eicher's schematization of Rahner's philosophical methodology only in that, in the interests of clarity and precision, we divide Eicher's first stage, viz. "the phenomenological explication of the act of knowing," into two: the vindication of the point of departure and its elaboration (*Die anthropologische Wende: Karl Rahners philosophischer Weg vom Wesen des Menschen zur personalen Existenz* [Freiburg (Schweiz): Universitätsverlag, 1970], 57). Materially, Eicher's first stage and our first two stages are identical.

effect that his chosen point of departure, the question, "What is the being of beings?"[102] satisfies these criteria.

i. Why these conditions? The nature of metaphysics itself, as Rahner conceives of it, demands that its point of departure be in some sense universal. For being itself is universal, and metaphysics is the science of being. "It is in precisely this way," explains Rahner, "that metaphysics differs from all other sciences. They inquire about some domain of beings...from a restricted point of view. Metaphysics inquires about all beings, insofar as they are. It inquires about the being of beings as such."[103]

The very universality of metaphysics' object, moreover, requires that its point of departure be in some sense necessary. For a metaphysical principle, if valid, must apply to all beings whatsoever necessarily. Yet, in Rahner's view, "the only meaning which the individual, taken simply as such, can convey is that of itself."[104] *A posteriori* experience of particular beings, accordingly, appears to Rahner "quite incapable of providing a basis for the validity of conceptions which are universal in a metaphysical sense, and so could be in turn the basis for an apodictic universality and validity of metaphysical propositions."[105]

For this reason, Rahner maintains that one can derive properly metaphysical principles only from "*transcendental reflection* upon that which is affirmed implicitly and simultaneously in the knowledge of the world."[106] In other words, Rahner believes that metaphysical principles are true solely because human beings universally and necessarily, albeit implicitly, affirm them. "The 'evidentness' of the first principles," he writes, "is the objective recognition that

---

[102] This question, superficial resemblances notwithstanding, is radically dissimilar to Heidegger's question of being. Robert Masson outlines the differences between the two questions in his "Rahner and Heidegger: Being, Hearing, and God," *Thomist* 37 (1973), 455–88.

[103] *Hearer*, 27–8; *Hörer*, *SW* iv, 58.

[104] "Thomas Aquinas on Truth," *TI* xiii, 23; "Die Wahrheit bei Thomas von Aquin," *SW* ii, 311.

[105] Ibid. 23–4; ebd.

[106] *Spirit*, 398; *Geist*, *SW* ii, 293.

in every judgment a human being makes as an act of cognition within the material world, the metaphysical validity of these principles is [implicitly] asserted."[107] Indeed, Rahner admits that if a human being could avoid implicitly affirming veritable metaphysical principles, they "would cease, so far as she was concerned, to have any claim to validity."[108] In order to authenticate any metaphysical principle at all, therefore, one must, according to Rahner, establish that human beings necessarily co-affirm it in each of their judgments. Rahner's principles dictate, accordingly, that if the point of departure from which such principles are to be inferred is not at least inextricably attached to some necessarily universal characteristic of human judgments, it will not suffice to undergird sound metaphysical conclusions.

The universality of metaphysics, furthermore, requires that its point of departure be irreducible, or presuppositionless. For, unlike merely regional sciences that confine their attention to limited sectors of being, metaphysics, as the science of everything in its fundamental constituents, can draw no premises from sciences other than itself. The metaphysician, therefore, must posit as a starting point that which, in some sense, validates itself if she is to reach any objectively certain conclusions whatever.

ii. Does Rahner's point of departure satisfy these conditions? The conformity of the question, "What is the being of beings?" to Rahner's three, self-imposed criteria for points of departure, seems relatively easy to establish.

That the question of the being of beings satisfies the criterion of universality is evident. Its universality, moreover, lends to the question a self-referential character that is crucial to Rahner's argument for the question's irreducibility. "This question about being in its totality," writes Rahner:

---

[107] "Thomas Aquinas on Truth," *TI* xiii, 26; "Die Wahrheit bei Thomas von Aquin," *SW* ii, 313.
[108] Ibid. 27; ebd.

is precisely that which cannot be so thought and so posed as though it were setting out to ask from a point "next to" or "outside" or "beyond" itself, which point itself would be given in unquestioned possession. Being in its totality can only be questioned as that which again constitutes in its turn every question about it (for the question certainly is not nothing). The being that is questioned is at once the being of the question and of the one questioning.[109]

The question about the being of beings, by including itself and everything else within its purview, thus precludes the possibility of its being answered on the basis of anything else. Yet it does supply the wherewithal for the questioner to find an answer. For the question of being itself, in Rahner's view, implies that the one who poses it knows something of the being of beings; one "must already know of being in its totality if she asks about it."[110] Rahner considers the question of the being of beings irreducible, therefore, not only in the sense that it takes its departure from nothing other than itself, but also in the sense that it constitutes a "solid positive starting point for metaphysics."[111]

In defense of the necessity of the question of the being of beings, Rahner argues that human beings implicitly pose and answer this question whenever they ascribe being to a being. "The question about being," he writes, "belongs necessarily to our existence, because it is implicitly contained in everything we think or say....Every statement [after all] is a statement about some being."[112] Rahner concludes, accordingly, that the question of the being of beings satisfies all three of his criteria for a starting point of metaphysics.

b. Elaborating the point of departure.

i. The Woher. After thus vindicating his point of departure, Rahner proceeds to reflect on the context, or *Woher*, out of which human beings ask the question of the being of beings. Human knowledge presupposes as its indispensable

---

[109] *Spirit*, 59; *Geist*, *SW* ii, 55.
[110] Ibid. 61; ebd. 56.
[111] *Hearer*, 25; *Hörer*, *SW* iv, 54.
[112] Ibid. 26; ebd. 56.

prerequisite, Rahner assumes, a conversion to the phantasms,[113] i.e. a turning of the intellect, by which one knows being as such, to particular beings of the world as present in human sensibility. "Intellectual knowing...is possible," writes Rahner, "only in an encounter with the material world (through sensibility)."[114] Again, in Rahner's words, "Spiritual knowing is possible only in an antecedent union of the intellectual act with the sentient act."[115]

In Rahner's view, accordingly, one cannot so much as ask the question of being, which presupposes a (logically) prior knowledge of being on the part of the questioner, without referring, at least implicitly, to a particular kind of sensible particulars, viz. "phantasms." Rahner also holds, however, that in every cognitive act, even if explicitly concerned exclusively with sensible particulars, the human being implicitly answers the question of being and so co-knows the being of beings itself. "Whenever we know anything," he writes, "we also possess an unexpressed...co-knowledge of being as the condition of every knowledge of single beings."[116] In Rahner's view, therefore, knowledge of earthly particulars is conditional on knowledge of being in its totality and vice versa.

ii. The unity of knowledge. In order to grasp the intrinsic possibility of this paradoxical unity of knowledge of the being of beings with knowledge of the particular things of the world, then, Rahner transposes the terms of the question. He writes:

What is united in this unity of knowledge? Knowledge of an existent in the world in its here and now and knowledge of being in its totality. If we say that sensibility is being with a thing in the here and now of the world, and that intellect is the knowledge of being in its totality, we can also say that it is a question of understanding the intrinsic possibility of the unity of sensibility and intellect.[117]

---

[113] A phantasm is "a formal determination of sensibility" that serves as "the *instrumental cause* of the agent intellect in spiritual knowing" (*Spirit*, 288–9; *Geist*, *SW* ii, 217).
[114] Ibid. 20; ebd. 27–8.
[115] Ibid. 279; ebd. 210.
[116] *Hearer*, 26; *Hörer*, *SW* iv, 56.
[117] *Spirit*, 66; *Geist*, *SW* ii, 60.

Next, in order to clarify the problem further, Rahner transposes the terms of the question again. "If we use the word *animality* instead of sensibility," he writes:

and *rationality* instead of intellect, then our question is about the unity of the rational and animal. Thomas treats this question formally in *In VII Metaph.* lect. 12. The question there is how genus (animal) and difference (rational) in the definition (rational animal) are one. They ought not to be thought of as two things which are grounded in themselves as their own possibility and come together only subsequently; in fact, they should not be considered as two "parts" of the human being in the first place. The genus already contains within itself the difference, just as that which is indeterminate, but which must be determined if it is to be at all, already contains its determination potentially.[118]

In other words, Rahner equates sensibility with animality and intellect with rationality in order to portray the unity of intellect and sensibility as analogous with that of genus and species. Now, a genus, although logically distinct from its various differences, cannot be instantiated without being determined by a specific difference. There are rational animals, viz. human beings, and there are irrational animals, viz. brute beasts; yet there are not and cannot be merely generic animals that neither possess understanding nor lack it.

In the real order, as Rahner recognizes, genus and difference are inseparable. It is not even admissible, as Rahner also notes, to distinguish between the two as parts of an individual. A human being is not part human and part animal, but entirely human and entirely animal, and so, Rahner concludes, an entirely sensible and entirely spiritual whole. "Neither sensibility nor thought as such," he writes:

can be met with in the concrete by itself; where they are found they are always already one...not in the sense [admittedly] that one could be reduced to or deduced from the other, but in the sense that each one is itself and different from the other only in its unity with the other.[119]

---

[118] Ibid.; ebd.

[119] Ibid. 67; ebd. 60–61. The cogency of Rahner's reasoning in this instance is somewhat questionable. For a real animal is not sensibility *simpliciter*, but a real being who possesses sensibility. Likewise, a rational being is not intellect *simpliciter*, but a real being who possesses an intellect. The identity of the animal and the rational being in the instance of a rational animal, therefore, implies only that the same being possesses both sensibility and intellect: not that the two might not constitute distinct parts of the same being. We are indebted for this argument to

This radical unity of intellect and sensibility implies, in Rahner's view, that one cannot adequately grasp the essence of human intelligence without simultaneously grasping the essence of human sensibility and vice versa. Since, then, "statements about sensibility and thought must be made one after the other, each further statement affects and modifies the sense of the previous statements. And all of them have their ultimate meaning only in the totality."[120] The permutations that the concepts of intellect and sensibility undergo in the remainder of our exposition bear out the wisdom of this recommendation.

iii. The knowability of being. The universal knowledge of being, which, in Rahner's view, human beings must possess in order merely to ask the question of the being of beings, implies that every being is intrinsically knowable and, in fact, at least partially known. "In view of the reality of the question about being," he writes, "the concept of a being unknowable in principle, in fact of a being even only factually (totally) unknown, is rejected as a contradiction. 'For whatever can be can be known.'"[121] This conclusion, which Rahner states rapidly and with little supporting argumentation in both *Geist in Welt* and *Hörer des Wortes*, seems to rest on at least three, distinct inferences. First, as we have seen, Rahner argues from the questionability of the being of beings as such to a universal, human knowledge of the being of beings. Second, Rahner reasons from human beings' universal knowledge of the being of beings to an imperfect knowledge in all human beings of all beings. Third and finally, Rahner reasons from human beings' actual, albeit incomplete, knowledge of all beings to all beings' inherent knowability.

The third conclusion manifestly follows from the second. The counterintuitive character of the second conclusion, however, might give one pause about the

---

Cornelio Fabro, *La svolta antropologica di Karl Rahner* (Problemi attuali; Milan: Rusconi, 1974²), 35–44.

[120] *Spirit*, 67; *Geist*, *SW* ii, 61.

[121] Ibid. 68; ebd. 62.

soundness of the first conclusion or the validity of the reasoning by which Rahner derives the second from the first. We shall defer critical evaluation, however, until after our summary of Rahner's gnoseology. In any event, it is crucial to note that, despite his paucity of argument on its behalf, the thesis that all beings are both knowable and known constitutes the key premise from which Rahner derives the chief principle of his ontology: that "being and knowing are the same."[122]

iv. The identity of being and knowing. The knowability of every being whatsoever, in Rahner's view, presupposes at least an original identity between being and knowledge. "Otherwise," Rahner writes:

> this relation of every being by itself to some knowledge might at most be a factual one, and not a feature of every being, belonging to the very nature of its being. An essential relation of correlativity between two states of affairs must, in final analysis, be founded in an original unity of both of them. For if they should be originally unconnected, i.e., if they were not by their very origin related to one another, their relation would never be necessary, but, at the most, factual and fortuitous.[123]

On the basis of this putative necessity, therefore, Rahner concludes that "being is *in itself* knowing, and knowing is the self-presence of being, inseparable from the makeup of being."[124] Again, in Rahner's words, "knowing is the being-present-to-self of being, and this being-present-to-self is the being of the existent."[125]

v. The analogy of being. Although this language is redolent of German idealism, Rahner sharply differentiates his metaphysics of knowledge from the idealistic systems of Fichte, Schelling, and Hegel. Anticipating the objection that he sympathizes overmuch with a panentheistic idealism, Rahner writes:

---

[122] Ibid. 69; ebd.
[123] *Hearer*, 29; *Hörer*, *SW* iv, 62.
[124] Ibid. 31; ebd. 66.
[125] *Spirit*, 69; *Geist*, *SW* ii, 62.

> If it belongs to the basic nature of being to be self-present, then it seems impossible that there may exist any being that is not at once knowing and known in identity. But then we have strayed into the basic assertion of the philosophy of German idealism, as it finds its peak in Hegel: Being and knowing are identical.[126]

In order to distance himself from the monism historically associated with this doctrine, Rahner returns to the starting point of his metaphysics, the question of the being of beings. The necessity with which human beings pose the question of being indicates, in his view, that human beings are not identical with being *simpliciter*; yet it would be absurd to conclude that they are not, therefore, beings. Rather, Rahner concludes, the human being "is deficient in its innermost ground of being."[127] Whereas God, the absolute being, is absolutely present to Godself, the human being, whose being is deficient, is only present to herself to the extent that she possesses being. In the case of the human being, Rahner writes, "Its intensity of being is finite, and therefore it must ask, therefore it is not absolutely present-to-itself."[128]

Only if Rahner allows a gradation of various intensities of being, it seems, can he reconcile the manifest variety of cognitive capacities, ranging from infinite to nil, in the universe of beings with the principle of the identity of being and knowing. He explicitly renounces, therefore, the notion of the univocity of being. "The concept of being itself," he writes, "proves to be variable in its content. It is not a univocally definable concept from which something unambiguous can be drawn,"[129] but rather a "fluctuating concept"[130] that encompasses manifold gradations of being and, therefore, of presence-to-self.

Rahner refines, moreover, the principle of the identity of being and knowing in order to take account of the radically analogous character of being. Now he asserts not merely that being is knowing, but that:

---

[126] *Hearer*, 35; *Hörer, SW* iv, 70, 72.
[127] *Spirit*, 72; *Geist, SW* ii, 64.
[128] Ibid.; ebd.
[129] Ibid.; ebd.
[130] *Hearer*, 37; *Hörer, SW* iv, 74.

the *degree* of self-presence, of luminosity for oneself, corresponds to the intensity of being, to the *degree* in which being belongs to some existent, to the *degree* in which, notwithstanding its non-being, a being shares in being. And the other way round: the degree of intensity of being shows in the degree in which the being in question is able to return into itself, in which it is capable, by reflecting upon itself, to be luminous for itself.[131]

Armed with this renovated principle of the proportional identity of being and knowing, then, Rahner answers the charge that his principles entail monistic conclusions. "True," he writes, "being is knowing. But only to the extent that a being is or has knowing. Now this being is an analogous concept....Hence not every being is 'knowing' or 'true' in the same sense and measure."[132] Rahner's principles thus allow for a radical diversity in grades of being and presence-to-self in the universe.

vi. Matter. One might object, nevertheless, that regardless of Rahner's success in accounting for diversity in presence-to-self among beings, his principles seem incapable of accommodating the existence of beings that are incapable of knowing. Rahner attempts to deflect this objection, however, by positing the existence of matter. "If," he writes:

according to experience...there is a being that does not know in any way, hence is in no way present-to-itself, then the being of this existent itself cannot be present-to-itself, it cannot belong to itself, it must be the being of "another." This "other" must on the one hand be real, but on the other hand it cannot have being in itself and of itself. This empty, in itself indeterminate "wherein"...of the being of an existent, in which a being is in such a way that it is not for itself but for that, and so is not "present-to-itself," is called...prime matter.[133]

In other words, the proportional identity of being and being's presence to itself need not preclude the existence of unintelligent creatures if it is permissible to posit the existence of a "wherein" in which the presence-to-self inherent in the being of unintelligent creatures disperses itself so that these creatures are not present to themselves, but to this "wherein." This "wherein," this "empty,

---

[131] Ibid.; ebd.
[132] Ibid. 39; ebd. 78.
[133] *Spirit*, 74; *Geist*, *SW* ii, 66.

undetermined possibility of being, really distinct from it,"[134] absorbs presence-to-self, as it were, so that presence-to-self increases proportionally with the degree of immateriality one naturally possesses.[135]

We include the word "naturally" in this assertion, incidentally, to distinguish Rahner's position from the absurd view that human beings could attain complete self-presence if only they could sever all relations with their bodies. In Rahner's view, rather, the human soul possesses merely potential self-presence on account of its finitude and, therefore, emanates materiality in order to gain self-presence *via* actual encounter with material beings. In his words:

> Human beings are spirits in such a way that, in order to become spirit, we enter...into otherness, into matter, and so into the world....Our human spirit is *receptive—anima tabula rasa—*and because of this receptivity, this spirit needs, as its own, indispensable means, produced by itself, a sense power [= among other things, a material medium in which it can encounter the material other] through which it may strive toward its own goal, the grasping of being as such.[136]

Although Rahner does conceive of matter as an index of the finitude of human beings, then, he does not regard matter as a cause of this finitude; indeed, he characterizes the body as a means employed by the human spirit to realize itself through self-transcendence towards common being. It seems, accordingly, that Rahner can reconcile the principle of the identity of being and knowing with the real existence of unknowing beings by positing the existence of matter.

c. Transcendental reduction. Having thus rebutted the charge that he narrows the range of beings to that of conscious beings, Rahner proceeds to address another, more substantial objection to his metaphysics of knowledge. It not at all clear how a human being can know anything other than herself if she can know, at least as proper object, only that which she herself is. Yet, as Rahner recognizes, "if being is primarily presence-to-self, then the real and original object of a

---

[134] *Hearer*, 101; *Hörer*, *SW* iv, 186.
[135] Cf. *Spirit*, 371; *Geist*, *SW* ii, 275. Cf. Maréchal's *Le point de départ de la métaphysique 5: Le Thomisme devant la philosophie critique* (ML.P 7; Brussels: L'Édition universelles, 1949²), 119.
[136] *Hearer*, 106; *Hörer*, *SW* iv, 194.

knowing being is that which it originally is: itself."[137] Rahner seeks, therefore, to determine how the other can constitute the first object of human knowledge by identifying the transcendental conditions of human knowledge of the other.

    i. Materiality. "If," Rahner reasons:

> only that which the knower itself is is known as proper object, and if, nevertheless, there is to be a knowledge in which this known as proper object is the other, then both of these can be understood as simultaneously possible only by the fact that *the knower itself is the being of the other.* The being of what intuits receptively must be the being of another as such.[138]

The knower who intuits receptively, in other words, must possess the capacity to become the being of another and, therefore, to be present, not to herself, but to this other. She must accomplish this, however, without so alienating herself from herself that something extrinsic to herself would become identical with the other rather than she. The knower, to state the matter simply, must be capable of presence-to-another without ceasing to be herself.

Such a feat is conceivable, Rahner holds, under two conditions. First, the other with which the knower becomes identical must belong to the ontological constitution of the knower herself. "This absolutely other," Rahner writes, "to which a being must be given away from the outset if it is to be able to have a receptive intuition of a definite other at all, must...be a real principle of the knower."[139] Second, however, this other must not consist in being, and therefore self-presence, *per se*; it "cannot itself have being in and of itself."[140] For, if it possessed being and so presence-to-itself of itself, Rahner claims, then the knower, by becoming identical with it, would experience presence-to-self rather than presence-to-another and so fail to experience the other precisely as other from itself. If the other possessed being in and of itself, Rahner writes:

---

[137] *Spirit*, 75; *Geist*, SW ii, 66.
[138] Ibid. 79; ebd. 70. Cf. Maréchal, *Le point de départ*, 110–21.
[139] *Spirit*, 80; *Geist*, SW ii, 70.
[140] Ibid.; ebd.

as being it would itself fall under the law that being means being-present-to-self. That being of the knower which would belong to another which exists of itself would then be conscious precisely as the being of that which is in itself present to itself, in other words, another *as such* could not be had in consciousness in this way.[141]

In sum, Rahner holds that the other with which a receptive knower becomes one must be intrinsic to the knower herself and yet not present-to-itself. Rahner recognizes, moreover, that that which is real, and yet is not present-to-itself, and yet constitutes, nonetheless, an "empty, indeterminate 'wherein'"[142] in which being that is not present to itself may be present to another, is nothing other than matter. "*That real non-being*," he writes, "*as the being in which a being is separated from itself, is called...prime matter.*"[143]

ii. *The sensible species.* Rahner holds, then, that the human person possesses a material principle of otherness by which she has always already invaded the empty "wherein" of matter. This principle, which Rahner designates "sensibility," does not, admittedly, in and of itself suffice to bring the human being to a real intuition of a distinct being. It does, however, supply a medium in which an external, material object can manifest itself to the human being.

Such a manifestation occurs, if it occurs at all, by means of a sensible species: sc. "a determination which the [intuited] thing produces as its own in that and insofar as it remains in the medium of sensibility."[144] This determination belongs to the reality of the intuited thing, in Rahner's view, only insofar as its being is dispersed in the matter of sensibility. In Rahner's words:

the ontological actuality which the object brings as its own into the medium of sensibility...is not simply and absolutely that which belonged to it before it became identical [*qua* species] with the

---

[141] Ibid.; ebd.
[142] Ibid. 74; ebd. 66.
[143] Ibid. 80; ebd. 70.
[144] Ibid. 88; ebd. 76.

sensibility but means a new self-actualization of the object through which the object has an influence upon sensibility.[145]

The species, then, begins to exist only when the intuited being projects itself into sensibility. In this medium alone, likewise, the species attains a consciousness of sorts. "The sense in act is the sensible in act," writes Rahner, "because on the basis of the general proposition about the identity of knowing and the actually known, what is actually knowable is by that very fact actually knowing."[146]

By the last statement, it is important to emphasize, Rahner does not mean to ascribe sentience *tout court* to the objects of human sensibility. Rather, he stipulates, first, that the sensible species can attain consciousness only in the medium of sensibility. The sensible object, he writes, "in this medium (and only in it) acquires...that intensity of being which implies consciousness."[147] Second, Rahner asserts, sensibility bestows on the sensible species that degree of being that implies consciousness. "The intensity of being which makes the self-realization of the sensible object in the medium of sensibility actually sensible must be bestowed upon it by sensibility itself."[148]

Rahner's views on the self-realization of material beings in human sensibility, therefore, seem quite remote from panpsychism. This is not to say, however, that his theory of sensibility entails no apparently paradoxical consequences. For, as Rahner recognizes, if the sensible species is to be simultaneously conscious and ontologically continuous with the object perceived, the selfsame species must constitute both the actuality of human sensibility and the actuality of the object perceived. As he explains:

on the one hand, the species, which is the actuality of the object itself, must be produced by the sentient knower herself, because otherwise it would not possess the intensity of being that implies

---

[145] Ibid.; ebd.
[146] Ibid. 93; ebd. 80.
[147] Ibid. 94; ebd.
[148] Ibid.; ebd. 81.

self-reflection; and, on the other hand, the species must be the self-realization of the sensible object itself, because otherwise this would not be intuited in its own self.[149]

One can account for the identity of the actuality of these two, ordinarily vastly differing entities, viz. human sensibility and the object sensed, Rahner argues, only if the following two assumptions hold true: a) that "a passive reception by the one receiving intrinsically includes, as such a reception, a production of this determination by the one receiving";[150] and b) that "a transient influence upon another as patient is also and essentially always a self-realization of the agent in the medium of the patient."[151] These claims, as we shall attempt to demonstrate in the next two sections, are roughly equivalent to the following: 1) all beings formally cause all determinations they receive from external, efficient causes; and 2) the action of every inner-worldly, efficient cause constitutes an exercise of intrinsic formal/material causality. The plausibility of Rahner's theory of human, sensible intuition, therefore, seems ultimately to depend on whether one can reasonably assert that every determination from without which a material being receives has two formal causes: the patient that receives the determination and the agent that effects it.

iii. Substantial forms and their determinations. The notion that the human body might be sustained by a substantial form distinct from the human soul appears absurd once one equates the referent of "body," considered in abstraction from the soul, with prime matter: an empty, indeterminate possibility of being that is precisely not being itself. Rahner, who takes this view of the subject, asserts, accordingly, that the human person possesses no actuality whatsoever that is not the actuality of the soul. In his words:

Whatever actuality of a material kind belongs to the human person is completely the actuality of the soul which enters into the empty potency of prime matter, and it does not receive this actuality

---

[149] Ibid. 92; ebd. 79. Cf. Maréchal, *Le point de départ*, 110–12.
[150] *Spirit*, 94; *Geist*, *SW* ii, 81.
[151] Ibid. 97; ebd. 82.

from the matter, although it can produce its own actuality only in matter and as the actuality of matter....Hence, every determination of an existent, even accidental determinations, is a determination of the substance insofar as it emanates from the substantial, continually and actively producing ground.[152]

Again, writes Rahner, "Something can be a determination of an existent only by the fact that it is produced by the substantial, ontological ground of the determined existent itself."[153] These conclusions, which do seem to follow from Rahner's conception of the soul as form of prime matter, imply, somewhat counterintuitively, that neither the soul nor any other form can suffer determination, at least in the strict sense of the term, by an external agent. "With regard to its form," Rahner asserts, "an existent cannot in principle suffer, in the sense of being determined by an inner-worldly cause."[154]

It is manifest, however, that some inner-worldly agents modify other existents. Such modification, Rahner reasons, is conceivable only if, and because, these existents consist not merely in form, but also in matter. If, that is to say, a being consists not merely in actuality, but also in a passive principle of potentiality, then an external influence could conceivably inhere in an existent without being a determination of the existent's form. Naturally, if the influence continued to inhere in the material aspect of a being, it would eventually modify it; it would do so, however, without determining the form as such, but rather by altering the disposition of the matter into which the form pours its actuality. In Rahner's words, "The 'giving-itself-out-of-itself-into-matter' of the form...*is* already essentially its being-determined by the matter....Thus the form 'suffers'...only by the fact that it actively informs."[155]

Rahner's thesis that forms necessarily actuate all of their determinations, therefore, in no way conflicts with the obvious truth that material agents determine the being of material patients. Unless one rejects Rahner's definition

---

[152] Ibid. 324–5; ebd. 242.
[153] Ibid. 341; ebd. 253.
[154] Ibid.; ebd.
[155] Ibid. 355; ebd. 263.

of matter or the unity of substantial forms, then, it seems unreasonable to deny Rahner's first assumption.

The second assumption, moreover, appears to follow straightforwardly from the first. For if each of a being's acts constitutes a determination of the acting being; and the form of each being sustains all of its determinations *via* formal causality; then every act on the part of any being must consist, at least partially, in an exercise of formal causality. Rahner concludes, accordingly, that every act of efficient causality in which a material agent influences a material patient consists in an act of formal/material causality. "The efficient causality of an agent causing from without," he explains:

> is only a tripartite mode of *intrinsic* causality. For, on the one hand, this efficient causality presents itself as a peculiar mode of a formal causality: the action as self-realization of the agent itself....On the other hand, it forms at the same time the specific mode of a material causality: the determinable matter of the patient as the "wherein" of the self-realization of the agent. And finally, it contains once again the aspect of a formal causality: the active self-realization of the patient as the actualization of precisely this matter.[156]

Given the assumption that one and the same modification of one substance by another can constitute the product of formal causality exercised by each of the substances, however, Rahner's claim that the sensible species in human sensation consists in the actuality of both the human knower and the object known no longer appears absurd. To the extent that Rahner does, indeed, establish that the inherence of such a species in human sensibility is prerequisite to human beings' intuition of material others, then, he seems successfully to identify the transcendental conditions of human sensation.

iv. The objectivity of knowledge. Nevertheless, Rahner himself denies that the human capacity for sensation suffices to account for the human being's ability to ask the question of being. For when the human person "asks about being in its totality," Rahner writes, "she places it in question comprehensively and in its

---

[156] Ibid. 357; ebd. 265.

totality (and thereby herself), and by doing this she places herself as the one asking in sharp relief against all the rest."[157]

Sensibility, however, which attains its end precisely by identifying itself with the objects of human knowledge, can hardly liberate human beings from subject-object unity. "Sensibility," asserts Rahner, "can...receptively accept the other, because it *is* the other, but it...cannot differentiate itself ontologically from the other."[158] Rahner, after unearthing *a priori* conditions for human intuition of material others, thus continues to probe for the conditions that enable human beings to pose the question of being. In order to grasp this question's possibility, Rahner explains, one must also account for:

> the capacity of the one human knowledge to place the other, which is given in sensibility, away from itself and in question, to judge it, to objectify it and thereby to make the knower a subject for the first time, that is, one who is present to herself and not to the other, one who knowingly exists in herself.[159]

Rahner, accordingly, first identifies and describes the elements of the human being's return to herself, which he designates "abstraction"; second, identifies and characterizes the "agent intellect" that accomplishes this abstraction; and, third, infers the existence of an athematic horizon of human intelligence that enables the agent intellect to effect a conscious distinction between the human knower and the objects of her intuition.

v. Abstraction. Rahner investigates abstraction under the rubrics of what he considers its three crucial moments: the universal concept, judgment, and truth. The term, "universal concept," in Rahner's parlance, signifies "the 'what' of a possible something,...a known intelligibility able to be synthesized with a possible subject."[160] Such a concept, he maintains, will inevitably metamorphose

---

[157] Ibid. 117; ebd. 98.
[158] Ibid. 226; ebd. 173. Cf. Maréchal, *Le point de départ*, 128.
[159] *Spirit*, 118; *Geist*, *SW* ii, 98–9.
[160] Ibid. 123; ebd. 102.

into a "this," sc. a mere subject that instantiates some universal concept, if it does not always already contain within itself a reference to potential subjects. "Just when the known content of the universal concept is supposed to be thought of by itself (for example, 'color' as such, independent of a possible colored thing)," he writes, "the universal concept is made into an individual thing which is itself again a synthesis of a universal and a subject."[161]

This is the case, Rahner maintains, because all knowledge whatsoever presupposes a conversion to the phantasm: i.e. an at least mediate reference to the singular existent apprehended in sensibility. Though such a conversion might appear superfluous to reasoning about universal concepts, Rahner insists that "all of these universalities too must always be thought of in a conversion."[162] As he explains:

> We apprehend the universal itself as object of our thought precisely when it is conceived *as universal*...in a concretizing conversion of the second order,...[i.e.] as an object which again is itself intrinsically structured as a known real object. Our known intelligibilities are similarly formed in all cases, and they are universal or concrete only by the fact that they are either related immediately and as such to the concrete thing given in sensibility, or only mediately. The singular concept always already contains in itself a universal ("this thing of this kind"), and the universal as such is still related to a "this" ("the kind of this thing"), or is itself conceived as a "this of this kind."[163]

This necessary reference of the universal concept to a possible subject lends to the universal concept itself the character of a possible synthesis, which Rahner refers to as a "concretizing" synthesis. It is "the possible synthesis of a universal with any 'this' at all."[164]

As Rahner conceives of it, then, the concretizing synthesis is in and of itself merely potential and bereft of any determinate reference. It receives both actuality and particularity of reference, however, in the judgment, or "affirmative synthesis," in which, Rahner asserts, the human being refers the quiddity of the

---

[161] Ibid. 121; ebd. 100.
[162] Ibid.; ebd. 101.
[163] Ibid.; ebd.
[164] Ibid. 124; ebd. 103.

concretizing synthesis to a particular subject distinct from the knower. "The concretizing synthesis," writes Rahner, "as possible is converted into one actually realized, insofar as it is no longer any 'this' at all that is held before the concretizing synthesis..., but that supposite already determined by the subject of the [judgmental] proposition."[165] Only in the judgment, then, does the concretizing synthesis become real and not merely potential; "*a concretizing synthesis occurs in real thought only as an affirmative synthesis.*"[166]

Only in the judgment, likewise, does the intellect attain truth. For, in Rahner's view, "truth is primarily a state of having reality before one in judgment, the process of applying the concretizing synthesis...to the reality as it is in itself";[167] and this is precisely what judgment accomplishes. Judgment, accordingly, seems to constitute the decisive moment in the human knower's liberating self-differentiation from the objects of her knowledge: the human being's return to self.

vi. The agent intellect. Having described the process whereby the human being returns into herself, Rahner proceeds to scrutinize its *a priori* condition of possibility: "the capacity to differentiate what is known universally from another existent, and by doing this to make possible for the first time an objectifying reference, by the knower, of the knowing to what is meant."[168] This capacity Rahner terms "agent intellect."

In order to apprehend a universal concept and thus achieve the first indication of abstractive presence-to-self, Rahner reasons, the agent intellect must enable the human being to derive from the material things of the world some universal intelligibility. Such intelligibility, in Rahner's view, lies latent in all material individuals insofar as a universal quiddity, i.e. a nature that can be instantiated in

---

[165] Ibid. 125; ebd.
[166] Ibid.; ebd.
[167] "Thomas Aquinas on Truth," *TI* xiii, 30; "Die Wahrheit bei Thomas von Aquin," *SW* ii, 316.
[168] *Spirit*, 134; *Geist*, *SW* ii, 110.

many individuals, appears as concretized by matter in every object of sensible perception. The role of the agent intellect, therefore, is to liberate the universal quiddity from its confinement in the matter of a particular thing.

Rahner cautions, however, that this "liberation" does not consist in a real, or even an intentional, detachment of the quiddity from materiality. "For if we wanted to...assume that there is question of an actual liberation...of the form from matter," he writes, "then abstraction would become intrinsically contradictory. For the form of a material thing as being and as known is intrinsically and essentially related to a 'this.'"[169] The agent intellect thus liberates the universal quiddity from matter not by abrogating its intrinsic reference to matter, but by manifesting the limitation of the universal form in the perceived material individual. "The form," writes Rahner, "must be known as limited by the 'this' whose form it is; only then can it be known that it is 'broader' in itself and so able to be related to other 'this's,'"[170] which is what Rahner means by universality.

The mere knowledge of the confinement of a quiddity in a material individual suffices to convey to the knower that the quiddity can be concretized in multiple instances, Rahner holds, because the agent intellect transcends the material object of sensibility so as to become athematically aware of a wider horizon of possibilities. "We must...ask," he writes:

how the agent intellect is to be understood so that it can understand the form as limited, confined, and thus as of itself embracing further possibilities in itself, as bordering upon a broader field of possibilities. Obviously this is possible only if, antecedent to and in addition to apprehending the individual form, it comprehends of itself the whole field of these possibilities and thus, in the sensibly concretized form, experiences the concreteness as limitation of these possibilities, whereby it knows the form itself as able to be multiplied in this field.[171]

The fundamental act of the agent intellect, which Rahner designates the *Vorgriff*, accomplishes the human being's abstractive return to herself, in other

---

[169] Ibid. 139; ebd. 113.
[170] Ibid. 140; ebd. 114.
[171] Ibid. 142; ebd. 115–16.

words, by stretching forth towards an unobjectivated horizon whose expanse exceeds the range of any sensible act of perception.

vii. The Woraufhin of the Vorgriff. This horizon, or *Woraufhin*, of the *Vorgriff*, inasmuch as it constitutes a condition of all objective, human knowing, must embrace all possible objects of human knowledge. Nevertheless, Rahner maintains, it cannot itself consist in an object or set of objects. For, Rahner asserts, "every represented object of human knowledge...is able to be apprehended itself only in a *Vorgriff*. If the *Vorgriff* itself attained to an object..., then this *Vorgriff* itself would again be conditioned by another *Vorgriff*."[172] If the *Vorgriff's Woraufhin* were an object, in other words, an infinite regress would ensue.

Rahner insists, however, that this *Woraufhin* cannot consist in mere nothingness. For, although a *Vorgriff* to nothingness might reveal the finitude of the sensible object perceived, it could never disclose the wider possibilities of the object's quiddity. A *Vorgriff* to nothingness, therefore, could not supply the human knower with a universal quiddity: the predicate of that affirmative synthesis whereby she distinguishes herself from the world.

If it is to ground the human knower's return to herself from her immersion in sensibility, Rahner holds, the *Vorgriff* must attain to quiddities. "What is 'form,'" he writes, "in other words, predicate in the affirmative and not merely concretizing synthesis, is what is first and fundamentally liberated [abstracted]."[173] Forms themselves, however are, in Rahner's view, mere limiting potencies for being or *esse*. Since, then: a) the form is objectified only in an affirmative synthesis in which one ascribes existence (*esse*) to some object at least logically distinguished from oneself; and b) the form itself, as potency for *esse*, cannot be conceived of without reference to *esse*; Rahner concludes that human

---

[172] Ibid. 143; ebd. 116.
[173] Ibid. 155; ebd. 124–5.

knowledge of forms presupposes a (logically) antecedent knowledge of *esse*. "The abstraction of *esse*," he writes, "is the condition of the possibility of the abstraction of form."[174]

The *Woraufhin* of the *Vorgriff*, then, is *esse*. This *esse*, it is important to note, does not consist in mere "entity" bereft of all determinations, the featureless being that Hegel identifies with nothingness[175] and Rahner designates *ens commune*. Unlike *esse*, writes Rahner, *ens commune*:

> is already a something that comes to be through a concretizing synthesis of *esse* with a quiddity emptied of all more precise determination, with an entity (as a material form). The word "entity," denoting the emptiest quiddity, could be translated as "any-quiddity." By this concretion *esse* is already limited in the sharpest way conceivable, so that determinations can be added to *ens commune*...in such a way that *ens commune* becomes thereby richer and fuller. Thus it is understood why among all concrete things, the merely existing (*aliquid, ens commune*) is the most imperfect, the emptiest.[176]

Rahner conceives of *esse*, by contrast, as the richest, fullest concept. "*Esse* itself," he observes:

> must be the absolute ground of all determinations: it is in itself "of all things the most perfect," fuller than anything else that can be thought of with a particular determination. It is in itself "the actuality of every form," "the actuality of every thing," the unified, generative ground of every conceivable quidditative determination.[177]

When one ascribes *esse* to an object in an affirmative synthesis, Rahner emphasizes, one ascribes this universal *esse* and not merely *esse* as contracted by the potency of a single quiddity. The knower who judges that the sky is blue, for example, ascribes to the sky an *esse* that contains within itself multiple quidditative determinations: skyness and blueness. She ascribes to the subject of an affirmative synthesis, that is to say, an *esse* that sustains multiple formal

---

[174] Ibid. 170; ebd. 135.
[175] *Wissenschaft der Logik 1: Die Lehre vom Sein* (ed. Friedrich Hogemann und Walter Jaeschke; Gesammelte Werke 21; Hamburg: Meiner, 1984), §132–4.
[176] *Spirit*, 176; *Geist*, *SW* ii, 139.
[177] Ibid. 177; ebd. 140.

determinations and thereby exhibits a universality that transcends the universality of form.

A knower may ascribe *esse* to two objects that share no quidditative notes in common, therefore, and, nonetheless, affirm precisely the same thing of each insofar as she predicates of each universal *esse*. "Insofar as all possible quidditative determinations are real through *esse*," writes Rahner, "in every judgment the same *esse* is *vorgreift*, in every judgment the same *esse* is simultaneously known."[178] The *Woraufhin* of the *Vorgriff*, consequently, must consist not merely in *esse* as limited by particular forms, but in *esse* as the original, united fullness of all forms cognizable by human beings.

d. Transcendental deduction. Through a process of transcendental reduction, Rahner thus locates the *a priori* conditions of human knowledge, or presence-to-self, in two aspects of the human being: sensibility and the agent intellect. Sensibility forms the human being's principle of otherness, that whereby she can unite herself with other material beings, as she must if she is to gain presence-to-self through knowledge of another. Agent intellect, by contrast, constitutes the principle whereby the human person distinguishes herself from the other to which she is united in sensibility by ascribing a universal quiddity to it in a judgment. The means by which the human being acquires this universal quiddity Rahner identifies as a *Vorgriff* by the agent intellect of an athematic horizon of *esse* from which it derives the formalities that it refers to a sensible object, thus accomplishing the human being's return to herself.

i. The expanse of the Woraufhin. It remains, therefore, to determine, *via* a transcendental deduction, the range of objects knowable to a human subject. One can determine this range precisely, it seems, only to the extent that one can discern the limits, if any, of the *esse* pre-grasped in the *Vorgriff*. The knowledge

---

[178] Ibid.; ebd.

that this *esse* transcends all, or virtually all, humanly knowable forms does not suffice to satisfy this inquiry, because the question is precisely which those forms are that are knowable, or perhaps unknowable, to a human being.

It might seem logical, Rahner realizes, to identify the *esse vorgreift* by human beings as that of material, and therefore divisible, being. This kind of being, *ens principium numeri*, is precisely co-extensive with the range of what Rahner regards as the primary object of the human intellect: the quiddities of material things. Rahner insists, nonetheless, that the *esse vorgreift* by human beings must be infinite, and defends his position by the following two arguments.

First, Rahner maintains, if one asserts that the *Vorgriff* attains to anything less than infinite *esse*, she implicitly asserts thereby that its *Woraufhin* is nothingness. "If the *Vorgriff* itself were to reveal the intrinsic finiteness of being," he writes, "this would be possible only by the fact that it 'pre-grasps' nothing."[179] For, in Rahner's view, one can speak of the *Woraufhin* of the *Vorgriff* only to the extent that she treats it as if it were an ordinary, cognitive object. Again, in Rahner's words:

when a condition of the possibility of objective knowledge is thematically made the object of a reflexive knowledge, this can only be done by this reflective knowledge itself subjecting itself to all the conditions of human knowledge. But among them [the conditions] belongs the concretion of the known "what" [the quiddity] with a something of which this "what" is affirmed in a conversion to the phantasm. In other words, the *Woraufhin* of the *Vorgriff*, if it is to be spoken of explicitly, must be conceived (designated) as an object, although not meant (affirmed) as such.[180]

A knower can distinguish herself from a cognitive object, either of the first or the second order, however, only insofar as she ascribes a quiddity to it in an affirmative synthesis; and she can ascribe a quiddity to an object only to the extent that she apprehends it in the context of a *Vorgriff* to some wider *Woraufhin*. In order to judge the *Woraufhin* finite, that is to say, one must apprehend it in the context of a larger *Woraufhin*.

---

[179] Ibid. 184–5; ebd. 145.
[180] Ibid. 143–4; ebd. 116–17.

The *Woraufhin* that one would judge finite constitutes, *ex hypothesi*, the totality of the possible objects of human cognition in their original unity. The only *Woraufhin* that could contain this all-encompassing *Woraufhin* within itself, it seems, would be an absolute void: nothingness. A human being can distinguish herself from a cognitive object, however, only to the extent that she can apprehend it as one among many possible instantiations of a quiddity; and she can so apprehend the object only within a *Woraufhin* whose *esse* exceeds that of the object itself.

One can judge the *Woraufhin* of the *Vorgriff* finite, then, only by conceiving of it as nothingness; yet a *Vorgriff* to nothingness would not suffice to enable one to judge it finite. The act of asserting the *Woraufhin* to be finite, and consequently nothing, in other words, involves the one who so asserts in a contradiction of a presupposition of the act whereby she asserts: viz. that the being of the *Woraufhin* exceeds the being of the subject of her assertion. "The...assumption...that *esse* [i.e. the *esse vorgreift* by the agent intellect] is intrinsically finite," Rahner writes, "goes against the implicit supposition of the assumption itself, which expresses a *Vorgriff* of *esse* and not of nothing."[181]

In this argument, Rahner emphasizes, he does not contend that the very concept of a finite *esse* is incoherent and that, therefore, the *esse vorgreift* by the agent intellect must be infinite. Such a contention, he writes, "would fall into the paralogism of the Anselmian argument for the existence of God."[182] Rahner argues, rather, by retorsion; sc. he argues that one cannot deny his conclusion without implicitly affirming it in the very act of denial. To this retorsive argument, then, Rahner appends a second rationale in *modus tollens*. He reasons:

1. If the *esse vorgreift* by the agent intellect were finite, this finitude would manifest itself in human consciousness.

---

[181] Ibid. 185; ebd. 145.
[182] Ibid.; ebd.

2. No such finitude manifests itself; therefore

3. The *esse vorgreift* by the agent intellect must, therefore, be infinite.

Insofar as Rahner's previous argument suffices to remove a *Vorgriff* to nothingness from serious consideration, the soundness of this argument seems to hinge on the truth of its first premise. In defense of this premise, accordingly, Rahner proffers a disjunctive argument. If the *Woraufhin* were finite, he asserts, it would consist in either: a) being in its totality as finite; or b) a segment of being in its totality. In the first case, Rahner asserts, a *Vorgriff* would necessarily transcend the postulated finite totality of being into nothingness. In this case, he writes:

It is not intelligible how there could be a *Vorgriff* of being in its totality without it manifesting itself as finite, since the supposition is that it is finite even in its totality, and without it being comprehended in its totality by the fact that the *Vorgriff* goes beyond the totality to nothing.[183]

In the second case, he asserts, the *Vorgriff's Woraufhin* would constitute the particular subject of a universal quiddity. As such, it would lack the capacity to ground human knowledge of such quiddities. Since he originally posited the existence of the *Vorgriff* in order to account for human knowledge of universal forms, Rahner reasons, the second assumption renders the very idea of a *Vorgriff* otiose. "The *Vorgriff* as such," he writes, "cannot attain to an object which is of the same kind as that whose knowledge it is supposed to make possible."[184] He concludes, accordingly, that the finitude of the *esse vorgreift* by the agent intellect could not be unconscious if this *esse* were, indeed, finite; b) that no such finitude is conscious; and c) that the *esse* pre-grasped in the *Vorgriff* must, therefore, be infinite.

---

[183] Ibid.; ebd. 146.
[184] Ibid. 186; ebd.

ii. The knowability of God. The infinite *esse* that one "pre-grasps" in the *Vorgriff*, Rahner holds, cannot be simply and undialectically identical with the absolute being, God. For, in order to enable the human knower to recognize the repeatability of particular concretions of material forms, the *esse vorgreift* by the agent intellect must contain at least virtually the essences of finite entities. It must, accordingly, be susceptible of limitation so that human beings can co-know finite, albeit universal, quiddities through it.

In Rahner's words:

> The *esse* apprehended in the *Vorgriff*...[is] known implicitly and simultaneously as able to be limited by quidditative determinations and as already limited, since the *Vorgriff*, if it is not to be a "grasp" (*Griff*), can only be realized in a simultaneous conversion to a definite form limiting *esse*....Hence insofar as this *esse* simultaneously apprehended in the *Vorgriff* is able to be limited, it shows itself to be non-absolute, since an absolute necessarily excludes the possibility of a limitation.[185]

Rahner refers to the *esse* to which the *Vorgriff* attains, then, not as *esse absolutum*, but as *esse commune*: that *esse* which contains all limited instantiations of *esse* virtually within itself. Now, Rahner reasons, when one predicates *esse commune* of a particular object in an affirmative synthesis, one co-affirms the existence of *esse commune* itself and thereby implicitly co-affirms the possible existence of anything that might appear within the horizon of *esse commune*. In the affirmative synthesis, writes Rahner, "any possible object which can come to exist in the breadth of the *Vorgriff* is simultaneously affirmed."[186]

Since the *Woraufhin* of the *Vorgriff*, viz. *esse commune*, is negatively infinite, then; it seems to Rahner that human beings, by implicitly affirming the full range of possible actualizations of this *esse*, co-affirm not merely the possibility of an infinity of limited concretizations of *esse commune*. Human beings also, in Rahner's view, co-affirm the possibility of a being in whom the fullness of being, indicated by *esse commune*, is actualized in a single instance. In co-affirming the

---

[185] Ibid. 180–1; ebd. 142.
[186] Ibid. 181; ebd. 143.

existence of *esse commune*, that is to say, human beings also co-affirm at least the possibility of *esse absolutum*.

Absolute being, however, if it existed at all, would exist necessarily. Rahner concludes, accordingly, that when the human knower co-affirms the possibility of all instantiations of *esse commune*, she simultaneous co-affirms the actuality, and not merely the possibility, of *esse absolutum*. "An absolute being," writes Rahner, "would completely fill up the breadth of this *Vorgriff*. Hence it is simultaneously affirmed as real (since it cannot be grasped as merely possible)."[187]

Rahner insists, however, that his gnoseological proof of the existence of God does not imply that human beings can intuit the divine being directly. "Insofar as in human knowledge, which alone is accessible to philosophy, the *Vorgriff* is always broader than the grasp of an object itself..., nothing," he asserts, "can be decided philosophically about the possibility of an immediate apprehension of absolute *esse* as an object of the first order."[188] Rahner does not compromise the supernaturality of the beatific vision, therefore, by constructing a putative proof of its objective possibility. Rather, he portrays the human person as a being naturally aware of God and, therefore, perhaps open to a supernatural fulfillment: one whose nature in no way anticipates the revelatory self-communication of God and, precisely for that reason, may receive it as a marvel of divine grace.

3. Criticisms. Rahner's metaphysics of knowledge, then, constitutes an imposing edifice that appears largely free from obvious defects. Before concluding this chapter, however, we should like to level two brief criticisms. First, Rahner's argument from the knowledge of all beings, which he ascribes to human beings, to the knowability of all beings seems premature at best. For it is by no means obvious that a human being's knowledge of being in general

---

[187] Ibid.; ebd.
[188] Ibid.; ebd.

involves a knowledge of every individual being in particular; and if one does not know that the human being knows every being, one can hardly infer the knowability of all beings from the human being's putative knowledge. First, Rahner seems to err when he characterizes the *Vorgriff* as an essential moment in human beings' acquisition of conscious distinctness from the objects of their experience. For the suffering of sensibility, when coupled with the intellect's inference that this suffering originates in something other than itself, appears abundantly sufficient to bring the subject-object distinction to thematic awareness.

Second, Rahner's inference of the identity of being and knowing from the knowability of all beings constitutes a patent *non sequitur*. A claim of such architectonic importance for Rahner's philosophy and theology as his identification of being and knowing merits more extensive argumentation. This identification, third, appears positively problematic insofar as it implies that a finite being is at least proportionally identical with one of its acts. For, as Aquinas explains:

> the action of an angel is not its being, neither is the action of any creature its being. For the genus of action is twofold.... One kind of action is that which passes into something exterior, inflicting passion on it: e.g. burning and cutting. Another kind of action...is that which does not pass into an exterior thing, but remains in the agent itself: e.g. sensing, understanding, and willing....It is manifest that the first kind of action cannot be the very being of the agent. For the being of the agent is...within the agent itself. Such action, however, is an *effluxus* from the agent into the act. The second kind of action, moreover, has infinity of its own nature, either simply or *secundum quid*. Such actions have as understanding, whose object is the true, and willing, whose object is the good, either of which [object] is convertible [or co-extensive] with being, have infinity simply...Knowing and understanding...are related to all things, and each also receives its species from its object. Sensing, moreover, is infinite *secundum quid*, because it is related to all things sensible, as sight is related to all things visible. The being of any creature, however, is limited to one genus and one species [*STh* I, 54, 2 corp.].

In other words, if a being consisted in one of its acts, such as its act of knowing, the constitution of the being itself would expand beyond the limits of its particular species. Admittedly, Rahner sometimes makes comments, which suggest that this implication does not trouble him. He writes, for instance, that "the very definition of the human person is her indefinability, i.e. precisely her transcendence as absolute openness to being in the absolute." [189] A metaphysical thesis that entails the infinite plasticity of all human and angelic subjects, however, surely strains credulity.

4. Conclusion. Rahner's philosophy, then, consists largely in a transcendentally grounded ontology of knowing, which, by virtue of Rahner's identification of being and knowledge, branches into metaphysics as well. It suffers from substantial limitations, however, in that two of its most central theses, viz. that objective human knowledge presupposes a *Vorgriff* to common being and that being and knowing are identical, appear, respectively, unfounded and implausible.

III. OUTLOOK

In the coming chapters, we hope to demonstrate the relevance of these conclusions to the evaluation of Rahner's theology of the Trinity. In particular, we should like, in Chapter 2, to outline Rahner's conception of revelation in general and then to discuss, in some detail, Rahner's *Grundaxiom*, "The economic Trinity *is* the immanent Trinity and vice versa," along with Rahner's understanding of the salvation history that the *Grundaxiom* is meant to interpret. After lodging a few fundamental criticisms, then, we intend, in Chapter 3, to examine three counterarguments to the objections raised in Chapter 2. In Chapter 4, then, we propose, for the sake of argument, to abandon our previous criticisms, presuppose that Rahner's overall position is correct, and then show that his suppositions lead to at least two conclusions that conflict with his nonnegotiable assumptions.

---

[189] "Immanent and Transcendent," *TI* x, 279; "Immanente und transzendente," *SW* xv, 548.

CHAPTER 2

In the present chapter, we should like, first, to set the stage for our discussion of the revelation of the Trinity by exploring Rahner's understanding of revelation as such. We intend, next, to explain and in some measure evaluate the *Grundaxiom* of Karl Rahner's doctrine of the Trinity, "The economic Trinity *is* the immanent Trinity and vice versa." Third and finally, then, we hope to describe and, to a limited extent, assess Rahner's understanding of the process whereby God reveals the mystery of the Trinity to human beings.

I. REVELATION AS SUCH

1. Transcendental experience. It is impossible adequately to convey the later Rahner's conception of divine revelation without taking account of what he calls "transcendental experience": sc. "the subjective, unthematic, necessary, and unfailing consciousness of the subject that is co-present in every spiritual act of knowledge."[190] Rahner's understanding of revelation, that is to say, is inextricably intertwined with the idea that the objects, which explicitly engage a human being's knowledge and will, are knowable and conable only within an unobjectivated horizon of experience, and that this horizon of experience is worthy of attention in and of itself.

We saw in the previous chapter that the young Rahner considers a *Vorgriff* towards the infinite horizon of *esse commune* indispensable to the human being's achievement of presence-to-self. The later Rahner retains this conviction. "The human person," he writes, "is a transcendent being insofar as all of her knowledge

---

[190] *Foundations*, 20; *Grundkurs*, *SW* xxvi, 26.

and all of her conscious activity is grounded in a *Vorgriff* of 'being' as such."[191] In his later career, Rahner supplements this conviction with the theological claim that human beings also apprehend the finite objects of their knowledge and will within a horizon that is objectively identical with God. "God," writes the later Rahner, "is the unexpressed, but real *Woraufhin* of...all spiritual and moral life."[192]

Although the human being cannot distinguish between the two horizons of her transcendence, the one natural and the other supernatural, Rahner maintains that the human person transcends herself in the direction of both in every thought and act. "For a metaphysics of knowledge," the later Rahner writes:

> there is no great difficulty in recognizing that transcendence towards being in general...cannot be clearly distinguished in subsequent reflexion from the supernatural transcendence...towards the God of eternal life....And this is true although both modes of transcendence, the formal object of the natural spirit and the formal object of the supernaturally elevated spirit, are both given in consciousness.[193]

The divine gift of a supernatural formal object, or *a priori* horizon, to the human subject, therefore, does not annul the subject's natural orientation towards common being; *gratia supponit, non destruit naturam.* Regrettably, however, the later Rahner fails to clarify the relation between the human being's two transcendental orientations. "The philosopher might," affirms Rahner in his closest approach to such a clarification, "give further reflection...to the question of how a transcendental relationship to...being, and a transcendental relationship to...God are related and how they are to be distinguished."[194] It appears, however, that transcendence towards God alone interests Rahner the theologian.

The datum that human beings experience God only as the transcendental horizon of their knowing and willing, Rahner maintains, implies that human beings can never adequately objectify the divine self-disclosure. For, first, one

---

[191] Ibid. 33; ebd. 37.
[192] "Nature and Grace," *TI* iv, 181; "Natur und Gnade," *ST* iv, 228.
[193] Ibid. 178–9; ebd. 225.
[194] *Foundations*, 60; *Grundkurs, SW* xxvi, 63.

can objectify an individual of a certain quiddity only by conceiving of it as one among many possible instantiations of that quiddity. Yet God is the only possible instance of God's quiddity, and, unlike all other subjects, is identical with it. Second, quiddities themselves manifest their distinctness from other quiddities only insofar as the knower transcends them in the direction of some horizon. As Rahner observes, however, "the horizon cannot be comprised within the horizon....The ultimate measure cannot be measured; the boundary which delimits all things cannot itself be bounded by a still more distant limit."[195] Every conception of the horizon as an entity distinct from others, therefore, must inevitably fall short of the horizon's reality and even convey a false impression of it to the extent that the knower fails to apply to the conception the appropriate analogical modifications.

According to Rahner, however, difficulties such as these, which inevitably beset human attempts to objectify God, by no means imply that one ought not to conceive of God as distinct from the finite existents that human beings perceive within the horizon of the divine being. Precisely that which renders conceptualization of God difficult, rather, demands, in Rahner's view, that one posit such a distinction. "The horizon of the transcendent," he writes:

since it is of immeasurable extent and thus provides the situation for the individual objects of knowledge and love, does indeed always differentiate itself essentially from all that comes within it as conceptual object. And so the distinction between God and all finite beings is not only clearly called for: it is even the condition of possibility for any distinction at all, both between objects in general and the horizon of transcendence, and between object and object.[196]

Rahner insists, nonetheless, that one ought not to conceive of the God-world distinction along the lines of a distinction between finite existents. For, in his view, God's self-manifestation to human beings as the all-embracing horizon constitutes an unveiling of God's being as it is in itself. To a hypothetical questioner who asks whether, in transcendental experience, one encounters only

---

[195] "The Concept of Mystery in Catholic Theology," *TI* iv, 36–73 at 51; "Über den Begriff des Geheimnisses in der katholischen Theologie," *SW* xii, 101–135 at 115–16.

[196] Ibid.; ebd. 115.

God *pro nobis*, as opposed to God *in se*, Rahner replies that on account of "the absolutely unlimited transcendentality of the human spirit,...such a radical distinction between...'God in Godself' and 'God for us' is not even legitimate."[197] Rahner asserts, accordingly, that God differs from the world "in the way in which this difference is experienced in our original, transcendental experience."[198]

Rahner recognizes, naturally, that God relates to created entities not only as their horizon, but also as their cause. He maintains, however, that this relationship of causality does not imply that one must distinguish between God and the world to the same extent and in the same manner that one distinguishes between a finite, efficient cause and its effect. For creation, in Rahner's view, constitutes a unique act, which cannot reasonably be considered a particular instance of the efficient causality observed in everyday life.

In everyday, efficient causality, explains Rahner, the causation itself presupposes some difference between agent and patient. In the divine act of creation, however:

the absolute being of God freely establishes us *for ourselves* as beings distinct from God *and* maintains this distinction in Godself because established by God alone. This means that for the absolute being of God the same distinction does not exist which God imposes on us as our mode of existence.[199]

In other words, Rahner conceives of confinement to undialectical difference from other entities as a creaturely imperfection to which God is not subject. Precisely because creation presupposes no already established distinction between God and creatures, then, God is free to render creatures distinct from each other and from Godself without imposing similar restrictions on the divine being. When rightly understood, therefore, the causal dependency of the world on God

---

[197] *Foundations*, 54–5; *Grundkurs*, *SW* xxvi, 58.
[198] Ibid. 62; ebd. 65.
[199] "An Investigation of the Incomprehensibility of God in St. Thomas Aquinas," *TI* xvi, 244–54 at 250; "Fragen zur Unbegreiflichkeit Gottes nach Thomas von Aquin," *ST* xii, 306–19 at 313.

does not exclude, but rather requires precisely the kind of radical unity-in-difference between God and world that obtains between the supernatural horizon of the human intellect, the human knower herself, and the objects of her knowledge (and will). God differs from the world "in the way in which this difference is experienced in our original, transcendental experience."[200]

In a lexicon article on "Panentheismus," therefore, Rahner proffers the following, extraordinarily sympathetic evaluation of panentheism.

> This form of pantheism does not want simply to identify the world and God monistically (God the "All"). It does, however, still wish to understand the "All" of the world "in" God as God's inner modification and appearance, even though God does not merge with it. The doctrine of such an "in-existence" of the world in God is then (and only then) false and heretical, when it denies the creation and the distinctness of the world from God (not only of God from the world).... Otherwise, it is a summons to ontology to think of the relation between absolute and finite being more deeply (i.e. understanding the two-sided condition of unity and differentiation growing in equal measure) and more precisely.[201]

Rahner's understanding of how human beings encounter the divine in transcendental experience thus engenders quite a robust understanding of divine immanence.

2. The universal history of revelation. Rahner's view of divine revelation is similarly all-embracing. The original, supernatural revelation, according to Rahner, which all other, secondary forms of revelation merely mediate and objectify, consists in the supernatural formal object of the human will and intellect. Since every categorical existent in some way mediates and objectifies this formal object or horizon, then, Rahner concludes that absolutely everything human beings experience constitutes, in some measure, a secondary form of supernatural, divine revelation. "Supernaturally elevated transcendentality," he writes, "is...mediated to itself by any and every categorical reality in which and

---

[200] *Foundations*, 62; *Grundkurs, SW* xxvi, 65.
[201] *KThW*[1], *SW* xvii/i, 744.

through which the subject becomes present to herself."[202] Therefore, "the history...of revelation is co-existent and co-extensive with the history of the world and the human spirit."[203]

It is difficult to conceive of a more comprehensive understanding of strictly supernatural revelation. By thus conceptualizing supernatural revelation, however, Rahner does not mean to exclude the possibility of particular histories of revelation such as those portrayed in the Old and New Testaments or the Qur'an. For, Rahner asserts, "the categorical history of the human being as a spiritual subject is always and everywhere the necessary but historical self-interpretation of...transcendental experience."[204] In other words, the human subject not only: a) mediates to herself categorically her transcendental experience of God's self-revelation in every act; but also b) constructs an objectifying interpretation or expression of her transcendental experience through the conduct of her life.

By this claim, Rahner does not mean to suggest that every human being develops, or need develop, an explicitly religious or philosophical account of her consciousness's *a priori* horizon. "The categorical, historical self-interpretation of what the human person is," he writes, "takes place not only, and not even in the first instance, by means of an explicit anthropology formulated in propositions."[205] Rahner maintains, nevertheless, that the dynamism of God's ontological self-communication to every human being drives categorical interpretations to become ever more explicit and religious.

Explaining why Rahner believes this to be the case requires some delving into his theological presuppositions. World history, as Rahner conceives of it, consists ultimately in an *exitus* and *redditus* from and to the deity. In the *exitus*, God establishes the world as distinct from Godself through a divine self-

---

[202] *Foundations*, 151; *Grundkurs*, *SW* xxvi, 149.
[203] Ibid. 153; ebd. 151.
[204] Ibid.; ebd.
[205] Ibid.; ebd.

communication. "Creation," writes Rahner, "can and should be conceived of as an element in, and prior setting for, the self-bestowal of God: that act in which God does not create something different from Godself and set it over against Godself, but rather communicates God's own reality to the other."[206] In the *redditus*, then, this creative self-communication realizes itself by empowering the world gradually to transcend the limitations of creaturehood until it achieves beatifying union with its origin. "In the outward movement of God's love," Rahner asserts, "God has inserted Godself into the world as its innermost *entelecheia*, and God impels the whole of this world and its history towards that point at which God...will be the innermost and immediately present fulfillment of our existence in the face-to-face presence of eternal beatitude."[207] Everything that occurs in the created realm, therefore, constitutes a moment in the world's "recapitulation into itself and into its ground."[208]

Rahner holds, accordingly, that the world as a whole evolves in the direction of more intimate union with God. This upward trajectory of cosmic evolution itself implies, in Rahner's view, that the human person's categorical interpretation of her transcendental experience of divine self-communication will also come to manifest this experience's nature and origins more successfully over time. "It will be ever more intensely," Rahner writes, "an explicitly religious self-interpretation of this supernatural, transcendental and revelatory experience of God."[209]

3. Particular histories of revelation. An interpretation of divine self-communication becomes ontologically and, at least with respect to a limited

---

[206] "Christology in the Setting of Modern Persons' Understanding of Themselves and of Their World," *TI* xi, 215–29 at 225; "Christologie im Rahmen des modernen Selbst- und Weltverständnisses," *SW* xv, 601–11 at 608.

[207] "The Position of Christology in the Church Between Exegesis and Dogmatics," *TI* xi, 185–214 at 200; "Kirchliche Christologie zwischen Exegese und Dogmatik," *ST* ix, 197–226 at 212–13.

[208] *Foundations*, 189; *Grundkurs*, *SW* xxvi, 184.

[209] Ibid. 154; ebd. 152.

population, functionally equivalent to the kind of interpretation objectified in the Christian Bible, Rahner maintains, when it satisfies two conditions. First, the interpretation must be such that "it knows itself to be willed positively and directed by God."[210] Second, asserts Rahner, such an interpretation must be "assured of the legitimacy of this knowledge in ways which are offered by this history."[211] Where these criteria are satisfied, he writes, one finds "the history of revelation in the sense which is usually associated with this word," or, as he more expressively describes it, "the full realization of the essence of both...transcendental and categorical revelation in the unity and purity of their essence."[212]

The criteria Rahner proffers lend themselves to misinterpretation by readers unaware of the later Rahner's antipathy to the idea of divine intervention within the categorical order. It is important to note, therefore, that the notion of God's disrupting the ordinary course of human events, for instance, by multiplying bread or literally resurrecting a corpse, strikes the later Rahner as implausible. For, first, the mature Rahner views divine intervention, at least in the sense of a violation of the laws of nature, as inconsistent with creation's character as a divine self-communication. As he explains:

> the creation of the other has to be understood to begin with as a moment within...divine self-communication to the other, a moment which God's self-communication presupposes as the condition of its own possibility....Looked at from this perspective, the laws of nature...must be understood to begin with as the structures of this precondition....There is no reason why this presupposition would...have to be abolished and suspended if God's self-communication is to come to appearance in its own presupposition, the very presupposition which this very self-communication creates for itself.[213]

In other words, it is self-contradictory to suppose that anything must negate its own presupposition *sine qua non* in order to actualize itself. If the laws of nature, therefore, constitute necessary conditions of divine self-communication, then, the

---

[210] Ibid. 155; ebd.
[211] Ibid. 155; ebd.
[212] Ibid. 155; ebd.
[213] Ibid. 261; ebd. 257.

supposition that divine self-communication must, or even can, violate them appears absurd.

Second, Rahner maintains, attempts to explain extraordinary events by invoking the idea of a divine violation of the laws of nature seem implausible in the light of contemporary humanity's experience of the world. Again, in his words:

> A person of today can no longer experience God so easily or so directly as a person of former ages believed to be possible....When within the context of our various experiences we fail to find an explanation for a particular phenomenon,...then we put a question-mark against it. We hope that in time some possible way of explaining it by the exact sciences may yet emerge. But what we do not say is this: 'Here God is at work in a special way.' We do not say: 'Here we find a special intervention of God in the world's course.' Nowadays we no longer want in any sense to have a God who has to be invoked as a stopper of the gaps so as to illumine to ourselves some point which still remains obscure, and to show its connection with the particular phenomena of our experience.[214]

Rahner operates on the presupposition, therefore, that miracles, in the sense of divine violations of nature's laws, simply do not occur. When Rahner asserts that a history of categorical revelation, such as that objectified in the Bible, must be directed by God and authenticated by factors intrinsic to itself, therefore, he does not mean to include divine intervention among the integral elements of such histories. "'Direction,'" he explains, "is understood here not as adventitious and coming from without, but rather as the immanent power of...divine self-communication";[215] and as for the requirement of self-authentication, Rahner appears to refer to nothing more than the inner certainty that accrues to the means whereby human beings genuinely come to experience God.

When historical self-interpretations of transcendental revelation satisfy these criteria, Rahner believes, one can reasonably speak of revelation in the same sense that one finds it in the Old Testament. Such histories, Rahner stresses, need not occur only within the bounds of the biblical narratives. "In the collective history

---

[214] "The Church's Commission to Bring Salvation and the Humanization of the World," *TI* xiv, 300; "Heilsauftrag der Kirche und Humanisierung der Welt," *SW* xv, 711–26 at 715.

[215] *Foundations*, 156; *Grundkurs*, *SW* xxvi, 154.

of humankind and in the history of its religion outside the economy of salvation in the Old and New Testaments," he writes, "there can be...brief and partial histories...of revelation in which a part of this self-reflection and reflexive self-presence of universal revelation and its history is found in its purity."[216] Rahner stresses, however, that nowhere, not even in the pre-history of the Christian church recorded in the Old Testament, does God utter an unconditional, irrevocable, unsurpassable, and therefore final word before God's definitive self-revelation in Christ.

4. The absolute savior. In this self-revelation, Rahner believes, God pledges the divine self to the world in such a radical way that it becomes objectively certain that the progress of divine self-communication will ultimately issue in the divinization of the cosmos as a whole. "The historical person whom we call Savior," writes Rahner, "is that subjectivity in whom this process of God's absolute self-communication to the spiritual world is *irrevocably* present as a whole."[217] No merely human prophet or set of words, in Rahner's view, could have sufficed to bring about this publicly tangible irrevocability, this ultimate self-commitment of God. For, as Rahner explains:

As long as this finite mediation of the divine self-manifestation...is not in the strictest sense a divine reality itself, it is basically transitory and surpassable...Hence if the reality in which God's absolute self-communication is pledged and accepted for the whole of humanity...is to be really the final and unsurpassable divine self-communication, then it must be said that it is not only posited by God, but is God.[218]

In other words, Rahner maintains that Christ's function as eschatological sign of the irreversibility of God's self-communication to the world requires that he be God and man in a single person. He himself, therefore, by being God and man in a single person, constitutes the ultimate revelation of God's will to communicate

---

[216] Ibid.; ebd.

[217] "Christology within an Evolutionary View of the World," *TI* v, 157–92 at 175; "Die Christologie innerhalb einer evolutiven Weltanschauung," *SW* xv, 219–47 at 233–4.

[218] Ibid. 182–3; ebd. 240.

Godself to humankind. After Christ, there is no new revelation properly speaking. One does, however, find the church, i.e. the social embodiment of Christ's continuing presence in the world, which sums up its experience of Christ in Scripture, which, in turn, forms the most specific and detailed of all kinds of revelation.

5. Scripture. "Scripture," Rahner writes, "[is] the inspired word of God...and not just debatable theology."[219] Yet specifying why and in what sense this thesis holds true, according to Rahner, "is not as easy as it might seem at first sight."[220] For the statements of Scripture, as proclaimed and heard, always contain, in his view, a moment of theology. In Rahner's words:

there is no *proclaimed* revelation except in the form of a *believed* revelation. A *believed*, i.e. heard, revelation always already includes also—insofar as it is a revelation understood, accepted and assimilated—a synthesis of the Word of God and the word of a particular human person....Every Word of God which is spoken by human beings is already, therefore, to a certain extent a reflected word, and to that extent also already a beginning of theology.[221]

This theology, this reflecting on a more primitive revelation, Rahner avers, occurs even in Scripture itself. "It would be absurd," Rahner writes, "to try to reduce the whole difference between for example the theology of the Synoptics or of the Acts of the Apostles and that of St. Paul to the intervention of a new, direct revelation of God."[222] One must instead suppose, according to Rahner, that the human authors of Scripture "ponder and reflect on the data of their faith already known to them" and respond to new questions, experiences, etc. "to the best of their ability in a theological reflection."[223]

---

[219] "Considerations on the Development of Dogma," *TI* iv, 6; Überlegungen zur Dogmenentwicklung," *SW* ix, 445.
[220] "What is a Dogmatic Statement?" *TI* v, 61; "Was ist eine dogmatische Aussage?" *SW* xii, 165.
[221] Ibid.; ebd. 166.
[222] "Theology in the New Testament," *TI* v, 28; "Theologie im Neuen Testament," *SW* xii, 197.
[223] Ibid.; ebd.

Indeed, in Rahner's view, the actual statements of Scripture constitute nothing more than a "conceptual objectification...[which] is secondary in comparison"[224] with a more "fundamental revelation [*Grundoffenbarung*]."[225] This revelation, in turn, as we have seen, he considers ultimately identical with a "pre-thematic and transcendental experience"[226] universally bestowed on human beings. "The express revelation of the word in Christ," he writes, "is not something that comes to us from without as entirely strange, but only the explicitation of what we already are by grace and what we experience at least incoherently in the limitlessness of our transcendence."[227] Rahner affirms, in fact, that "the totality of the message of the Christian faith is in a real sense already given in...transcendental experience."[228] The specific difference between Scripture and other forms of theological discourse, therefore, most definitely does not, in Rahner's view at least, "lie in the fact that in the former there is as it were the pure Word of God alone and in the latter only human reflection."[229]

The real distinction between the two, Rahner claims, derives from "the peculiar and unique position of Holy Scripture,"[230] which Rahner attempts to articulate in his "Catholic principle of *sola-scriptura*."[231] Such a principle need not conflict with the defined doctrines of the Catholic Church, according to Rahner:

provided that we understand...it to involve also [1] an authoritative attestation and interpretation of holy scripture by the living word of the Church and her magisterium, and [2] an attestation of

---

[224] Ibid. 39; ebd. 206.

[225] Ibid. 40; ebd. 207.

[226] "Contemporary Sciences," *TI* xiii, 97; "Heutigen Wissenschaften," *SW* xv, 707.

[227] "Anonymous Christians," *TI* vi, 390–98 at 394; "Die Anonymen Christen," *ST* vi, 545–54 at 549.

[228] "Methodology," *TI* xi, 109; "Methode," *ST* ix, 122. Likewise, writes Rahner, "Christianity is none else but the deepest reality of the transcendental experience" ("Ideology and Christianity," *TI* vi 43–58 at 51; "Ideologie und Christentum," *SW* xv, 395–408 at 402).

[229] "Dogmatic Statement," *TI* v, 61; "Dogmatische Aussage," *SW* xii, 166.

[230] Ibid. 62; ebd. 167.

[231] "Scripture and Tradition," *TI* vi, 98–112 at 108; "Heilige Schrift und Tradition," *ST* vi, 121–38 at 132.

scripture itself and its authoritative interpretation which cannot be replaced by scripture itself...presupposing, of course [3]...that one does not interpret this principle of the *sola-scriptura* as meaning a prohibition of a living development of the faith of the Church.[232]

The self-understanding of the Catholic Church, in fact, requires such a principle, Rahner contends, for at least three reasons. First, Rahner explains, "by herself testifying absolutely...that the Scriptures are absolutely authoritative:"[233] that they are just as authoritative, in fact, as the Church's infallible teaching office, "the Church seems to involve herself in a contradiction."[234] For, it seems, one of the authorities cannot but render the other superfluous. If the Church recognizes an infallible and intelligible Bible, "she evacuates the force of her own authoritative 'infallible' magistery in favour of the Bible, as the infallible Word of God."[235] If the Church retains the plenitude of her authority, however, "she subjects the Scripture to her own magisterial interpretation; it is she who decides what the Scriptures can do and say."[236]

One cannot dispose of the latter difficulty, moreover, by claiming "that the Bible cannot interpret itself, that it needs an infallible interpreter."[237] The person who reasons thus, Rahner avers, "is in effect saying that the Bible can claim no priority over other [ecclesiastical] traditions when it comes to finding out just what is of divine revelation; both are equally in need of a teaching authority if the divine revelation in them is to be unerringly discerned."[238] In such an event, an infallible book would be superfluous. The "Two-Source Theory,"[239] therefore, according to which Scripture and tradition constitute two, independent sources of doctrine, seems to involve the Catholic theologian in an insoluble dilemma: "why

---

[232] Ibid. 107–8; ebd.
[233] "Inspiration in the Bible," *Studies in Modern Theology* [*SMT*] (W. J. O'Hara et al, tr.; London: Burns & Oates, 1965), 7–86 at 31; "Über die Schriftinspiration," *SW* xii, 3–58 at 24.
[234] Ibid.; ebd.
[235] Ibid.; ebd.
[236] Ibid.; ebd. 25.
[237] Ibid. 32; ebd.
[238] Ibid.; ebd.
[239] Ibid. 36; ebd. 28.

an infallible teaching authority if there is an infallible Scripture? Why an infallible Scripture if there is an infallible teaching authority?"[240]

Rahner believes that he can resolve this dilemma by developing a new theory of inspiration, which implies, in turn, a less problematic understanding of the relation between Scripture and tradition. According to Rahner, "inspiration does not of itself require an immediate divine intervention into the interior of the human will; it is possible for the will to be moved mediately, by means of created impulses arising within...the author's concrete empirical experience."[241] Rahner contends, rather, that one can do justice to the traditional doctrine of inspiration simply by asserting that "God wills and produces the Scripture as a constitutive element in the foundation of the Apostolic Church, because and to the extent that it is precisely in this way that God wills and effects the Apostolic Church's existence."[242] God constitutes the divine author of Scripture, in other words, insofar as God wills the existence of the church.

God's willing of the church's existence makes God the "author" of Scripture, according to Rahner, because "the concrete, fully realized essence of the Church includes the Scriptures: they are a constitutive element of her."[243] "A fundamental character of the Scriptures," Rahner explains, "is the fulfillment of the role...[of] the Apostolic Church as distinct from the later Church: to be not only the earliest phase in time, but also the permanent source, the Canon and norm for the Church of later eras."[244] Before the Church possessed the entire canon of Scripture, therefore, it constituted "an *église naissante*, the Church in the process of birth."[245] By her "production of the Scriptures," however, "she constituted herself the normative law for the Church's future course"[246] and thus

---

[240] Ibid. 31; ebd. 25.
[241] Ibid. 22–3; ebd. 19.
[242] Ibid. 58–9; ebd. 40–41.
[243] Ibid. 50; ebd. 36.
[244] Ibid. 51; ebd.
[245] Ibid. 47; ebd. 34.
[246] Ibid. 51–2; ebd. 36.

brought about the "self-constitution,"[247] the "self-realization"[248] and, indeed, "the completion of the Apostolic Church."[249]

This understanding of Scripture as the Church's self-produced and self-imposed doctrinal standard implies, according to Rahner, that "the inspiration of Holy Scripture is nothing else than God's founding of the Church."[250] This thesis, in turn, suggests a means of conceiving of the relation between Scripture and the Church's teaching authority in such a way that neither renders the other superfluous: the "Catholic *sola-scriptura* principle." Such a principle, according to Rahner, if conceived in terms of his understanding of inspiration, actually confers on the magisterium and Scripture a status of mutual priority.

Insofar as Scripture constitutes "the enduring and unsurpassable *norma normans, non normata* for all later dogmatic statements,"[251] the magisterium must remain utterly subservient to it. Yet Scripture, according to Rahner, proceeds, to a degree at least, from that very magisterium. "The New Testament authors *were*," Rahner writes, "on this showing, organs of the Church's self-expression."[252] In yielding to the authority of Scripture, therefore, the magisterium merely conforms to its own previous edicts. "The infallible teaching authority of the Apostolic Church, in her function for the future, consists in the capacity for creating the Scriptures, while the infallible teaching authority of the later Church consists in the authentic interpretation of the Scriptures."[253]

Rahner's "Catholic principle of *sola scriptura*" with its concomitant view of inspiration, therefore, vindicates his church's self-understanding, first, in the sense that it maintains the authority of both Scripture and tradition while giving no impression of conflict between the two. It thus endows, in Rahner's view, the

---

[247] Ibid. 51; ebd.
[248] Ibid. 69; ebd. 48.
[249] Ibid. 79; ebd. 53.
[250] Ibid. 53; ebd. 37.
[251] "Dogmatic Statement," *TI* v, 62; "Dogmatische Aussage," *SW* xii, 167.
[252] "Inspiration," *SMT*, 76; "Schriftinspiration," *SW* xii, 51.
[253] Ibid. 77; ebd. 52.

Catholic understanding of Scripture and tradition with "that measure of intelligibility which...is needed for a solid and enduring faith on the part of the majority of human beings."[254]

Rahner's principle sustains his church's self-understanding, second, to the extent that it engenders "a less embarrassed attitude toward the datum of comparative religion, that non-Christian religions of a high cultural level also have their holy books."[255] Embarrassment at this datum, Rahner thinks, arises from a mythological understanding of inspiration that he intends for his theory of inspiration, including the "Catholic *sola scriptura* principle," to replace. According to Rahner's theory, the Bible does not consist in miraculously dictated messages from heaven: the kind of literature one would expect to find only in Christ's mystical body. Instead, Rahner holds, the Bible consists in a document written by the church to define the church's beliefs: the kind of writing one would expect to find in any literate religious group. In Rahner's words:

> a community will almost necessarily establish itself as historically founded and enduring into the future through the medium of books. It could even be suggested that the origin of books lies here, rather than in the need for private communication. Possession of sacred books is [therefore] something to be expected *a priori* in any religion which possesses a certain level of culture and claims to be a bearer of historical revelation.[256]

For one who accepts Rahner's understanding of inspiration, therefore, "the non-Christian analogies to the Christian Scriptures are no longer a cause of unease,"[257] and, to that extent, Rahner's theology of Scripture sustains the credibility of Christianity.

Third, and, for Rahner, probably quite significantly, his understanding of Scripture's inspiration retains key elements of a traditional, Christian doctrine without invoking divine intervention: a concept Rahner rejects as mythological. If one presupposes his theology of inspiration, Rahner writes, "it is possible...to

---

[254] Ibid. 34; ebd. 26.
[255] Ibid. 81–2; ebd. 55.
[256] Ibid. 82; ebd. 55.
[257] Ibid.; ebd.

understand all statements of the Christian faith about the Holy Scripture of the Old and New Testaments, in such a way that the statements about God's authorship of Holy Scripture, about the inspiration, the normativity, [and] the inerrancy of Scripture do not smack of the miraculous [*einen miraculösen Beigeschmack haben*], which today is no longer assimilable. it seems to me that all that is being said [by the church] about the Sacred Scripture of the Old and New Testaments — about God as the main author of Scripture, about inspiration, about Scripture as norm, about the inerrancy of Scripture — can be understood without recourse to the miraculous, which does not find credence today."[258]

Rahner's theology of Scripture and tradition also concedes to historic Protestantism the material sufficiency of Scripture as a source of Christian doctrine.[259] He does not, however, in so doing adopt a Protestant understanding of the relation between ecclesiastical authority and Scripture. For he maintains: a) that only the church can identify precisely which books belong to the canon of Scripture; b) that the church herself not only receives, but actually produces the Scriptures; and c) that "the very fact that the Church proclaims a teaching according to the norms of her office...guarantees that the Scriptures are being rightly interpreted."[260] Rahner's theory of inspiration, as we have seen, confers on the magisterium and Scripture a status of mutual priority. "The infallible teaching authority of the Apostolic Church, in her function for the future, consists in the capacity for creating the Scriptures, while the infallible teaching authority of the later Church consists in the authentic interpretation of the Scriptures."[261]

---

[258] "Buch Gottes—Buch der Menschen," *ST* xvi, 278–91 at 284. Joseph Donceel's translation of this passage in *TI* xxii, 219 correctly conveys Rahner's overall position, but strays unnecessarily from the literal sense of Rahner's words.

[259] That Rahner can concede this point to historic Protestantism without contravening the decrees of the Council of Trent and Catholic tradition in general appears doubtful. For a thorough discussion of the relevant historical data, cf. José Saraiva Martins, "Escritura e tradição segundo o Concilio de Trento," *Divus Thomas* (Piacenza) 67 (1964), 183–277.

[260] "Inspiration," *SMT*, 77; "Schriftinspiration," *SW* xii, 52.

[261] Ibid. 77; ebd.

In Rahner's view, then, the teachings, which the post-apostolic church (excluding the question of the canon) deems infallible, derive, in some sense, from Scripture. Scripture, in turn, derives from the experience of the biblical authors, whose experience derives from certain historical events, which, while they provide the material content of categorical revelation, do not, in and of themselves, contain its ultimate and authoritative meaning. This deeper meaning, in Rahner's view, subsists entirely in the divine self-revelation bestowed at all places, in all times, and on all persons in humanity's transcendental experience.

This brief etiology seems to sum up at least the essential elements of Rahner's view of divine revelation. On this understanding, particular truths, like the doctrine of the Trinity, demand the assent of Christians only to the extent that their meaning is contained implicitly in the former levels of revelation.[262] In particular, their meaning must be implicitly contained in transcendental experience: the sole origin of the indispensable and formal, as opposed to the dispensable and material, content of revelation.

A "recourse to this originating reality of faith," i.e. transcendental experience, "is [therefore] wholly suitable," in Rahner's view, "to provide a critical criterion for determining the exact meaning and the limitations of a theological statement."[263] Whatever in a dogma reflects this "originating reality" must, in Rahner's view, remain absolutely normative. All else he considers dispensable: "time-conditioned amalgams" with "no claim to permanent validity."[264]

One might object, of course, that this kind of interpretation of dogma "might lead eventually to the elimination of what is 'really' meant, a process of elimination leading ultimately to the destruction of any real meaning of a religious

---

[262] Cf. Rahner, "The Congregation of the Faith and the Commission of Theologians," *TI* xiv, 98–115 at 107; "Glaubenskongregation und Theologenkommission," *ST* x, 338–57 at 348–9.

[263] "Yesterday's History of Dogma and Theology for Tomorrow," *TI* xviii, 3–34 at 20–21; "Dogmen- und Theologiegeschicte von gestern für morgen," *ST* xiii, 11–47 at 31.

[264] "Magisterium and Theology," *TI* xviii, 68; "Lehramt und Theologie," *ST* xiii, 85.

statement."[265] Rahner, however, seems to consider such fears unfounded. Of this difficulty, he writes:

> it need only be said that a religious statement points not to what is drained of meaning, but to the ineffable mystery that we call God....In other words, these processes of elimination are basically continually recurring events pointing to that mystery and must occur over and over again in the history of abiding religious truth, since this liberating and hopeful approach to the mystery of God must take place in the light of continually new historical situations of truth.[266]

As long as the dogma continues effectively to mediate the transcendental experience of God, Rahner holds, it *ipso facto* retains its true meaning. Rahner identifies, then, the certain, irreducible content of Christian revelation with human beings' universal, athematic, and transcendental experience of divine grace.

II. THE REVELATION OF THE TRINITY

1. Introduction. Rahner's view of the content of Christian revelation renders the doctrine of the Trinity, as traditionally understood, quite problematic. For, in the traditional view, the acts of the Trinitarian persons *ad extra* are absolutely indistinguishable so that neither creation nor grace engenders elements in human experience from which one can legitimately infer the existence of the immanent Trinity. In order for human beings to possess any certain knowledge at all about the tripersonality of God, the traditional view holds, God must reveal this tripersonality to them through a conceptual, and even verbal, revelation. In Rahner's non-miraculous understanding of Christianity, however, the kind of divine intervention necessary for the conveyance of such a revelation simply does not occur. "Every real intervention of God in God's world," Rahner writes, "is always only the becoming historical and...concrete of that 'intervention' in which God as the transcendental ground of the world has from the outset embedded

---

[265] "History of Dogma," *TI* xviii, 16; "Theologiegeschicte," *ST* xiii, 26.
[266] Ibid.; ebd.

Godself in the world as its self-communicating ground."[267] In contrast to those who insist on the necessity of a verbal revelation for human knowledge of the Trinity, therefore, Rahner insists that the revelation of the immanent Trinity must be strictly identical with its ontological self-communication to the world. "The revelation of the Trinity as immanent," he writes, "can only be conceived of as occurring thus. The immanent Trinity is communicated in the *act* of divine grace as such [in der göttlichen Gnaden*tat* als solche]; sc. the immanent Trinity becomes the Trinity of the economy of salvation."[268]

The very idea of a revelation of something unrelated to humanity, which utterly and completely transcends human beings and their world, moreover, strikes Rahner, on philosophical grounds, as absurd. For his theory of the unity of being and knowing, as we have seen, entails the abandonment of any theory of knowledge according to which the known remains simply external to the knower. As Rahner explains: "Every knowledge of another by a human being is a mode of her self-knowledge, of her 'subjectivity'; the two are not merely extrinsically synchronized, but intrinsic moments of the one human knowing....This holds also for human knowledge of God."[269]

Even if a verbal revelation could occur, therefore, it would suffice, in Rahner's view, only to convey an unintelligible and insignificant doctrine about the Trinity to human beings. In order for human beings to know the Trinity itself, Rahner holds, they must experience God's triune nature in some way in the depths of their own being; indeed, the Trinity must become, in some sense, an aspect of their being. If this "economic Trinity," the Trinity that communicates itself to human beings, does not relate in a very intimate way to the "immanent Trinity," i.e. God as God exists *in se* from all eternity, then, in Rahner's view, human

---

[267] *Foundations*, 87; *Grundkurs*, *SW* xxvi, 88.

[268] "Trinität," *SM* iv, *SW* xvii/ii, 1337–49 at 1342. In Rahner's view, writes Klaus Fischer, "the Trinity is...the revelation itself" (*Der Mensch als Geheimnis: Die Anthropologie Karl Rahners*, [Ökumenische Forschungen 2.5; Freiburg: Herder, 1974], 341).

[269] *Spirit*, 183; *Geist*, *SW* ii, 144.

beings cannot know of the immanent Trinity. Now, the dogmas which Rahner, the theologian, must uphold dictate, among other things, that certain human beings at least do know explicitly of the immanent Trinity. Such a relationship must, therefore, in his view, exist. In order to assert, explain, and defend the existence of this relationship, then, Rahner develops: 1) a complex and original account of the process whereby God discloses the Trinitarian structure of the intra-divine relations to human beings; and 2) an *a priori* rule[270] that warrants inferences from God's Trinitarian self-revelation to the doctrine of the immanent Trinity.

2. Rahner's Grundaxiom. The rule in question, of course, is Rahner's famous *Grundaxiom*: "the economic Trinity *is* the immanent Trinity and vice versa,"[271] Since, in Rahner's view, this *a priori* dictum constitutes the principle of intelligibility of God's Trinitarian self-revelation, it seems reasonable to examine its meaning and grounds before discussing the revelation of the Trinity itself.

a. Four misconstruals. In order the more precisely to determine what Rahner's *Grundaxiom* means, we shall first eliminate four, possible misconstruals.

i. Trivially obvious identity. First and above all else, Rahner does not posit his *Grundaxiom* in order to affirm a trivially obvious identity of the Trinity with itself. In the words of Philip Cary:

Rahner must be claiming more than just the identity of the Father, Son, and Holy Spirit of salvation-history with the three persons of the immanent Trinity; for that is an identity already written into the Creed, which no Trinitarian theology could possibly want to contest....The

---

[270] We refer, of course, to Rahner's *Grundaxiom*. Commenting on its apriorism, J. A. Colombo writes, "It is precisely at this point that a danger arises, for it appears that the speaker has taken up a position *ab aeterno* and abandoned the historicity of his own starting point" ("Rahner and His Critics: Lindbeck and Metz," *Thomist* 56 [1992], 71–96 at 79, n. 19).

[271] "Oneness and Threefoldness," *TI* xviii, 114; 'Einzigkeit und Dreifaltigkeit," *ST* xiii, 139. In the following sentence, Rahner writes: "I do not know exactly when and by whom this theological axiom was formulated for the first time."

distinction between the economic Trinity and the immanent Trinity has never implied that there were two separate Trinities, but only that there is a difference between describing God *in se* and describing the work of God in the economy of salvation.[272]

ii. Absolute identity. Second, however, Rahner also does not intend for his *Grundaxiom* to affirm an identity so absolute that it renders the distinction between the immanent and the economic Trinity superfluous. "The 'immanent' Trinity," Rahner's writes, "is the necessary condition of the possibility of God's free self-communication":[273] not that self-communication *simpliciter*.

iii. Copy theory. Nor does Rahner, third, regard the economic Trinity as a mere manifestation of the immanent Trinity through the divine acts of salvation history. God's "threefold, gratuitous, and free relation to us," in Rahner's view, "*is* not merely a copy or an analogy of the inner Trinity."[274] Rahner characterizes the economic Trinity much more as the self-gift of the immanent Trinity to humanity. "God has given Godself so fully in...absolute self-communication to the creature," he writes, "that the 'immanent' Trinity becomes the Trinity of the 'economy of salvation.'"[275] Again, "because God...and not some created representation of God is involved in the free self-gift of God as mystery, the three-fold form belongs directly to God in his relation to human beings. Thus the economic Trinity of salvation is *ipso facto* the immanent Trinity."[276]

The economic Trinity, then, does not, in Rahner's view, correspond to the immanent Trinity as, for instance, a picture corresponds to the reality it portrays.

---

[272] "On Behalf of Classical Trinitarianism: A Critique of Rahner on the Trinity," *Thomist* 56 (1992), 365–405 at 367.

[273] *Trinity*, 102, n. 21; "Der dreifaltige Gott," *MS* ii, 384, Anm. 21. As Joseph Wong explains, "If the economic Trinity simply *is* the immanent Trinity, then Rahner's repeated assertion that the immanent self-expression of God [the Trinitarian processions] is the *presupposed condition* for the free self-utterance *ad extra* [the economy of salvation] would lose its meaning" (*Logos-Symbol in the Christology of Karl Rahner* [BSRel 61; Rome: LAS, 1984], 211). Cf. the similar remarks of Ludger Oeing-Hanhoff in his "Die Krise des Gottesbegriffs," *TQ* 159 (1979), 285–303 at 301.

[274] *Trinity*, 35; "Der dreifaltige Gott," *MS* ii, 337.

[275] "Mystery," *TI* iv, 69; "Geheimnis," *SW* xii, 132.

[276] "The Hiddenness of God," *TI* xvi, 227–43 at 240; "Über die Verborgenheit Gottes," *ST* xii, 285–305 at 301.

It corresponds to the immanent Trinity, rather, as a person who spends herself for the good of another corresponds to herself as she would exist whether or not she undertook this labor. The economic Trinity, as Rahner understands it, is the immanent Trinity pouring itself out in grace.

iv. Merely de facto identity. Rahner, fourth and finally, does not consider this correspondence between the eternal Trinity and the Trinity which communicates itself to humanity as merely *de facto* and unnecessary in itself. Although Rahner allows for and, indeed, insists upon some change in God's being when God communicates the divine self to others, he nonetheless regards God's triune, internal relatedness as a principle of divine identity which necessarily perdures even through the process of divine self-communication. Rahner denies the possibility, therefore, of a self-communication of God whose internal distinctions differ in any way from those of the immanent Trinity. In his words, "if...there is a real *self*-communication with a real distinction in that which is communicated as such, hence with a real distinction 'for us,' then God must '*in se*' carry this distinction."[277]

b. Rahner's actual meaning. By the statement, "the economic Trinity *is* the immanent Trinity, and vice versa," then, Rahner does mean that divine self-communication "can, *if* occurring in freedom, occur only in the intra-divine manner of the two communications of the one divine essence by the Father to the Son and the Spirit."[278] In other words, the immanent constitution of the Trinity

---

[277] *Trinity*, 36, n. 34; "Der dreifaltige Gott," *MS* ii, 338, Anm. 34.
[278] Ibid. 36; ebd. 338. The words "*if* occurring in freedom" are worthy of note. As Luis Ladaria justly remarks, "The 'is' in the second part of the axiom is not equivalent to that in the first. In the first, it concerns a necessary reference to the foundation and principle of the economy of salvation; in the second, it indicates a divine presence in sovereign liberty" ("La teología trinitaria de Karl Rahner: Un balance de la discusión," *Greg* 86 [2005], 276–307 at 283).

forms a kind of *a priori* law for the divine self-communication *ad extra* such that the structure of the latter cannot but correspond to the structure of the former.[279]

c. Rahner's arguments for the Grundaxiom. That such a correspondence must obtain, however, is by no means self-evident. Rahner, after all, famously admits that "the one who is not subject to change in Godself can *Godself* be subject to change *in something else.*"[280] If God could alter other facets of God's being in something else, it seems, *prima facie*, that God could also alter the relations between God's modes of subsistence.[281] God's simplicity,[282] as classically understood, moreover, would seem to dictate that changes in other facets of God's being could not leave the Trinitarian relations untouched. For, if God is simple, i.e. absolutely uncomposed, then every aspect of God's being is essentially, though not necessarily relatively, identical with every other; hence the slightest change in any aspect of a simple God would transform every aspect of that God. It seems, then, that the relations between Father, Son, and Holy Spirit could hardly escape the comprehensive metamorphosis entailed by divine becoming. Such becoming, however, seems to form an indispensable prerequisite to divine self-communication as Rahner conceives of it: : i.e. "the act whereby God goes

---

[279] "The Trinity as present in the economy of salvation," Rahner writes, "necessarily embodies also the Trinity as immanent" ("Methodology," *TI* xi, 108; "Methode," *ST* ix, 120).

[280] *Foundations*, 220; *Grundkurs*, *SW* xxvi, 212.

[281] Rahner explicitly affirms the objective identity of each divine person with the divine essence (*Trinity*, 72–3; "Der dreifaltige Gott," *MS* ii, 364). When he speaks of the Trinitarian persons as "modes of subsistence," accordingly, he means to refer to the persons *qua* distinct, i.e. according to their personal properties, and not to reduce the persons to those properties (cf. ibid. 74, n. 27, 109–10; ebd. 365, Anm. 26, 389).

Rahner explicitly states, moreover, that the Trinitarian persons are really (i.e. in fact and not merely in conception), eternally, and necessarily distinct ("Dreifaltigkeit," *KThW*[1], *SW* xvii/i, 535–8 at 536–7). One cannot, therefore, reasonably consider him a Sabellian, or "modalist." For a more extensive defense of Rahner against this charge, cf. Marc Pugliese, "Is Karl Rahner a Modalist?" *IThQ* 68 (2003), 229–49.

[282] Rahner endorses the doctrine of divine simplicity (cf. *Trinity*, 69, 102, n. 21; "Der dreifaltige Gott," *MS* ii, 362, 384, Anm. 21), but interprets it in an unconventional sense (cf. ibid. 103; ebd. 384).

out of Godself into 'the other' in such a way that God bestows Godself upon the other by becoming the other."[283]

i. The argument from divine self-communication. Rahner contends, nevertheless, in his only explicit argument for the *Grundaxiom*, that precisely because God communicates the divine self, the relations intrinsic to that communication necessarily correspond to the eternal relations within the immanent Trinity. "The differentiation of the self-communication of God...must," he writes, "belong to God 'in Godself,' or otherwise this difference...would do away with God's *self*-communication."[284] Rahner, indeed, seems to regard asymmetry between God's eternal relations and God's communicated relations as self-evidently incompatible with a genuine, divine self-communication and, accordingly, never responds explicitly to the difficulty raised above about the implications of change in a simple being. To his credit, however, Rahner does display awareness of a related objection to his position: viz. that even if he could identify an authentically Trinitarian superstructure of religious experience; and even if he could plausibly argue that this superstructure characterizes the God who communicates Godself to human beings; Rahner could not, it seems, establish that the structure in question 1) characterized this God even before God communicated the divine being, and 2) would have characterized this God even if God had never communicated this being.

---

[283] "Mystery," *TI* iv, 68; "Geheimnis," *SW* xii, 131. In particular, Rahner asserts that God must change in order to accomplish the most radical instance of divine self–communication, the Incarnation. Although, he writes:

we must maintain methodologically the immutability of God,...it would be basically a denial of the incarnation if we used it [i.e. the divine immutability] to determine what this mystery could be. If, to expedite the mystery, one transferred it into the region of the creature alone, one would really abolish the mystery in the strict sense....The mystery of the incarnation [therefore] must lie in God...: in the fact that God, although unchangeable 'in Godself', can become something 'in another'" ("On the Theology of the Incarnation," *TI* iv, 105–20 at 114, n. 3; "Zur Theologie der Menschwerdung," *SW* xii, 309–22 at 317, Anm. 3).

[284] *Trinity*, 99–100; "Der dreifaltige Gott," *MS* ii, 382. Cf. *Foundations*, 137; *Grundkurs*, *SW* xxvi, 135–6; and "The Mystery of the Trinity," *TI* xvi, 255–9 at 258; "Um das Geheimnis der Dreifaltigkeit," *ST* xii, 320–25 at 323.

In the following passage, for instance, one can discern a preliminary response to the criticism that, if God is not immutable, God's inner structure after God communicates Godself need not mirror God's structure before, or prescinding from, this communication. "The Λόγος ἐνδιάθετος," he writes:

> is the condition of the possibility of the Λόγος προφορικός. This does not make of the Logos a mere principle of creation. For if the *verbum prolativum*...is uttered *freely*, *thus* having its condition in the Father's immanent Word, it must have an "immanent" sense and a meaning for the Father himself. Otherwise the Father's self-expression *ad extra* would either no longer be a free grace, or no "immanent" word could pre-exist in relation to it as the condition of its possibility.[285]

Rahner recognizes, in other words, that one could reasonably conceive of the Logos as "a mere principle of creation" under one, or possibly both, of two conditions. The Logos could constitute a mere principle of creation if: a) the self-communication involved in creation were not a free grace; or b) the Logos did not exist prior to creation. It is the second possibility that interests us here.

By raising the possibility that God first differentiates Godself into Father and Logos when God wishes to communicate the divine self *ad extra*, Rahner displays his awareness that a differentiation within a mutable God's self-communication need not imply a differentiation within this God prior to, or irrespective of, the communication. He acknowledges, in fact, that "here lies the critical point of the whole question. Why is the Son as the word of the free self-expression of the Father to the world necessarily also the Λόγος ἐνδιάθετος of the Father? Why does the possibility of the Father's self-expression to the world, even as a mere possibility, already imply an inner 'differentiation' in Godself?"[286]

Rahner seems, then, clearly to understand the problem: if God can change in communicating Godself, why should one assume that the communicated God corresponds to God as God existed before, or as God would have existed without, the self-communication? He attempts, moreover, to supply a rudimentary answer, which, due to the importance of the matter at hand, we quote at length:

---

[285] *Trinity*, 64; "Der dreifaltige Gott," *MS* ii, 358–9.
[286] Ibid. 64–5; ebd. 359.

93

First, we may simply point out that the experience of the absolute proximity of the God who communicates Godself in Christ is already interpreted in this way by the theology of the New Testament. This theology knows already of a descent Christology [*Deszendenzchristologie*] as an interpretation of an ascent Christology [*Aszendenzchristologie*] in the Synoptics and in the discourses of the Acts of the Apostles. But *how* and *why* did such an interpretation arise—a "theology" developed within the very framework of the history of revelation? Taking a leaf from this biblical interpretation itself we may say: Jesus knew of himself in a peculiar way as the "Son" *as well* with respect to the Father *as also* with respect to human beings. But this would be impossible if he were simply the Father making himself present and giving himself in a human reality. Let us suppose that...we should, in some kind of Sabellian way, allow the human reality to subsist hypostatically in the Father. In that case we could still in this humanity conceive of a spiritual, free, created subjectivity which might also refer to the Father in adoration, obedience, and so on....It might call this origin in which it subsists "Father." But as the concrete presence of the Father it could not with respect to *humanity* experience and express itself as the *Son* of the Father.[287]

These remarks, which Rahner himself characterizes as "brief and stammering words,"[288] do, of course, contain significant moments of truth. The central claim of the first half of Rahner's statement, nonetheless, seems partially gratuitous; and the central claim of the second half seems largely, albeit not entirely, immaterial.

The gratuitous aspect of the first half, naturally, does not consist in Rahner's acknowledgment of a robust descent Christology in the New Testament, especially in the Johannine literature and the epistles of Paul. The gratuitous aspect of Rahner's statement lies rather in the undefended assumption that this descent Christology constitutes "an interpretation of an ascent Christology...in the Synoptics and in the discourses of the Acts of the Apostles." For, first, the New Testament writers themselves do not claim that they reached their descent Christology by drawing conclusions from earlier, more modest claims. On the whole, they either: a) ascribe their Christology to Jesus' words delivered on earth (Matt 28:19; John 3:13; 8:23, 42, 58; 10:30; 12:45; 14:9; 16:15; 17:5, etc.) and from heaven (Gal 1:11-12; Rev 1:8, 11, 17; 22:13, etc.); or b) simply give no account of their Christology's origins.

If Rahner wishes to assert that the New Testament writers inferred the pre-existence of Jesus as a distinct divine person from some source other than verbal

---

[287] Ibid. 65; ebd.
[288] Ibid.; ebd.

testimony, moreover, he should explain how this could have occurred.[289] In the passage quoted above, however, which represents Rahner's principal effort to meet this challenge, Rahner explains, on the basis of Christ's filial consciousness, not how Jesus' followers could have recognized him as the pre-existent Son of God, but how they could have recognized him as the Son of God after the decisive event of divine self-communication.

That, however, is not at all to the point. For the question at hand is not how the disciples could have recognized Jesus as the intra-divine Logos, but rather how the disciples could have known, without simply being told, that the God who, according to Rahner, can and even must metamorphose when communicating the divine self, must have possessed a Logos prior to this self-communication. Rahner seems, then, not to substantiate his claim that Christ's disciples did, or even could have, inferred the eternal pre-existence of the Logos from their experience of Jesus and his resurrection without explicit, divinely authenticated, verbal testimony; and Rahner does not explain how the early community could have discovered the pre-existence and personality of the Holy Spirit.

It seems doubtful, moreover, that Rahner could explain how the disciples could reasonably have inferred these doctrines from their experience. What experience, short of the beatific vision, would suffice to justify, of itself, an inference to such subtle conclusions? What reason, short of a verbal revelation, moreover, could suffice to prove that a mutable God could not alter the structure of the intra-divine relations when communicating Godself in such a way as to render it impossible for human beings to infer the relational structure of God's inner being before God communicated the divine self from the structure God exhibits in the communication? Rahner seems to supply insufficient evidence for this last proposition, which is equivalent to the *Grundaxiom*; and, if one disallows a verbal revelation, it is difficult to imagine in what such evidence might consist.

---

[289] Cf. Rahner's remarks in ibid. 66, n. 18; ebd. 359, Anm. 18.

Rahner's argument for the *Grundaxiom* from divine self-communication, therefore, seems to face practically insuperable objections.

ii. The methodological rationale. Although Rahner explicitly proposes only one full-fledged argument for the *Grundaxiom*, viz. that from self-communication, a second concern seems to underlie both Rahner's vigorous advocacy of the *Grundaxiom* and the theological public's enthusiastic embrace of it. Rahner seeks, with the aid of the *Grundaxiom*, to place Trinitarian theology on a new methodological footing. Unlike neoscholastic theologians who consider the doctrine of the Trinity a datum revealed primarily through words and without foundation in ordinary, human experience, Rahner contends that "the mystery of the Trinity is the last mystery of our own reality, and...it is experienced precisely in this reality."[290] Though he cautions that "this does not imply...that we might, from this experience, by mere individual reflexion, conceptually objectivate the mystery,"[291] Rahner insists that when "we experience that the divine self-communication is given in two distinct ways, then the two intra-divine processions are already co-known as distinct in this experience of...faith."[292] In Rahner's view, accordingly, "we may...confidently look for an access into the doctrine of the Trinity in Jesus and in his Spirit, as we experience them through faith in salvation history."[293]

Instead of relying on putatively revealed propositions in the manner of the neoscholastics, therefore, Rahner seeks to elucidate the doctrine of the immanent Trinity by showing how it originates ultimately in the human experience of the economic Trinity. The following remarks of Rahner about the concepts of "substance" and "essence" reflect his approach to Trinitarian theology as a whole.

---

[290] Ibid. 47; ebd. 346.
[291] Ibid.; ebd.
[292] Ibid. 119; ebd. 396.
[293] Ibid. 39; ebd. 340.

> These concepts...always refer back to the origin from which they come: the experience of faith which assures us that the incomprehensible God is really, as he is in himself, given to us in the (for us) twofold reality of Christ and the Spirit....Hence insofar as the *dogmatically* necessary content of both concepts is concerned, nothing should be introduced into them except that which follows ultimately from our basic axiom, that which comes *from the fact* that the "economic" Trinity is *for us* first known and first revealed, that it is the "immanent" Trinity and that of it [i.e. the immanent Trinity] we can know with dogmatic certitude only what has been revealed about the former.[294]

According to Rahner, then, the *Grundaxiom*, in light of which the economic Trinity reveals the immanent Trinity,[295] is or at least can be the sole formal foundation of the doctrine of the immanent Trinity; and the human experience of the economic Trinity is or at least can be its sole material foundation, its genuine "*Ursprungsort-für-uns.*"[296]

d. Conclusion. In Rahner's view, then, one can: a) discern from one's experience of divine self-communication as objectified in Scripture that this communication contains irreducibly distinct, inseparable, and definitely ordered modes of subsistence; and b) by virtue of one's knowledge of the necessary correspondence between οἰκονομία and θεολογία expressed by the *Grundaxiom*, reasonably infer that these modes of subsistence correspond precisely and, indeed, are identical to those of the immanent Trinity. In the foregoing, we have expressed serious reservations about the *a priori* rule by which Rahner seeks to establish the soundness of such an inference.

We have not yet discussed in any detail, however, Rahner's account of the revelatory event which this *a priori* rule allows one to interpret as a revelation of the immanent Trinity: an account, which, as we shall see, proves quite complex

---

[294] Ibid. 55; ebd. 352.

[295] In Rahner's view, writes Mário de França Miranda, "the basic principle of Trinitarian theology, which acknowledges the economic Trinity and the immanent Trinity as identical, must be maintained on penalty of our knowing nothing of God, as God is in Godself" (*O mistério de Deus em nossa vida: a doutrina trinitária de Karl Rahner* [Coleção fé e realidade 1; São Paulo: Edições Loyola, 1975], 109).

[296] "Dogmen– und Theologiegeschichte," *ST* xiii, 32. In Rahner's view, writes Josep M. Rovira Belloso, "only [*tan sólo*] from the economy of salvation...is it possible to enter into the mystery of the Trinity...Only from here can we 'ascend' towards the Trinity in itself." ("Karl Rahner y la renovación de los estudios sobre la Trinidad," in *La teologia trinitaria de Karl Rahner* [Nereo Silanes, ed.; Koinonia 20; Salamanca: Ediciones Secretariado Trinitario, 1987], 95–109 at 103).

and, in some respects at least, quite as problematic as Rahner's defense of the *Grundaxiom*. Before proceeding to this topic, we would simply like to note that this account, no less than the *Grundaxiom* itself, plays an essential role in justifying Rahner's overall understanding of how God reveals the doctrine of the Trinity. A consistent application of the *Grundaxiom* itself, that is to say, could yield radically unorthodox conclusions if the economy of salvation did not display the proper relational structure. The account of the revelatory event and its Trinitarian structure summarized and critiqued in the next segment, therefore, constitutes an integral aspect of Rahner's case for a revelation of orthodox Trinitarianism mediated through divine self-communication.

3. The Trinitarian structure of the revelatory event.

a. Rahner's objective. Rahner seeks to demonstrate that divine revelation displays a Trinitarian structure by analyzing the concept of divine self-communication. In his words, he desires to show "how the Incarnation and the descent of the Spirit can, in the properties we know about them through revelation, be so 'conceptualized' [*auf den 'Begriff gebracht'*], or understood that they look like moments of the *one* self-communication of God, hence as *one* economic Trinity, and not merely as two 'functions' of two divine hypostases, which might be exchanged at will."[297]

b. Dual modalities of divine self-communication. Rahner seeks, more specifically, to conceive of divine self-communication in such a way that the very idea implicitly contains within itself dual modalities, corresponding to the missions of the Spirit and the Son, that: a) characterize such a self-communication necessarily; b) are irreducible to each other; and c) relate to each other in a certain τάξις that corresponds to the τάξις of the Son and the Spirit within the

---

[297] *Trinity*, 87; "Der dreifaltige Gott," *MS* ii, 373–4. Cf. ibid. 84–5; ebd. 372.

immanent Trinity. In this way, Rahner hopes to render credible his claim that the structure of God's self-communication necessarily mirrors the structure of God's inner life.

By divine self-communication, Rahner means, here as elsewhere, "the act whereby God goes out of Godself into 'the other' in such a way that God bestows Godself upon the other by becoming the other."[298] In Rahner's view, moreover, divine self-communication includes creation as a moment within itself and renders God "the very core of the world's reality"[299] and "the innermost constitutive element of the human person."[300] In consequence, Rahner reasons, one may characterize divine self-communication in terms of human beings' experience of it without fear of projecting the merely creaturely into the divine. Such a procedure, he writes, "does not necessarily imply that we add something to this self-communication, which would be extrinsic to it in itself, insofar as it comes from God."[301]

Rahner believes, therefore, that he possesses some basis for speaking of divine self-communication on the basis of human experience, prescinding from the testimony of Scripture and, in fact, produces quite a detailed account of God's self-communication from precisely this perspective. "Once we presuppose this concept of the self-communication of God," he writes, "it reveals to us a fourfold group of aspects: (a) Origin—Future; (b) History—Transcendence; (c) Invitation—Acceptance; (d) Knowledge—Love."[302] By opposing the first of each pair of aspects to the second and understanding the resultant "correlative axes"[303]

---

[298] "Mystery," *TI* iv, 68; "Geheimnis," *SW* xii, 131.

[299] "Specific Character," *TI* xxi, 191; "Eigenart," *ST* xv, 190.

[300] *Foundations*, 116; *Grundkurs*, *SW* xxvi, 116.

[301] *Trinity*, 89; "Der dreifaltige Gott," *MS* ii, 375.

[302] Ibid. 88; ebd. 374. Anthony Kelly, apparently following Rahner, employs virtually the same set of dyads to clarify the structure of divine self-communication in his *The Trinity of Love: A Theology of the Christian God* (New Theology Series 4; Wilmington, Del.: Michael Glazier, 1989), 105–6.

[303] We borrow this term from Emmanuel Durand, "L'autocommunication trinitaire: Concept clé de la *connexio mysteriorum* rahnérienne," *RT* 102 (2002), 569–613 at 587.

as unities, Rahner holds, one can gain knowledge of the "specific character"[304] of the "two basic manners [*Grundweisen*] of the self-communication of God"[305] and, therefore, of the nature and relationships of the two divine processions of the Son and Spirit.

c. Rahner's dyads.

i. Introduction. In order to evaluate Rahner's schematization of the human experience of divine self-communication adequately, it seems, one must, first, gain some sense of why Rahner considers the dyads, origin—future, history—transcendence, invitation—acceptance, and knowledge—love, correlative opposites that correspond to the processions of the Son and the Spirit; and, second, ask whether, given the presuppositions of Rahner's larger theology, these dyads constitute apt representations of the relations between the two divine processions.

ii. Origin—future. "Origin" and "future" belong among the correlative modalities of divine self-communication as experienced by *viatores*, according to Rahner, insofar as: a) divine self-communication possesses "a beginning, in which the addressee of a possible divine self-communication is constituted by the will which decided this self-communication;"[306] and b) "this beginning or origin aims at a future (the total communication of God), which should not be considered as that which develops naturally from the beginning, but as something which, despite the latter's finalization towards the future, stands opposed to the beginning as the other moment of something radically new, something separated by a real history of freedom."[307]

---

[304] *Trinity*, 94; "Der dreifaltige Gott," *MS* ii, 378.
[305] Ibid.; ebd.
[306] Ibid. 91; ebd. 376.
[307] Ibid.; ebd.

In other words, Rahner identifies: 1) the beginning of divine self-communication with creation itself, either of the individual or of the cosmos or possibly both; and 2) the future of divine self-communication with "the total communication of God," by which Rahner presumably means either the finalization of one's fundamental option for God achieved in death[308] or the "recapitulation" of the cosmos into God at the eschaton[309] or, again, possibly both.

If one prescinds from Rahner's knowledge that, according to dogma, the Son's procession logically precedes that of the Spirit, it is difficult to see why Rahner associates "origin" with the procession of the Son rather than that of the Spirit. An understanding of the atonement as a satisfaction of divine justice would, admittedly, guarantee a priority of the Son's work in the economy over the Spirit's insofar as the Son's appeasement of divine wrath would, on such a theory, constitute a prerequisite of God's bestowal of grace on repentant sinners by the Holy Spirit. Rahner, however, pointedly rejects all theories of the atonement that portray Christ's death as a satisfaction or substitution,[310] choosing, instead, to conceive of Christ as savior only to the extent that he constitutes: a) salvation's perfect exemplar, and so its final cause;[311] and b) the sign of divine self-communication's eschatological irreversibility, and so salvation's "sacramental" cause, which causes salvation by signifying it.[312] In "origin" and "future," then, Rahner finds aspects of the human experience of divine self-communication that do seem both correlative and opposed. Their correspondence to the processions of the Son and Spirit respectively, however, seems far from obvious.

---

[308] Cf. e.g. "Dogmatic Questions on Easter," *TI* iv, 121–133 at 128; "Dogmatische Fragen zur Osterfrömmigkeit," *SW* xii, 323–34 at 329.

[309] Cf. *Foundations*, 189; *Grundkurs*, *SW* xxvi, 184.

[310] Cf. e.g. "Reconciliation and Vicarious Representation," *TI* xxi, 255–69 at 265–6; "Versöhnung und Stellvertretung," *ST* xv, 251–64 at 261.

[311] Cf. e.g. "Jesus Christ in the Non-Christian Religions," *TI* xvii, 39–50 at 46; "Jesus Christus in der nichtchristlichen Religionen," *ST* xii, 370–83 at 377.

[312] Cf. e.g. "The Christian Understanding of Redemption," *TI* xxi, 239–54 at 250–1; "Das christliche Verständnis der Erlösung," *ST* xv, 236–50 at 246–7.

iii. History—transcendence. History and transcendence form the second pair of modalities identified by Rahner as constitutive of the human experience of divine self-communication. "There belongs to the human person," writes Rahner:

> essentially the following open difference which we indicate with these two words: the difference (in knowledge and in action) between the concrete object and the "horizon" within which this object comes to stand, between the *apriori* and the *aposteriori* of knowledge and freedom, between the way in which knowledge and activity reach the well-determined concrete here and now (*so* and *not* otherwise) and the open range which knowledge and action anticipate, from whose vantage point, by limiting themselves, they ever again establish the "object," while ever again discovering its contingency.[313]

In this, in itself rather cryptic, sentence, Rahner seems to appeal to his metaphysics of knowledge to endow the terms "history" and "transcendence" with unconventional meanings. If this is the case, one can reasonably identify the "history" to which Rahner refers as the human experience of concrete particulars within the infinite, athematic horizon opened up by the dynamism of the human spirit towards the totality of possible objects of its knowledge and love.

This dynamism, likewise, which is presumably what Rahner means here by "transcendence," constitutes human beings as knowing subjects over against the particular things of the world by enabling them to perceive themselves and the objects of their sensation as distinct and limited concretizations of the *esse commune* that (along with *esse absolutum* according to the later Rahner) constitutes: a) the horizon within which human subjects experience particular things of the concrete world; and b) the term of their athematic, and yet both conscious and free, primal striving.

"History" and "transcendence," thus understood, correspond to the missions of the Son and Spirit, as Rahner conceives of them, in that: a) Rahner considers the Incarnation merely the most profound among many manifestations of the same, transcendental, divine self-communication responsible for creation and all events of human history; and b) he identifies the indwelling of the Holy Spirit with the

---

[313] *Trinity*, 91–2; "Der dreifaltige Gott," *MS* ii, 377.

divine endowment of all human intellects with a supernatural, formal object: i.e. an *a priori* horizon of consciousness that consists not merely in *esse commune*, but in God.

In Rahner's view, then, just as, according to Christian proclamation, one accepts God's offer of grace poured out in the Holy Spirit through faith in the Son, so one correctly aligns oneself vis-à-vis one's supernatural, formal object by faithfully responding to the categorical particulars encountered in concrete experience. Just as "no one can say 'Jesus is Lord' except by the Holy Spirit" (1 Cor 12:3), likewise, Rahner believes that categorical particulars can mediate the experience of grace to persons only insofar as these particulars are experienced within a supernaturally elevated, transcendental horizon. One who accepts Rahner's transcendental-anthropological formulation of the gospel, therefore, cannot reasonably question the aptness of "history" and "transcendence" as characterizations of the divine missions as experienced by human beings.

iv. Offer–acceptance. Rahner supplies few details, at least in *Mysterium Salutis*, about the third pair of aspects he identifies as constitutive of the human experience of divine self-communication: offer and acceptance. "If," he writes, "the human person is the being with the one duality of origin and future, if she is history in (into) transcendence, and *thus* the free being, then God's self-communication must also mean the difference between *offer* and *acceptance* (the *third* couple of aspects) of this self-communication."[314]

Rahner seems to think, then, that offer and acceptance evidently characterize the human experience of divine self-communication and that they do so in a way that corresponds to the missions of the Son and Spirit if one understands this experience and those missions in the terms in which Rahner describes them. It seems difficult, moreover, reasonably to dispute this verdict. If, as Rahner claims,

---

[314] Ibid. 92; ebd.

103

"God has really and in a strict sense offered *Godself* in Jesus,"[315] after all, "offer" seems an eminently appropriate way to characterize the modality of Christ's presence to the world. Likewise, if the light of faith, through which one accepts God's offer of salvation in Christ, is "brought about by the Spirit and ultimately identical with the Spirit,"[316] then one can fittingly describe the Holy Spirit as present to human beings in the modality of "acceptance."

v. Knowledge—love.

α. The problematic. The fourth and final dyad of modalities identified by Rahner as constitutive of human beings' experience of divine self-communication consists in "*knowledge* and *love*, [i.e.] actuation of truth and actuation of love."[317] Although the words, knowledge/truth and will/love, constitute traditional characterizations of the Son and Spirit, Rahner assigns unconventional senses to his terms in order to render them suitable for employment in his transcendental-anthropological account of divine self-communication.

β. Truth. Specifically, Rahner insists that truth, properly understood:

is not first the correct grasping of a state of affairs. It consists first [rather] in letting our own personal essence come to the fore, positing ourself without dissimulation, accepting oneself and letting this authentic nature come to the fore in truth also in the presence of others....This true "revealing"—letting our nature come to the fore in the presence of others— is (when it includes a free commitment to the other) what we call "fidelity." Hence truth is first the truth which we *do*, the deed in which we firmly posit ourself for ourself and others.[318]

The clearest defense of this understanding of truth in Rahner's corpus appears not, as one might expect, in his early investigations into the metaphysics of knowledge, but in one of Rahner's spiritual writings: the essay, "Über die

---

[315] *Foundations*, 280; *Grundkurs*, SW xxvi, 267.
[316] "Considerations on the Development of Dogma," *TI* iv, 25; Überlegungen zur Dogmenentwicklung," *SW* ix, 461.
[317] *Trinity*, 93; "Der dreifaltige Gott," *MS* ii, 377.
[318] Ibid. 95–6; ebd. 379–80.

Wahrhaftigkeit." In the first of three stages of a particular argument about the nature of truth in this essay, Rahner asserts:

> Reality is essentially not the objective status of things which cognitive being is 'set over against' as something independent, alien and separate....Reality is ultimately spirit and person, and in the measure that a given reality is not this, is incapable of realizing itself, is not objectified to itself, is not apparent to itself, in the same measure the being of this reality is itself as such weak and lacking in ultimate validity.[319]

In other words, Rahner postulates at the outset of his argument the understanding of being as being's-presence-to-itself that he achieves in his early writings on the metaphysics of knowledge. On this basis, then, Rahner asserts in the second stage of his argument: 1) that truth considered as a characteristic of being rather than as a property of statements, consists fundamentally in self-awareness; and 2) that truthfulness in its most primordial sense thus consists in the accurate self-disclosure of one's being to oneself. In Rahner's words:

> Truth, as the givenness of a thing to itself, is an intrinsic element in reality itself, so that a given being has being and exists to the extent that it...discloses to itself the truth that is its own nature. From this point of view, therefore, truthfulness is not, in the first instance, a virtue, a moral prescription which regulates human intercourse, but...the self-confrontation of a reality in so far as this self-confrontation is faithful and really reproduces this 'being to itself' clearly and luminously, undistorted and really achieved, expressed and really accepted.[320]

Rahner presumably includes acceptance among the criteria of truthfulness, because, in his view, knowledge and freedom are, at least in their most primordial senses, identical.[321] According to Rahner, then, one can truly know oneself only to the extent that one accepts oneself.

In the third and final stage of the present argument, then, Rahner introduces the notion of truthfulness to others and states explicitly a conclusion implicit in the previous citation: that truth and truthfulness are ultimately identical. Referring back to the last sentence of the previous bloc quote in which he describes interior

---

[319] "On Truthfulness," *TI* vii, 229–59 at 257; *SW* x, 447–68 at 466–7.
[320] Ibid. 257–8; ebd. 467.
[321] Cf. *Hearer*, 83, 126 (*Hörer*, *SW* iv, 152, 154, 224); "Incomprehensibility," *TI* xvi, 254 ("Unbegreiflichkeit," *ST* xii, 319).

truthfulness as "the self-confrontation of a reality in so far as this self-confrontation is faithful," Rahner writes:

> It is here, then, that truthfulness towards others as well has its source. It imparts to the other person only what the individual herself is. It makes her own unique personality emerge from its hidden background and appear before that other pure and undistorted. This truthfulness is in the first instance the free self-disclosure of one's personal being as rendered present to one's self, made available to others, the conveying of one's own personal truth to others. And for this reason it is true that truth and truthfulness are at basis the same: the act of uttering one's own truth faithfully to others. Truth is in origin not the emergence of any kind of thing, but the self-bestowal of being upon itself. As such it is essentially personal, and truthfulness is the disclosure precisely of this personal being to others in freedom and love.[322]

In other words, Rahner claims that just as truthfulness towards oneself consists in accurate self-disclosure of one's being to oneself, so truthfulness towards others consists in accurate disclosure of one's being to others. Why Rahner, in this passage, identifies the first kind of truthfulness with truth itself seems relatively clear: one possesses self-awareness, i.e. what Rahner means in this context by truth, to the extent that one faithfully discloses one's being to oneself. How truth, in the sense of self-awareness, can be identical with truthfulness towards others, as Rahner also claims in this passage, seems, by contrast, obscure.

The obscurity dissolves, however, when one realizes that, in Rahner's view, truthfulness towards others is a necessary consequence of the self-awareness and self-acceptance that constitute truthfulness towards oneself. It is nothing more than truthfulness towards oneself, that is to say, as this truthfulness manifests itself to other persons. That Rahner does, in fact, understand truthfulness towards others in this manner appears from the following remarks, also taken from the essay "Über die Wahrhaftigkeit," about lying and liars. "What is a liar?" Rahner asks, "or, more precisely: Who finds it necessary to lie?"

> Evidently it is she who feels herself insecure,...who has something to hide which in her opinion would, if it were known, lower her in the esteem of others. The liar attaches value to this esteem as if it were something vitally necessary to her existence. In this sense the lie appears as a weapon, presumed to be necessary, in the struggle for self-assertion....Considered in this light, as a weapon necessary for one's self-assertion, the lie must seem, in the long run, unavoidable to

---

[322] "On Truthfulness," *TI* vii, 258; "Über die Wahrhaftigkeit," *SW* x, 467.

anyone who has not been interiorly liberated from herself in interior truthfulness, and found the absolute courage she needs in order to discover her true nature in the infinite mystery of truth....Only one who has hidden her own true and ultimate selfhood in God, and delivered it into God's protection, only one who has thereby become secure and unassailable in a truly ultimate sense, finds it no longer necessary...to defend herself. And only one who no longer has to defend herself can in all cases be truthful to her neighbour.[323]

Precisely how this quotation resolves the obscurity in the previous citation might, admittedly, seem obscure. Again, however, the obscurity dissolves when one realizes that Rahner identifies self-acceptance, which on account of the presumed identity of knowing and willing constitutes self-awareness and interior truthfulness, with the athematic acceptance of the self-communication of God. "Anyone who really accepts *herself*," Rahner writes, "accepts a mystery in the sense of the infinite emptiness which is humanity. She accepts herself in the immensity of her unpredictable destiny and—silently, and without premeditation—she accepts the One who has decided to fill this infinite emptiness (which is the mystery of humanity) with God's own infinite fullness (which is the mystery of God)."[324]

In Rahner's view, accordingly, the person who is truthful to others is precisely the person who accepts God; and the person who accepts God is the person who accepts herself. If, then, the person who accepts herself is precisely the person who is interiorly truthful, the person who is interiorly truthful is, likewise, truthful to others: in which case truthfulness to others constitutes nothing other than interior truthfulness as it manifests itself in interpersonal relations. Now, if exterior truthfulness is interior truthfulness, and interior truthfulness is truth itself, then it seems that truth does consist in "letting our own personal essence come to the fore, positing ourself without dissimulation, accepting oneself and letting this authentic nature come to the fore in truth also in the presence of others."[325] Given Rahner's presuppositions, then, his definition of truth seems quite accurate.

---

[323] Ibid. 240; ebd. 454–5.
[324] "Thoughts on the Possibility of Belief Today," *TI* v, 3–22 at 7–8; "Über die Möglichkeit des Glaubens heute," *SW* x, 574–89 at 578.
[325] *Trinity*, 95–6; "Der dreifaltige Gott," *MS* ii, 379–80.

γ. *Love.* Rahner says relatively little, by comparison, in his two, principal statements about love as a modality of divine self-communication. In the first statement, by which Rahner seeks to refute the view that the human spirit possesses three basic modalities rather than two, Rahner writes, "If we understand will, freedom, 'good' in their true and total essence, that is, above all, not only as a mere drive but as love for a person, a love which does not simply strive towards this person but rests in her full goodness and 'splendor,' *then* we can see *no* reason for adding a third and higher power to this duality."[326]

In the second statement, by which Rahner seeks to vindicate the appropriateness of placing love alongside "transcendence—futurity—acceptance of the future"[327] on the axis representing characteristics of the Spirit's mission, Rahner writes, "The self-communication which wills itself absolutely and creates the possibility of its acceptance and this acceptance itself, is precisely what is meant by love. It is the specifically divine 'case' of love, because it creates its own acceptance and because this love is the freely offered and accepted self-communication of the 'person.'"[328]

These brief remarks about the nature of love seem self-explanatory. In their similarities and contrasts with Rahner's statements about truth, however, they are rife with implications. The concern Rahner evinces in the first remark for demonstrating that truth and love require no complement, for instance, may explain why Rahner employs an expansive definition of truth, encompassing truth as a characteristic of being, truthfulness towards oneself, truthfulness towards others, and even, in a secondary sense, truth as correspondence between thought and reality.[329] Rahner's second statement about love, in which he seeks to

---

[326] Ibid. 93–4; ebd. 378.
[327] Ibid. 97; ebd. 381.
[328] Ibid. 97–8; ebd.
[329] Cf. ibid. 95, n. 14; ebd. 379, Anm. 14.

characterize the "specifically divine 'case' of love," however, at least hints at the limitations of Rahner's definition of truth.

δ. Criticism. This definition's principal limitation seems to consist in Rahner's failure to distinguish between truth's notional and essential senses. Rahner defines truth, and to a lesser extent love as well, that is to say, without regard to the distinction between essential properties, which the divine persons possess in common and which correspond to created analogates; and notional properties, i.e. the purely relative properties that distinguish the divine persons and which, as purely relative, have no created counterparts. In one sense, admittedly, Rahner is quite justified in ignoring this distinction. For: a) the divine relations being objectively identical with the divine essence, one can never experience one in the concrete without also experiencing the other;[330] and b) as Rahner himself, somewhat surprisingly, notes, "a 'personal,' 'notional' concept of the word and 'inclination' of love cannot be derived from human experience."[331]

To the extent that Rahner describes the modalities of divine self-communication precisely in order to show how the economic Trinity that human beings experience corresponds to the immanent Trinity, however, Rahner's failure to differentiate between essential and notional properties defeats his purpose. For Rahner admits that the "Father, Son, and Spirit are only 'relatively' distinct":[332] "the persons are distinct," he writes, "only through their *esse ad*."[333] He admits, moreover, that in all other aspects of their being, including knowledge (= self-presence) and love (=will), the divine persons are absolutely identical: "there

---

[330] "In both 'economic' self-communications of God," Rahner writes, "God is given in God's (essential) fullness" (ibid. 116; ebd. 394).
[331] Ibid. 19; ebd. 326.
[332] Ibid. 68; ebd. 361.
[333] Ibid. 71; ebd. 363.

exists in God," he writes, "only *one* power, *one* will, only one self-presence, a unique activity, a unique beatitude, and so forth."[334]

Rahner implicitly acknowledges, therefore, that if one equates the distinction between the Logos and the Spirit *qua* communicated with the distinction between divine knowledge and divine love *simpliciter*, one posits a non-relative distinction between the divine persons in the economy of salvation. Now, the existence of such a distinction in the economy of salvation would imply one of two consequences, neither of which is acceptable to Rahner: either a) non-relative distinctions must exist within the immanent Trinity; or b) the economic Trinity does not correspond precisely to the immanent Trinity.

It would be unfair, of course, to claim that Rahner equates the modalities of the Son's and the Spirit's communication *ad extra* with divine knowledge and love *simpliciter*. As we have seen, Rahner takes particular care to depict the love that constitutes a modality of the Spirit's communication *ad extra* in such a way that one can neither equate it with the love of God *in se* nor with a merely human, interpersonal love. Nevertheless, Rahner does seem to operate with global conceptions of knowledge and love, whose essential and notional moments remain undifferentiated. It seems, therefore, that one can reasonably apply to Rahner a criticism he levels against scholastic theologians who, like himself, attempt to correlate the divine processions with knowledge and love. The scholastic theologians' "Augustinian-psychological speculations on the Trinity," Rahner writes:

result in that well-known quandary which makes all of their marvelous profundity look so utterly vacuous: for they begin from a human philosophical concept of knowledge and love, and from this concept develop a concept of the word and 'inclination' of love; and now, after having speculatively applied these concepts to the Trinity, they must admit that this application fails, because they have clung to the 'essential' concept of knowledge and love, because a 'personal,' 'notional' concept of the word and 'inclination' of love cannot be derived from human experience.[335]

---

[334] Ibid. 75; ebd. 366.
[335] Ibid. 19; ebd. 326.

Rahner's unwillingness to distinguish between notional and essential senses of knowledge and love, therefore, renders the dyad "knowledge—love," as Rahner characterizes it at least, inapt for the task to which Rahner puts it: viz. specifying the process by which the relations of Son and Spirit in the economy of salvation mirror their relations in the immanent Trinity.

vi. Evaluation. Rahner neglects, in fact, to distinguish between the notional and the essential significance of any of his four dyads. It seems, accordingly, that one can reasonably generalize our unfavorable conclusions about Rahner's treatment of knowledge and love to each of the four dyads, at least as Rahner unfolds their content.

d. Results. Rahner's attempt to generate a concept of divine self-communication that manifests how such a communication contains two correlative and irreducible modalities that relate to each other precisely as the processions of the Son and Spirit relate to each other in the immanent Trinity, therefore, seems unsuccessful. Rahner's lack of success in this endeavor, nonetheless, in no way invalidates his *Grundaxiom*. The weaknesses of his systematic conception of divine self-communication as Trinitarian indicate at most, rather, that Rahner's treatment of the relation between the Son and Spirit in the economy of salvation would have benefited from attention to certain "subtle considerations of school theology,"[336] such as the distinction between notional and essential truth, which Rahner chooses to ignore.[337]

---

[336] Ibid. 81; ebd. 370.

[337] Cf. Ghislain Lafont's more pointed criticisms of Rahner along the same lines in his *Peut–on connaître Dieu en Jésus–Christ?* (Cogitatio Fidei; Paris: Cerf, 1969), 202–5, 208–9, 216.

III. CONCLUSION

Both Rahner's *Grundaxiom* and his account of the event of Trinitarian self-revelation, therefore, face formidable difficulties to which he supplies no unambiguously satisfactory response. These difficulties, however, by no means render the critique of Rahner's *Grundaxiom* mounted in the following two chapters superfluous. For one could plausibly argue that an implicit answer to our concerns about change in a simple being appears in Rahner's dialectical understanding of God's immutability in Godself and mutability in another and/or in his equally dialectical understanding of divine self-communication. We intend to address these possibilities, accordingly, in chapter three.

Likewise, one could plausibly argue that the *Grundaxiom*, or a close analogate of it such as Eberhard Jüngel's "God corresponds to Godself,"[338] possesses, if not unmistakable warrant, at least sufficient plausibility to serve as a basis for the theology of the Trinity in the absence of a verbal revelation. In chapter four, therefore we intend to show that, even if one granted the soundness of the *Grundaxiom*, one could not derive the orthodox, Latin doctrine of the Trinity from the economy of salvation with its aid, because: a) Rahner's explicit statements about the orthodox doctrine of the Trinity preclude the possibility of the Trinitarian persons' indicating their distinctness by their actions; and b) the New Testament accounts of Christ's anointing with the Holy Spirit, when interpreted in accordance with the *Grundaxiom*, seem to entail consequences that Rahner would find unacceptable. The brief, preliminary criticisms of this chapter, therefore, convey some sense of why one might question the soundness of Rahner's *Grundaxiom*. They hardly suffice, however, for a comprehensive refutation.

---

[338] Eberhard Jüngel, *The Doctrine of the Trinity: God's Being is in Becoming* (Horton Harris, tr.; SJTh.OP; Edinburgh: Scottish Academic Press, 1976), 24.

CHAPTER 3

I. INTRODUCTION

In the previous chapter, we introduced Rahner's views on the revelation of the Trinity while leveling two preliminary criticisms of his idea of the identity of the economic and the immanent Trinity. First, we argued, if God is simple, as Rahner admits, then the slightest change in any aspect of the divine being would effect more or less radical changes in every aspect of God's being. It seems, then, that if God must change in order to communicate Godself, as Rahner maintains God must, then the intra-Trinitarian relations of God as communicated must differ in some measure from those relations as they subsist eternally and necessarily in the immanent Trinity

We also noted that Trinitarian patterns within the experience of divine self-communication and its objectification in salvation history seem not, by themselves, to warrant inferences to the doctrine of the immanent Trinity. For, if God could alter the very divine being, then it would seem difficult, if not impossible, to distinguish novel from permanent aspects of that being on the basis of mere religious experience. We examined Rahner's response, to the extent that he supplies one, to this criticism in the last chapter, moreover, and found it wanting in crucial respects.

We have yet to explore the resources offered by Rahner's theology for a response to the first criticism. It seems vitally necessary for us to explore these resources, however, insofar as a successful rebuttal of the first criticism would seem to blunt the force of the second considerably. If one assumed, that is to say, that God reveals Godself only through the experience of divine self-communication, then one would have reason to suspect that the relational structure of the divine being as communicated in time corresponds rather exactly to that which characterizes God in eternity. Admittedly, one could not deduce the point, but if: 1) the experience of divine self-communication did constitute the sole medium of revelation; and 2) if one could vindicate Rahner's vision of becoming in a simple being from the charge of absurdity; then, it seems, 3) one could reasonably hope that one's experience of God *pro nobis* corresponds in some analogous way to God's being *in se*. There is a certain intrinsic plausibility to the dictum, "God corresponds to Godself."[339]

In the remainder of this chapter, therefore, we shall: a) rehearse some of Rahner's emphatic statements in favor of both classical and quasi-Hegelian understandings of the divine attributes in order to illustrate the tension in Rahner's thought exploited by the second criticism; b) analyze Bert van der Heijden's argument that Rahner's views on divine self-communication, when correctly interpreted, do not ultimately conflict with the doctrine of divine immutability; and c) assess an indirect argument concerning sanctifying grace and the Incarnation for the compatibility of the doctrines of divine immutability, simplicity, etc. with Rahner's views on divine self-communication.

II. DIVINE TRANSCENDENCE AND SELF-COMMUNICATION

1. Introduction. We intend in this section, as we just announced, to document the tension in Rahner's thought between divine transcendence and divine self-communication as Rahner conceives of it and thus to demonstrate the relevance of the first criticism in the context of an immanent critique of Rahner's position.

2. Rahner's acknowledgement of divine transcendence. Throughout his corpus, Rahner upholds, at least guardedly and with qualifications, at least six elements of classical theism that might seem to exclude his understanding of divine self-communication peremptorily.

---

[339] Ibid.

a. Simplicity. Rahner states, first, that "God...is absolutely 'simple' precisely because of God's infinite fullness of being (because every differentiation in a common dimension of being is an indication of reference to another and so bespeaks finitude), so that everything (not merely relatively) plural, antagonistic, and contradictory is an indication of non-divine worldliness."[340] In other words, "God...is absolute and simple spirit."[341]

b. Immutability. Rahner affirms in various places, second, that "God is and remains unchangeable in Godself."[342] Christians, Rahner writes, and "all really theistic philosophers...proclaim God as the 'Unchangeable', the one who simply is—*actus purus*—who...possesses from eternity to eternity the absolute, unwavering...fullness of what God is."[343] They proclaim these things, moreover, "not," in Rahner's view, "only under the tyranny of a rigid metaphysics of infinity"; they "say it because we need someone who is not as we are, so that we may be redeemed in that which we are."[344] Rahner, in fine, affirms in no uncertain terms God's immutability.

c. Atemporality. Rahner, third, avows his belief in God's atemporality. "Christian theology must hold firm," he writes, "to the 'immutability' and 'eternal' timelessness of God 'in themselves.'"[345]

d. Impassibility. He does not shrink, moreover, fourth, from affirming God's impassibility even in the death of the God-Man on the cross. "Jesus' fate," he writes, "does not impinge upon God's own life, with its metahistorical character and its freedom from suffering and its beatitude without guilt, since God's reality

---

340 "Gott V. Die Lehre des kirchl. Lehramtes," *LThK*² iv in *SW* xvii/i, 264–7 at 266.
341 "Immanent and Transcendent," *TI* x, 287; "Immanente und transzendente," *SW* xv, 555.
342 "Christology Today," *TI* xxi, 220–27 at 222; "Christologie heute," *ST* xv, 217–24 at 219.
343 "Incarnation," *TI* iv, 112; "Menschwerdung," *SW* xii, 315.
344 "Current Problems," *TI* i, 149–200 at 178; "Probleme," *SW* xii, 261–301 at 283.
345 "Theological Observations on the Concept of Time," *TI* xi, 288–308 at 307; "Theologische Bemerkungen zum Zeitbegriff," *SW* xv, 622–37 at 636.

and Jesus' creatureliness remain unmixed."[346] Even through the darkness of Golgotha, Rahner affirms, the eternal Logos "has remained eternally the same, untouched."[347] Rahner, in other words, seems at times to evince a firm and uncompromising faith in the impassibility of God.

e. No real relations to the world. Indeed, fifth, Rahner endorses that perennial quarry for critics of classical theism, the doctrine that God has no real relations to the world. The deity, he writes, "cannot experience itself as defined in relation to another or limited by another."[348] God possesses, according to Rahner, "infinite and abiding unrelatedness."[349]

f. Distinctness from the world. Sixth and finally, Rahner maintains that God "inexpressibly transcends everything that is or can be thought outside Godself."[350] He insists on "a radical distinction between God and the world."[351]

Rahner, then, admits that God transcends the world in at least six respects. God does not partake of its: 1) composition; 2) mutability; 3) temporality; or 4) passibility. Indeed; 5) God does not even possess real relations to it so that one can justly consider God 6) radically distinct from it. Rahner, in sum, endorses, at

---

[346] "Jesus Christ—The Meaning of Life," *TI* xxi, 208–19 at 215; "Jesus Christus—Sinn des Lebens," *ST* xv, 206–16 at 212.
[347] "Current Problems," *TI* i, 178; "Probleme," *SW* xii, 283.
[348] *Foundations*, 74; *Grundkurs*, *SW* xxvi, 75.
[349] "Incarnation," *TI* iv, 114; "Menschwerdung," *SW* xii, 317. When classical theists claim that God has no real relations to the world, they mean to assert that God is in no way dependent on the world. As Aquinas explains:

Whenever two things are referred to each other, one also depends on the other, but not *e converso*; in that which depends on the other, there is a real relation. Yet in that on which it depends, there is no relation except in thought….Since all creatures depend on God, but not *e converso*, in creatures there are real relations by which they are referred to God. Yet in God there are corresponding relations only in thought (*De ver.* q. 4, a. 5 corp.).

For a more extensive explanation and defense of the claim that God has no real relations to the world, cf. Martin J. De Nys, "God, Creatures, and Relations: Revisiting Classical Theism," *JR* 81 (2001), 595–614.

[350] "Priest and Poet," *TI* iii, 294–317 at 309; "Priester und Dichter," *SW* xii, 421–40 at 433.
[351] "Specific Character," *TI* xxi, 191; "Eigenart," *ST* xv, 190.

least occasionally and with, as we shall see, severe qualifications, a fairly traditional understanding of divine transcendence.

3. Absolute self-communication. Rahner expresses views on divine self-communication, however, that seem to conflict with his guarded endorsements of classical theism.

a. "God becomes world." Rahner's avowals of divine transcendence notwithstanding, for instance, he insists on the existence of an "immediate self-communication of God in quasi-formal causality"[352] to human beings. As he explains:

> When we speak of God's self-communication, we should not understand this term in the sense that God would say something *about* Godself in some revelation or other. The term "self-communication" is really intended to signify that God in God's own most proper reality makes the divine self the innermost constitutive element of the human person.[353]

In Rahner's view, this implies that humanity constitutes "the event [*Ereignis*] of God's absolute self-communication."[354] "When God 'lets *Godself* go out of Godself'," he writes, "then there appears the human person."[355] Again, "if God wills to become non-God, the human being comes to be."[356] Rahner seems very much to consider humanity the product of God's "self-alienation"[357] and "self-exteriorization."[358]

By no means, moreover, does he restrict this radical self-communication of God to human beings. "There is no problem," he writes, "in understanding what is called creation as a partial moment in the process in which God becomes

---

[352] "Mystery," *TI* iv, 66; "Geheimnis," *SW* xii, 129.
[353] *Foundations*, 116; *Grundkurs, SW* xxvi, 116.
[354] Ibid. 119; ebd. 119.
[355] "Thoughts on the Theology of Christmas," *TI* iii, 24–34 at 32; "Zur Theologie der Weihnachtsfeier," *SW* xiv, 97–105 at 103.
[356] "Incarnation," *TI* iv, 116; 'Menschwerdung," *SW* xii, 319.
[357] "Current Problems," *TI* i, 176, n. 1; "Probleme," *SW* xii, 282, Anm. 28.
[358] "Symbol," *TI* iv, 239; "Symbols," *SW* xviii, 439. Cf. also "Nature and Grace," *TI* iv, 176; "Natur und Gnade," *ST* iv, 222.

world."[359] God, according to Rahner, "has inserted Godself into the world as its innermost *entelecheia*"[360] and as such propels it towards a final "recapitulation into itself and into its ground."[361] By divine self-communication, then, Rahner seems to mean an act which renders "God...the very core of the world's reality."[362]

b. Real relations to the world. When speaking of the Incarnation, which he considers a singularly potent instance of divine self-communication, furthermore, Rahner seems to contradict his endorsements, in a different context, of divine unrelatedness. "We, scholastics," he states, "we say frequently that God has no real relations *ad extra*. This formula expresses something true, but, nevertheless, who is this God who has no real relation to me? This is absurd."[363] Rahner affirms, then, that his idea of divine self-communication, at least in this instance, nullifies any straightforward assertion of divine unrelatedness, and, accordingly, declares "the assertion of...the lack of any real relation between God and the world" a "dialectical statement."[364]

---

[359] *Foundations*, 197; *Grundkurs*, *SW* xxvi, 190. Cf. "Christianity and the 'New Man,'" *TI* v, 135–53 at 147; "Das Christentum und der 'Neue Mensch,'" *SW* xv, 138–53 at 148.
[360] "The Position of Christology in the Church," *TI* xi, 200; "Kirchliche Christologie," *ST* ix, 213.
[361] *Foundations*, 189; *Grundkurs*, *SW* xxvi, 184.
[362] "Specific Character," *TI* xxi, 191; "Eigenart," *ST* xv, 190.
[363] "Débats sur le rapport du P. Rahner," in Henri Bouëssé and Jean-Jacques Latour, ed. *Problèmes actuels de Christologie: Travaux du Symposium de L'arbresle 1961* (Bruges: Desclée de Brouwer, 1965), 407.
[364] "Current Problems," *TI* i, 181, n. 3; "Probleme," *SW* xii, 286, Anm. 32. Dialectical statements, it is important to note, are subject to grave abuse. If the premises of an argument, after all, include p and ~p, then, on the basis of p, one can validly deduce "p or q": even if q is obviously false. Then one can combine "p or q" with the premise ~p and thereby validly infer the obvious falsehood q. Any absurd proposition q, accordingly, can be justified by a set of premises that are dialectically juxtaposed.

Likewise, the acceptance of dialectical statements tends to render theories immune to criticism. For, in order to refute any system of thought, one must show that it contradicts itself or some datum independent of it. Yet, if the proponent of the theory in questions admits the legitimacy of juxtaposing contradictory statements dialectically, she can argue that contradictions between her own statements or her statements and some other truths do not disprove her theory. Such contradictions need not be unacceptable, she might reason, if one's logic is tolerant of dialectical assertions. We are indebted for this argument and the former to Karl Popper, "What is Dialectic?" *Mind* 49 (1940), 403–26, esp. 408–9 and 417.

c. Temporality. Similarly, in the context of the Incarnation understood as self-communication, Rahner asserts that "God...undergoes history, change, and so too time; the time of the world is God's own history"[365] and thus seems to contradict his affirmations of divine atemporality.

d. Passibility. Likewise, Rahner insists on affirming the "death *of God*,"[366] i.e. not merely the death of God's human nature, in Christ's crucifixion: a sentiment difficult to reconcile with his statements quoted above in support of divine impassibility.

e. Mutability. Rahner does not attempt, moreover, pellucidly to reconcile his understanding of divine self-communication with the dogma of divine immutability. He rests satisfied, instead, with the paradoxical formula: "The one who is not subject to change in Godself can *Godself* be subject to change *in something else.*"[367] This statement, he admits, "is not intended to offer a positive insight into the compatibility of the dogma of God's immutability and the possibility of becoming in the eternal Logos, nor a positive solution to the duality of this fundamental Christian assertion. It is [merely] a formulation which clearly and seriously maintains both sides of it.[368]

---

[365] "Concept of Time," *TI* xi, 307–8; "Zeitbegriff," *SW* xv, 636.
[366] *Foundations*, 305; *Grundkurs*, *SW* xxvi, 290.
[367] Ibid. 220; ebd. 212.
[368] Ibid.; ebd. Rahner conceives of God as the world's quasi-form, as we have just seen, and therefore presumably also regards the world as God's quasi-matter. Rahner also believes, as we saw earlier (cf. Chapter 1, section II.2.c.iii), that a created form: a) can be unchangeable in the sense that it is always agent and never patient; and yet b) indirectly suffer determination from without by virtue of its relation to matter. Rahner holds, that is to say, that every created form whatsoever is, in a meaningful sense, unchangeable in itself and yet changeable in the "other" of matter. Since this seemingly impossible juxtaposition occurs constantly in nature, Rahner appears to think, it is not unreasonable, especially given the Incarnation, to suspect that it might occur in the supreme *coincidentia oppositorum*, God: that God might be unchangeable in Godself and yet changeable in the quasi-matter of the world. Rahner's formula, therefore, is not simply nonsense.

4. Conclusion. Rahner does, then, seem to say that God changes radically in at least some respects. In view of his emphatic endorsement of divine simplicity (cf. 2a. above), then, the first criticism, viz. that if God is simple, then any divine becoming would alter every aspect of God and thus guarantee that the interpersonal relations in the economic Trinity do not correspond to those of the immanent Trinity, seems to exploit a genuine inconsistency in Rahner's thought.

III. BERT VAN DER HEIJDEN

1. Introduction. Bert van der Heijden admits this inconsistency in Rahner's thought insofar as he recognizes that Rahner intends dialectically to ascribe both a radical immutability and a radical mutability to God. In Van der Heijden's view, however, Rahner so neglects the personal aspect of divine self-communication that he ultimately, if only implicitly, denies any real mutability in God. Van der Heijden argues, that is to say, that if one interprets Rahner's endorsements of divine mutability in terms of his larger theology, they affirm nothing more than God's ability to unite changeable realities to Godself: a kind of "mutability" not incompatible with the doctrine of God's absolute unchangeableness.

Van der Heijden himself, incidentally, considers Rahner's putative failure to ascribe thoroughgoing mutability to God a glaring weakness of his thought. In the context of our investigation, however, Van der Heijden's interpretation of Rahner's views on divine self-communication will function as a defense of Rahner against the first criticism.

2. Van der Heijden's argument.

a. Selbstmitteilung vs. Seinsmitteilung. Van der Heijden attributes what he perceives as Rahner's failure fully to thematize the reality of divine becoming principally to a lack of reflection on the personal element in divine self-communication. "The personal as such in Rahner," he writes:

> scarcely becomes thematic. He can, therefore,...with a sense of unproblematic self-evidentness convert the revealed datum of the self-communication of God into the thesis, that the divine being [*Sein*] is communicated to the created spirit....[But] is the divine "self" precisely the same as the divine being [*Sein*]? Rahner does not expressly reflect on this problematic. Hence his two theological basic concepts—self-communication and formal causality—remain ambiguous: do they concern a communication of God's being [*Sein*] or the Person (or "self") of God? Are they both the same? If not, then what can the immanent difference between the divine being [*Sein*] and the divine "self" be?[369]

This ambiguity, this failure of Rahner's to "distinguish expressly between being-self and being-being [*Selbstsein und Sein-Sein*],"[370] leads him, in Van der Heijden's view, to commit fundamental errors when treating each of what Van der Heijden describes as the three *Hauptakzenten* of Rahner's theology: "the identity of being and being's-presence-to-itself, the struggle against monophysitism, and the struggle against tritheism."[371] The errors Van der Heijden detects, which we discuss in inverse order, constitute, in turn, the proximate causes of what Van der Heijden regards as Rahner's implicit, but decisive, denial of any real mutability in God.

b. Der Kampf gegen Tritheismus. In the third *Hauptakzent* of Rahner's theology, his in itself justified struggle against the obvious error of tritheism, Rahner goes to what Van der Heijden regards as the unjustified extreme of claiming that "there can be no inner-Trinitarian relations which are 'personal' in what is today the normal sense of that term."[372] As Van der Heijden explains, in Rahner's view, "the Logos does not differentiate himself from the Father through a personal, I-Thou relation. That is to say, he is a...relative mode of subsistence

---

[369] *Karl Rahner: Darstellung und Kritik seiner Grundpositionen* (Einsiedeln: Johannes, 1973), 12.
[370] Ibid. 124.
[371] Ibid. 410.
[372] Ibid. 409.

that has the fullness of being's-presence-to-itself."[373] This implies, Van der Heijden concludes, that "one can make no [real] differentiation between Logos and divinity:"[374] i.e. that person and nature do not really differ in God. By identifying the divine persons as relations, of course, Rahner intends, in Van der Heijden's view, only to combat tritheism. According to Van der Heijden, however, by affirming the strictly relative character of the intra-Trinitarian distinctions and, therefore, implying the real, though not quidditative, identity of the Logos and the divine essence, Rahner indirectly implies the impossibility of meaningful change in God.

For, as Van der Heijden notes, correctly, "mutability cannot be in God if God is understood...as essence or nature. That would mean the destruction of metaphysics and the theological truth of the fulfilled perfection of God."[375] Rahner's decision to posit a merely relative distinction between the divine persons thus constitutes, in Van der Heijden's view, an implicit endorsement of the doctrine of absolute divine immutability.

c. Der Kampf gegen Monophysitismus. In the second *Hauptakzent* of his theology, i.e. the "struggle against monophysitism," Rahner, likewise, according to Van der Heijden, carries an in itself legitimate concern to unwarrantable extremes. Reacting against what he perceives as monophysitic tendencies within conventional theology, Rahner characterizes Christ's human nature, in Van der Heijden's words, as "a human person, when one understands 'person' in the sense normal today, namely as a conscious subject as such."[376] Van der Heijden, moreover, considers such a stance perfectly justified on the basis of both "Christological dogma" and "the Gospel image of Christ [*die evangelische Christusgestalt*]."[377]

---

[373] Ibid. 405.
[374] Ibid. 411.
[375] Ibid. 381.
[376] Ibid. 402.
[377] Ibid.

Van der Heijden objects, however, when Rahner ascribes to this human subject autonomy even over against the divine Logos. For, in that case, Van der Heijden reasons, one could not truthfully assert that "the person—'in the modern sense'—of Jesus is the Logos;"[378] and, in that case, the flesh of Christ which others see and touch would constitute not the expressive symbol of the Logos, but the expressive symbol of a mere human subject. If Rahner correctly ascribed autonomy over against the Logos to Christ's humanity, Van der Heijden explains, logic would dictate that: "when Jesus expresses himself, he speaks out his being-present-to-himself: i.e. the same human being that we also have."[379]

The presence of such a mere, human subject in the world does not establish the radically supernatural, personal relationship which, in Van der Heijden's view, can alone bring about salvation. In order to attain to truly supernatural communion with God, Van der Heijden believes, human beings need, rather, "a relation of God to us that corresponds in a special measure to our mode of being."[380] "The basic correspondence," Van der Heijden elaborates, "consists herein, that divine love also acquires categoriality as its self-expression and self-communication, as its personal, real symbol, in a similar way as we exist and encounter one another through categoriality."[381]

The Logos, as Rahner understands it, cannot assume categoriality in this way, according to Van der Heijden, because it does not possess itself as a subject distinct from the divine essence and, therefore, capable of independent action. Instead, it constitutes a *Subsistenzweise*, a mode of subsistence of the divine essence which as such partakes of its perfections, including immutability. The Logos, as Rahner understands it, can thus serve at most, in Van der Heijden's view, as "a mere *suppositum* of an autonomous human nature."[382]

---

[378] Ibid. 411.
[379] Ibid. 410.
[380] Ibid. 382.
[381] Ibid.
[382] Ibid. 411.

In his Christology as in his doctrine of the Trinity, then, Rahner, as Van der Heijden interprets him, identifies essence and person in God in such a way as implicitly to deny that the divine persons can change in the ways that Heijden thinks essential to any genuinely supernatural communion between God and human beings; and, as we have seen, Rahner thus identifies essence and person in God, at least according to Van der Heijden, in order sharply to distinguish his own position from viewpoints he considers monophysitic or tritheistic.

d. Sein = Beisichsein. In Van der Heijden's view, nonetheless, Rahner possesses in the first *Hauptakzent* of his theology a more basic reason for identifying essence and person in God, one not tinged, like the others, by specifically polemical motives. Rahner believes, on philosophical grounds, that *Sein* is *Beisichsein*: that being *is* being's-presence-to-itself. If *Sein* and *Beisichsein*, at least in God, are strictly identical, then the God who possesses only one *Sein* can possess only one *Beisichsein*, or personality in the Cartesian sense, and God's *Sein* and God's personality must be strictly identical.

Van der Heijden, therefore, in explicating what he considers the Rahnerian idea of grace as a new relation to the *Deus unus*, writes, "This conception corresponds to Rahner's identification of *Sein* and *Beisichsein*: a divine *Sein*, also a divine *Beisichsein* = a divine self or person."[383] Likewise, Van der Heijden explains, in Rahner's view, "the personal [in the Cartesian sense] is in God an *essentiale*, not something that differentiates the persons. For *Sein* is *Beisichsein* and *Beisichsein* is *Sein*."[384]

The first *Hauptakzent* of Rahner's theology, the identity of *Sein* and *Beisichsein*, thus renders unthinkable any real distinction between self and being in God. On this presupposition, "self-communication, love, personal relation,"[385] etc., the sort of things Van der Heijden considers indispensable to a higher, more

---

[383] Ibid. 409.
[384] Ibid. 403.
[385] Ibid. 412.

personal relation to God than that given with creation, become "identical with the metaphysically immutable and absolute essence of God."[386] Van der Heijden concludes, therefore, that Rahner effectively denies the possibility of God's so exteriorizing Godself as actually to change in a finite, material other; and he interprets Rahner's formula, "The one who is not subject to change in Godself can *Godself* be subject to change *in something else*,"[387] accordingly.

e. Rahner's immutability formula. "The formula," he writes:

is situated in the background of the conception of the human person as being-present-to-oneself in being-present-to-another. The human being is as "she herself" transcendence, openness to the fullness of being, remaining "I." She exists thus, however, only in "another," i.e. in the lower degree of being that belongs to her: in her material mode of being and in the formal principle of *materia prima*....This fact is transferred to God. Also God has the "other from Godself:" the immanent Logos and the sub-divine that is assumed in the Incarnation. This is God's own. Insofar as it changes, it unites God to a becoming. God "Godself," however, does not change. For God Godself is—in contrast to ourself—the already fulfilled and, consequently, unchangeable being.[388]

Van der Heijden does not, it is important to note, believe that Rahner interprets his own formula in this way. He understands Rahner to mean, rather, that "the Incarnation is before all else the becoming of God"[389] and quotes Rahner to the effect that the Incarnation constitutes "*die Selbstentäußerung, das Werden, die Kenosis und Genesis Gottes selbst*"[390] to substantiate his claim. Van der Heijden explicitly and repeatedly states, moreover, that Rahner's ideas of divine self-communication and the absolute savior presuppose "a relational becoming strictly immanent in God."[391] In Van der Heijden's view, however, "Rahner does not reflect thematically on this strictly immanent becoming of God."[392]

---

[386] Ibid.
[387] *Foundations*, 220; *Grundkurs*, *SW* xxvi, 219.
[388] *Karl Rahner*, 380.
[389] Ibid. 373.
[390] "Menschwerdung," *SW* xii, 317 as quoted in *Karl Rahner*, 373. We reproduce the quote exactly as it appears in Van der Heijden's text. Cf. "Incarnation," *TI* iv, 114.
[391] *Karl Rahner*, 382.
[392] Ibid.

Likewise, Van der Heijden recognizes that Rahner considers his immutability formula "an ontological ultimate," i.e. a paradox which does not admit of further clarification. He holds, nevertheless, that this belief of Rahner's manifests Rahner's failure adequately to reflect on the meaning of the term "self" in his formula. "If the formula, 'God Godself changes in another without Godself changing,'" Van der Heijden writes, "is not supposed to be a contradiction, 'self' cannot mean precisely the same thing both times. The unreflected ambiguity of this word of Rahner's appears here very plainly. For this reason he can believe, with this formula, 'to have reached an ontological ultimate.'"[393]

Van der Heijden seeks to dispel this mistaken belief by eliminating all "unreflected ambiguity" in Rahner's terms. "Godself/self [*sich/Selbst*] in this formula," he writes "is understood on the one side as absolute being and on the other side as the self of humanity differentiated from absolute being."[394] This twofold meaning of "self" notwithstanding, Van der Heijden argues, the personal relation of God to human beings which Rahner unsuccessfully attempts to describe through his immutability formula does, when properly understood, require some becoming on the part of God. Nonetheless, Van der Heijden writes, Rahner's "attention goes immediately to the acquisition of a sub-divine being of which, then, it must naturally be said: God does not become a sub-divine being, but remains transcendent being [*Sein*]."[395] In a variation of what constitutes a virtual refrain throughout Van der Heijden's work, he writes that in Rahner's theology, "the personal determination of God, to which the acquisition of determined categoriality corresponds and that really adds to what we understand as the essence of God, is neither in its concrete meaningfulness nor in its distinction from this essence thematically reflected."[396] Van der Heijden believes, in other words, that Rahner does not delve sufficiently deeply into his own

---

[393] Ibid. 380–1.
[394] Ibid. 381.
[395] Ibid. 382.
[396] Ibid.

thought and words and that, if he did, he would recognize the necessity, according to his own principles, of unambiguously ascribing mutability to the "self" of God.

3. Response. In response to all of this, one can truthfully say, first, that Van der Heijden unquestionably launches the lengthiest and most sophisticated argument ever presented for the view that Rahner denies that God changes in the Incarnation. One can also truthfully say, however, that it is surprising that someone with the extensive knowledge of Rahner's corpus that Van der Heijden evidently possesses would defend such a thesis. For, at least from the perspective of the history of ideas, Van der Heijden seems inaccurately to portray Rahner's thought.[397]

Van der Heijden's purpose, however, seems to consist not so much in accurately recounting Rahner's claims as in eliciting from Rahner's ideas unspoken presuppositions and consequences and evaluating them from his own radically personalist perspective. Van der Heijden's interpretation of Rahner's theology, in fact, resembles in this respect Rahner's own work on the gnoseology of Aquinas in which Rahner attempts to "relive the philosophical event...in Thomas"[398] without paying unnecessary attention to historical details.

a. Selbstmitteilung vs. Seinsmitteilung. In any event, it seems quite possible to exculpate Rahner at least partially from each of the charges Van der Heijden levels at him. Van der Heijden's first and principal charge, viz. that Rahner does not thematize the distinction between "self" and "being" in God, for instance, seems palpably false. In his essay, "Theos in the New Testament," for instance, Rahner writes that "God is never appealed to in the New Testament as simply Being, God's entitative infinity is never mentioned. It is not so much to the

---

[397] For further criticism of Van der Heijden along these lines, cf. Klaus Fischer's "Kritik der 'Grundpositionen'? Kritische Anmerkungen zu B. van der Heijdens Buch über Karl Rahner," *ZKT* 99 (1977), 74-89.

[398] *Spirit*, li; *Geist*, *SW* ii, 13.

Absolute and Necessary—and thus easily impersonal and abstract—that the New Testament turns its gaze...; its eyes are upon the *personal* God in the *concreteness* of God's free activity."[399] One reads in the same essay, likewise, that "love is not the emanation of a nature but the free bestowal of a person."[400] These are not, to say the least, the words of one for whom "*Selbst=Seinsmitteilung.*"[401]

Van der Heijden may be correct, of course, in his judgment that, in Rahner's thought, "the difference between a natural relation to the creative *ipsum esse* and the self-communication of God is not thematized."[402] This seems to be the case, however, not because Rahner allows for no genuine self-communication at all, but rather because divine self-communication so permeates the universe, in Rahner's view, that one cannot adequately distinguish, on the basis of experience, between the natural and the supernatural: i.e. between aspects of life which reflect the relations that must obtain between creatures of a particular sort and God and aspects of life owing particularly to God's free, but universally effective, will to communicate Godself to creation. Rahner finds himself unable to distinguish unambiguously between nature and supernature, then, not because he systematically reduces the supernatural to the natural, but because he considers the supernatural so all-encompassing that he shrinks from attributing virtually any aspect of reality to nature alone. Rahner does not reduce God's self to God's being, therefore, either in God's interior life or in God's self-communication *ad extra*; if anything, he so emphasizes the supernatural, personal aspect of God that it overshadows almost completely God's natural and necessary being.

b. Persons and essence. Van der Heijden's second charge, viz. that Rahner, by characterizing the divine persons as relations of opposition, identifies them with the divine essence in such a way that they share its immutability, would convict

---

[399] *TI* i, 79–148 at 114; "Theos im Neuen Testament," *SW* iv, 346–403 at 375.
[400] Ibid. 123; ebd. 383.
[401] Van der Heijden, *Karl Rahner*, 384.
[402] Ibid. 128.

Rahner of denying the divine persons' mutability if, like Van der Heijden, Rahner unambiguously ascribed immutability to the divine essence. Rahner, however, seems nowhere, at least in his mature works, explicitly to affirm the divine essence's immutability without also qualifying this immutability dialectically. The very idea that God could consist in a necessarily changeless essence really, and not merely rationally, distinct from three radically mutable persons, moreover, seems highly questionable. If the persons lacked any of the perfections of the divine essence, for instance, how could they qualify as fully divine? If the divine essence did not constitute an at least incompletely subsistent,[403] individual nature,[404] but rather a non-subsisting οὐσία δευτέρα instantiated by three, distinct individuals, how could one intelligibly speak of only one God?

Rahner avoids such imposing difficulties of which Van der Heijden seems scarcely aware, by positing a rational, but not a real distinction between the divine persons and the divine essence. This does not mean, as we have already noted, that for Rahner, *Selbst=Seinsmitteilung*. It implies, rather, that, just as grace presupposes nature, so, in Rahner's view, communication of the divine self (or selves?)[405] presupposes communication of the divine being. The objective

---

[403] The divine essence is incompletely subsistent in that it possesses existence, individuality, and the capacity for action, sc. three of the four traditional notes of subsistence, and yet lacks the fourth, viz. incommunicability to multiple supposita. We derive these criteria from Charles René Billuart, *Cursus Theologiae: Tomus II: De Trinitate: De Angelis: De Opere Sex Dierum et Pars Prima de Incarnatione* (Paris: LeCoffre, 1878), 101b.

[404] John of Damascus distinguishes between three senses of the term "nature:" the purely intentional, universal nature that does not inform any individual; the universal nature that informs every individual included under its aegis; and the individual nature, i.e. the universal nature as determined by individuating features. In his words:

Nature is either understood in bare thought (for in the same it does not subsist); or commonly in all hypostases of the same species uniting them, and [in this case] it is said to be considered in the species; or entirely the same, having received accidents in addition, in a single hypostasis, and [in this case] it is said to be nature considered in an individual (*Expositio Fidei* 55 in *Die Schriften des Johannes von Damaskos* 2 [Bonifatius Kotter, ed.; PTS 12; Berlin and New York: Gruyter, 1973], 131).

[405] Elmar Salmann correctly observes that the identity of the *"Selbst"* in *"Selbstmitteilung,"* as Rahner employs the term, seems, at times at least, quite ambiguous. (*Neuzeit und Offenbarung: Studien zur trinitarischen Analogik des Christentums* [StAns 94; Rome: Pontificio Ateneo S. Anselmo, 1986], 38). "What does *Selbstmitteilung* now mean?" Salmann asks. "Which self

identity of the divine essence with the divine persons, in any event, does not entail, according to Rahner, those persons' absolute immutability.

c. Autonomy of Christ's humanity. Van der Heijden's third charge, viz. that Rahner, by ascribing radical autonomy to the humanity of Jesus, logically precludes its functioning as the self-expression of the Logos, seems justifiable only if one dismisses, or misinterprets, Rahner's repeated statements to the effect that "autonomy...does not decrease, but increases in direct proportion to dependence on God."[406] Rahner emphatically denies that:

> God's grace and mastery and the...exercise of freedom are realities encroaching upon one another—in the sense, for instance, of a Pelagian synergism—as if they were realities of which the one could assert itself or grow only at the expense of the other. The divine freedom and mastery [rather] are experienced from the outset as the reason for the possibility of the creature's...freedom, so that both grow in equal and not in inverse proportion.[407]

Given this presupposition, one cannot reasonably claim that the Logos could exteriorize itself in a human nature only if it subjected that nature to total control. One could object, of course, that the idea of dependence and autonomy growing in equal, and not inverse, proportions seems self-contradictory. Yet Rahner, here as elsewhere, thinks that he can justify such dialectical statements without establishing their harmony with the law of non-contradiction. In resolving the inconsistency between dependence and autonomy in Rahner's Christology in favor of autonomy, then, Van der Heijden seems more to obscure than to clarify Rahner's actual meaning.

d. Unity and distinction in God. Van der Heijden's fourth and final charge, viz. that by equating *Sein* with *Beisichsein*, Rahner implicitly depreciates

---

communicates what? Does God communicate—God, hence his nature, his knowledge and will? Or the Father (who in no case can communicate his fatherhood) his loving knowledge in the form of the Logos and Pneuma?"
[406] *Foundations*, 79; *Grundkurs*, *SW* xxvi, 81.
[407] "Guilt—Responsibility—Punishment," *TI* vi, 197–217 at 200; "Schuld—Verantwortung—Strafe," *ST* vi, 238–61 at 242.

multiplicity in God seems, like the previous charge, reasonable only if one ignores or misunderstands Rahner's statements concerning the dialectical relationship between unity and distinction in and with God. Rahner explicitly states that "here [i.e. in 'being *as* such, and hence *as* one'] unity and distinction are correlatives which increase in like proportions, not in inverse proportions which would reduce each to be contradictory and exclusive of the other."[408]

As we shall see in section IV.3.d.i, moreover, the idea of being as being's-presence-to-itself requires, in the view of the later Rahner, a certain plurality intrinsic to every being and especially to God. In order to attain presence-to-itself, every being, to the degree that it possesses being, must, according to Rahner's theory, produce an internal other simultaneously identical with and distinct from itself so that one can intelligibly describe the being as present to itself. In Rahner's view, then, the identity of *Sein* and *Beisichsein*, so far from eradicating the multiplicity in God affirmed by the doctrine of the Trinity, actually requires such multiplicity as an indispensable prerequisite of God's presence-to-self.

As before, Van der Heijden could point out that the idea of unity and distinction between two realities in the same respect increasing in direct proportion seems flatly self-contradictory; and he would, perhaps, be abundantly justified in so doing. He is not justified, however, in ignoring, or explaining away, one of two seemingly incompatible positions Rahner holds and then criticizing Rahner as if he unequivocally affirmed one of the two contradictory positions and just as unequivocally rejected the other. Rahner, in any event, rejects the idea that one can truthfully posit a real distinction between an immutable essence and one or more mutable selves in God; he does not explicitly rule out, in fact, the possibility that every aspect of God is just as immutable and/or mutable as every other. Rahner, therefore, rejects the premise on which Van der Heijden's fourth objection is based: viz. that God's essence is immutable

---

[408] "Symbol," *TI* iv, 228; "Symbols," *SW* xviii, 429–30.

to such an extent that, if God changes, God must possess a "self" in some way extrinsic to that essence.

4. Conclusion. Van der Heijden succeeds, then, in proving neither: a) that Rahner denies, implicitly or explicitly, the mutability of the Logos in the Incarnation; nor b) that Rahner's formula, "The one who is not subject to change in Godself can *Godself* be subject to change *in something else*,"[409] coheres with an unqualified doctrine of divine immutability. His arguments, though strikingly original and obviously grounded in thorough research, thus seem insufficient to neutralize our first criticism of Rahner's *Grundaxiom*.

IV. CONCILIAR AUTHORITY AND THE CONSISTENCY OF RAHNER'S VIEWS

1. Introduction. A counterargument to the first criticism, it seems, might be drawn from Rahner's confidence in the teaching authority of ecumenical councils in union with the Pope. One might argue, that is to say: a) that Rahner considers the teachings of such councils, when approved by the Pope and when intended as definitive statements of faith, infallibly true; b) that such councils, in union with the Pope, have definitively affirmed the doctrine of divine immutability, the reality of sanctifying grace, the Incarnation of the Logos, and Christ's "absolute saviorhood"; c) that Rahner demonstrates the integrality of divine self-communication, in his sense of that term, to sanctifying grace and/or the Incarnation and/or Christ's "absolute saviorhood"; d) that the charism of infallibility precludes the possibility of self-contradiction in definitive teaching; e) that Rahner's understanding of divine self-communication and the doctrine of divine immutability, therefore, must be compatible; and f) that any criticism of

---

[409] *Foundations*, 220; *Grundkurs, SW* xxvi, 212.

Rahner's *Grundaxiom* that presupposes the incompatibility of divine self-communication as Rahner conceives of it with divine immutability, as our first criticism does, must, consequently, be invalid.

In the context of a strictly immanent critique, such an argument seems practically invincible. For one cannot reasonably call Rahner's belief in the infallibility of definitive, conciliar teaching definitively authorized by the Pope into question. In a 1976 lexicon article on "Unfehlbarkeit,"[410] for instance, Rahner, after identifying "an ecumenical council together with the Pope"[411] as one of the "bearers of infallibility,"[412] writes:

The historicity of a dogma does not mean...that the infallibility of the church must be interpreted thus: God guarantees an eschatological perseverance of the church in the truth, while dogmas of the magisterium or statements of Scripture could always also be erroneous. The perseverance in the truth realizes itself *also* in true propositions; every ultimate *Grundentscheidung* of the human person, which (through the grace of God) establishes her in the truth, expresses itself always and necessarily in true propositions. The church as a tangible substance [*Größe*] would not persevere in the truth if the objectivations of its perseverance in the truth, viz. its actual propositions of faith as the concrete form of its perseverance in the truth, were erroneous.[413]

It seems, however, that one can reasonably question the cogency of Rahner's arguments for the integrity of divine self-communication as he understands it to sanctifying grace, the Incarnation, and Christ's status as "absolute savior." In the following, accordingly, we intend to ask whether, and in what degree, Rahner actually demonstrates that the doctrines of sanctifying grace, the Incarnation, and Christ's absolute saviorhood presuppose or imply the reality of divine self-communication in his sense of the term. We intend, in other words, to test the soundness of premise c) in the above counterargument to our first criticism: the only premise of this counterargument, in our view, that admits of challenge within the context of a strictly immanent critique.

2. Sanctifying grace.

---

[410] *KThW*[10], 425–7.
[411] Ibid. 425.
[412] Ibid.
[413] Ibid. 426–7.

a. Introduction. Few Christians deny, of course, that God communicates the divine self to at least some human beings by a certain uncreated grace insofar as God sanctifies and dwells within the souls of the justified.[414] In this section, accordingly, the issue in dispute is not whether sanctifying grace necessarily involves divine self-communication and uncreated grace; it is, rather, whether these realities constitute "the act whereby God goes out of Godself into 'the other' in such a way that God bestows Godself upon the other by becoming the other."[415] The issue in dispute, in other words, is whether these realities ought to be conceived of in Rahnerian terms. In order to resolve this issue, we intend, for the remainder of this section: first, to outline Rahner's arguments for the identity of the uncreated aspect of sanctifying grace with divine self-communication in his distinctive sense of that term; and, second, to respond to those arguments by evaluating their adequacy for this purpose.

b. Rahner's arguments. In order to establish that sanctifying grace in its uncreated aspect consists in divine self-communication as he understands it, Rahner proposes two, basic arguments: one from the believer's possession of the

---

[414] "Grace," writes Adolphe Tanquerey, "is said to uncreated or created: (**a**) *uncreated* grace is God Godself communicating Godself to the intellectual creature; (**b**) *created* grace is the gratuitous gift distinct from God and, as it were, the effect of divine love" (*Synopsis theologiae dogmaticae specialis* 2 [Paris: Desclée, 1914[14]], §8, p. 24. Uncreated and created grace, Tanquerey explains, constitute the two elements of habitual grace, which, "as it is *uncreated* grace, is a special union of God with the soul in which God dwells, and, insofar as it is *created* grace, is a supernatural quality, permanently and intrinsically inhering in the soul through which we are made partakers of the divine nature" (ibid. §11, p. 25).

Protestants, incidentally, do not deny that God infuses created grace into the regenerate. The Synod of Dordt specifically condemns those "who teach...that in the true conversion of the human person no new qualities, powers or gifts can be infused by God into the will....For thereby they contradict the Holy Scriptures, which declare that God infuses new qualities of faith, of obedience, and of the consciousness of his love into our hearts" (Canons of Dordt, Chapter III-IV, Rejection of Errors, paragraph 6 in *The Creeds of the Evangelical Protestant Churches* [Philip Schaff, ed. and tr.; London: Hodder & Stoughton, 1877], 569–70).

[415] "Mystery," *TI* iv, 68; "Geheimnis," *SW* xii, 131.

Holy Spirit as the "earnest of our inheritance" (Eph 1:14; cf. 2 Cor 1:22 and 5:5)[416] and another from the priority of uncreated to created grace.

i. Uncreated grace as presupposition of the beatific vision.

α. Introduction. In the first, Rahner contends that, because "the possession of the Pneuma (and thus primarily uncreated grace) is conceived of in Scripture as the homogeneous germ and commencement of the beatific vision,...we have the right to apply to uncreated grace in this life the concepts of formal ontology relating to the possession of God in the *visio beatifica*."[417] In other words, if uncreated grace, the possession of the Holy Spirit, constitutes the earnest of the life of glory, whose principal blessing is the beatific vision, then this uncreated grace must constitute, in some sense, a presupposition of that vision. In such a case, Rahner reasons, one could determine something of the essence of uncreated grace by determining the ontological presuppositions of the beatific vision. Indeed, he seems to consider such delving into the presuppositions of the beatific vision the only viable method for determining the essence of uncreated grace. "Uncreated grace," he writes, "is only to be determined in terms of the *visio*."[418]

Rahner reasons, in other words: a) that the uncreated grace bestowed on the blessed constitutes an ontological presupposition of the beatific vision; b) that, according to the testimony of Scripture, the uncreated grace in which God communicates Godself to the *viator* is of the same kind as that in which God

---

[416] The NRSV's rendering of ἀρραβών τῆς κληρονομίας ἡμῶν as "pledge of our inheritance" suggests that Paul means in Eph 1:14 to identify the Holy Spirit as he dwells in the righteous on earth as a temporary and inferior substitute for the joys of heaven of which he constitutes the pledge. In extra-biblical usage, however, the term ἀρραβών almost always signifies *"earnest money*...[i.e.] a real part of the object of contract, given in advance both to insure final payment and also to contribute to it" (Barnabas Ahern, "The Indwelling Spirit, Pledge of Our Inheritance (Eph 1:14)," *CBQ* 9 [1947], 179–89). We think it appropriate, therefore, to translate ἀρραβών as "earnest" rather than "pledge."

[417] "Some Implications of the Scholastic Concept of Uncreated Grace," *TI* i, 319–46 at 334; "Zur scholastischen Begrifflichkeit der ungeschaffenen Gnade," *ST* i, 347–76 at 362.

[418] Ibid. 335; ebd. 363.

communicates Godself to the blessed; and c) that whatever characterizes the uncreated grace of the blessed insofar as it constitutes a presupposition of the beatific vision must, therefore, characterize equally the uncreated grace received already by the *viator*. Acting on these assumptions, then, Rahner seeks to prove that God must communicate Godself to the blessed in the way that Rahner envisions in order to endow them with the beatific vision; and that God, therefore, already communicates Godself in the radical, Rahnerian sense of that term to *viatores*. To this end, specifically, Rahner employs two arguments: one from the nature of knowledge itself and another from the absolute immediacy of the beatific vision.

β. Being and knowing. In the first, Rahner contends that, because "knowing, in its first and original sense, is the self-presence of being,...something is known to the extent that it becomes in its being identical with the knowing subject."[419] One cannot know God, therefore, according to Rahner, unless one becomes, in some measure, identical with the divine being. Hence, in Rahner's view, human beings cannot know God in the beatific vision or even in this life unless "God goes out of Godself into 'the other' in such a way that God bestows Godself upon the other by becoming the other;"[420] unless, that is to say, God communicates the divine self in the Rahnerian sense of the term. "Knowledge," writes Rahner, "cannot at its ultimate basis consist in a state of having something intentionally 'over against' one as an object; the only way still open to us to conceive of it is as a state...in which the knower in the true sense and the known in the true sense are one and identical in being."[421] If Rahner is correct in so concluding, it seems, something like the beatific vision can, indeed, occur only if God communicates Godself to human beings in the Rahnerian sense of those words.

---

[419] *Hearer*, 32–3; *Hörer*, *SW* iv, 68.
[420] "Mystery," *TI* iv, 68; "Geheimnis," *SW* xii, 131.
[421] "Thomas Aquinas on Truth," *TI* xiii, 29; "Die Wahrheit bei Thomas von Aquin," *SW* ii, 315.

γ. *God as impressed species.* In his second argument for the indispensability of divine self-communication, as he understands it, to the beatific vision, Rahner asserts that God, in the beatific vision, does not manifest Godself to the blessed through a created, impressed species, but rather absolutely immediately, "face to face" (1 Cor 13:12). Rahner, upon the authority of Aquinas, moreover, claims that in order to compensate for the lack of a created, impressed species, ordinarily a *sine qua non* of human knowledge, "God's essence itself takes the place of the *species* (*impressa*) in the created mind."[422]

Rahner admits, of course, that God's transcendence prevents God from informing the human intellect in precisely the same way that a created, impressed species, in other instances, informs it. Yet he also maintains that God, the divine transcendence notwithstanding, exercises "an active formal causality (*eine formale Wirkursächlichkeit*)"[423] on the minds of the blessed.

Rahner concedes, again, that, on account of the uniquely transcendent nature of God, one could reasonably refer to this causality as merely *"quasi-formal."*[424] Yet he insists:

all this 'quasi' implies is that this 'forma', in spite of its formal causality, which must be taken really seriously, abides in its absolute transcendence (inviolateness, 'freedom'). But it does *not* imply that the statement, 'In the beatific vision God occupies the place of a *species* in virtue of a formal causality', is a mode of speech lacking all binding force; on the contrary, it is the *quasi* which must be prefixed to every application to God of a category in itself terrestrial.[425]

Rahner again attempts to moderate his position, however, by associating the quasi-formal causality which he ascribes to God with the scholastic idea of an "actus *terminans,*"[426] which he correctly, although only partially, defines as "that which in itself is and remains a perfect reality in spite of and prior to the act of determination."[427]

---

[422] "Uncreated," *TI* i, 327; "Ungeschaffene," *ST* i, 355.
[423] Ibid.; 330; ebd. 358.
[424] Ibid.; ebd.
[425] Ibid.; ebd. 358–9.
[426] Ibid. 331, n.1; ebd. 359, Anm. 1.
[427] Ibid.; ebd.

Now, an *actus terminans*, or terminative cause, at least as commonly understood, influences a reality distinct from itself only in the sense that a point influences a line; i.e. it serves only as an object or a limit, and nothing more.[428] Louis Billot does not err in the slightest degree, therefore, when he explains that God, *qua* terminative cause of the beatific vision, "informs not physically, but merely intentionally."[429]

Rahner, however, declares that if Billot means "that God is in fact an 'intentional' *known object*, the whole explanation is false, for it is a question here precisely of an ontological (hence 'physical') *presupposition* of knowledge."[430] Rahner cannot, therefore, mean merely to assert that God must exert a terminative causality in order to bestow the beatific vision upon the souls of the blessed. Rahner states quite clearly, rather, that he regards a *"communication* of the divine being taking place *by way of formal causality* to the created spirit...[as an] *ontological presupposition* of the *visio.*"[431]

"The reality of the mind in the beatific vision," he writes, "so far as such a reality in itself is due to a *species* as the means of knowledge, is the very Being of God."[432] The beatific vision, then, cannot occur, in Rahner's view, without "the one self-communication of God to the creature, which is essentially the act whereby God goes out of Godself into 'the other' in such a way that God bestows Godself upon the other by becoming the other."[433]

On the basis of this argument and the former, then, Rahner concludes that one cannot deny the reality of divine self-communication as he conceives of it without also implicitly denying that the saints departed enjoy an immediate and beatifying vision of God: something which few Western Christians would wish to do.

---

[428] Cf. Reginald Garrigou-Lagrange, *Christ the Savior: A Commentary on the Third Part of St. Thomas' Theological Summa* (Bede Rose, tr.; St. Louis and London: Herder, 1950), 39–42.
[429] *De Deo Uno et Trino: Commentarius in Prima Parte S. Thomae* (Prati: Giachetti, 1910^5), 146.
[430] "Uncreated," *TI* i, 331, n. 1; "Ungeschaffene," *ST* i, 359, Anm. 1.
[431] Ibid. 335; ebd. 363.
[432] Ibid. 332; ebd. 360.
[433] "Mystery," *TI* iv, 68; "Geheimnis," *SW* xii, 131.

δ. Conclusion. In his first argument for the necessity of divine self-communication in the distinctively Rahnerian sense of that term to uncreated grace, then, Rahner argues: a) that the uncreated grace of the blessed constitutes an ontological presupposition of the beatific vision; b) that the uncreated grace of the *viator*, according to Scripture, differs in no essential respect from that of the blessed; c) that whatever must be true of the uncreated grace of the blessed in order for it to function as an ontological presupposition of the beatific vision must, therefore, be equally true of the uncreated grace of the *viator*; d) that the identity of being and knowing and the absolute immediacy of the beatific vision imply that the uncreated grace of the blessed must consist in divine self-communication as Rahner understands it; and e) that the uncreated grace of the *viator* as well, consequently, must consist in divine self-communication in the Rahnerian sense.

ii. The priority of uncreated over created grace.

α. Introduction. In his second argument to the effect that a proper understanding of grace entails a belief in divine self-communication as he conceives of it, Rahner contends that if one denies that uncreated grace consists fundamentally in such divine self-communication, one thereby implicitly denies the ultimate priority of uncreated to created grace. Such a denial, Rahner contends, places one in conflict with the plain sense of Scripture and the overwhelming consensus of the Fathers.

"For St. Paul," Rahner asserts, "the human being's inner sanctification is first and foremost a communication of the personal Spirit of God, that is to say, in scholastic terms, a *donum increatum*; and he sees every created grace, every way of being πνευματικός, as a consequence and manifestation of the possession of this uncreated grace."[434] Likewise, Rahner affirms, "the Fathers (especially the

---

[434] "Uncreated," *TI* i, 322; "Ungeschaffene," *ST* i, 349–50.

Greek Fathers) see the created gifts of grace as a consequence of God's substantial communication to justified human beings."[435]

β. The "scholastic" view of uncreated grace. The scholastic theories of the relation between created and uncreated grace, however, in Rahner's view at least, teach precisely the opposite. "However diverse they may be among themselves," he writes, "all the scholastic theories...see God's indwelling and God's conjunction with the justified human being as based exclusively upon created grace."[436] As he summarizes the scholastic viewpoint, "In virtue of the fact [*dadurch*] that created grace is imparted to the soul God imparts Godself to it and dwells in it."[437]

Rahner, moreover, thinks this putative departure from scriptural and traditional teaching entirely understandable, albeit regrettable. From the perspective of the scholastic theologians he criticizes, Rahner explains, the "new *relation* of God to the human person"[438] brought about by the indwelling of the Holy Spirit "can only be conceived of as founded upon an absolute entitative modification of the human person herself."[439] For God cannot change, and one cannot speak of a new relation between two terms at all if neither changes in any way.

Yet, in Rahner's view, such an understanding of human salvation fails satisfactorily to account for the presence of uncreated grace in human beings, and that in two respects. First, Rahner holds, it manifestly reduces uncreated grace to "a function [*eine abhängige Funktion*] of created grace"[440] and thus opposes the view of Scripture and the Fathers. Second, and perhaps even more importantly, Rahner contends that it, implicitly and unintentionally, denies that sanctifying grace effects a new relationship with God at all. For, according to Rahner:

---

[435] Ibid.; ebd. 350–1.
[436] Ibid. 324; ebd. 352.
[437] Ibid.; ebd.
[438] Ibid.; ebd.
[439] Ibid.; ebd.
[440] Ibid.; ebd.

an accidental modification, from without, of the creature's being in itself and with regard to itself,...could not be the basis for a fundamentally and essentially new 'relationship' of God to the creature....The only fresh feature such an accidental absolute modification of the creature could bring with it is that relation to God which is a constituent [*mitgesetzt ist*] of any creaturely being, namely the transcendental reference of absolute finite being to God as to its cause.[441]

Recalling his discussion of uncreated grace as the ontological presupposition of the beatific vision, Rahner insists also that "here it is a question precisely of a 'relation' which does not immediately imply an absolute created determination; for otherwise the *species* of the beatific vision would ultimately be yet again a created quality."[442]

γ. Rahner's alternative. In articulating his own perspective, however, Rahner does not wish to claim that uncreated grace does not bestow created grace as its concomitant effect; for, if he claimed such a thing, he too, no less than the scholastics whom he opposes, would render himself unable to "say with St. Paul that we possess our pneumatic being [*Pneumatischsein*] (our 'created sanctifying grace') because we have the personal Pneuma of God."[443] In such a case, furthermore, Rahner could also not consistently affirm that divine self-communication stands in a relationship of mutual causality to the created *lumen gloriae*,[444] as he himself explicitly states.[445]

When Rahner asserts that "here it is a question precisely of a 'relation' which does not immediately imply an absolute created determination,"[446] then, he seems to mean that uncreated grace, although unrealizable apart from created grace, engenders a new relation between a human being and God in a sense in which this created grace does not. In such an event, the new relation would depend directly

---

[441] Ibid. 328–9; ebd. 357.
[442] Ibid. 329; ebd.
[443] Ibid. 322; ebd. 350.
[444] "The *lumen gloriae*," writes Adolphe Tanquerey, "is a supernatural habit that perfects the intellect of the blessed and renders him proximately capable of seeing God intuitively" (*Synopsis* 2, §1014, p. 720).
[445] "Uncreated," *TI* i, 333; "Ungeschaffene," *ST* i, 361.
[446] Ibid. 329; ebd. 357.

on uncreated grace as its formal cause and only indirectly on created grace as uncreated grace's necessary complement. In this sense and in this sense only, then, does Rahner mean to assert that the new relation between human beings and God established by uncreated grace "does not immediately imply an absolute created determination."

Rahner does not, therefore, declare the indwelling of the Holy Spirit absolutely and in every respect logically prior to the presence of created grace in the soul.[447] He does, however, distinguish sharply between: a) the relation engendered directly by uncreated grace in virtue of which one can reasonably claim that a soul possesses the Holy Spirit; and b) any relation constituted by created grace *simpliciter* or by some uncreated grace bestowed solely for the purpose of imparting created grace. By so distinguishing, Rahner implicitly pronounces every form of merely extrinsic, divine causality insufficient to the task of effecting a divine indwelling in justified souls.

For God, in Rahner's view, cannot through efficient causality or exemplary causality or final causality bestow anything whose value does not depend, in some degree at least, on the value of its created effects. If, as Rahner holds, the uncreated grace that effects divine indwelling must possess some significance irrespective of its created effects, it must, then, consist in some supra-categorical assimilation to God. It must consist, in Rahner's words, in "a taking up into the ground":[448] which is precisely what Rahner intends to signify by the term quasi-formal causality.

δ. *Conclusion.* Rahner, in sum, concludes in this second argument from the reality of sanctifying grace to the reality of divine self-communication as he understands it that one who does not equate the uncreated grace which effects

---

[447] "The point which we must not lose sight of in this," Rahner writes, "is the unity which exists between uncreated grace considered as *causa quasiformalis* and created grace as the necessary prior condition and at the same time the consequence of the uncreated grace" ("Immanent and Transcendent," *TI* x, 282; "Immanente und transzendente," *SW* xv, 551.

[448] "Uncreated," *TI* i, 329; "Ungeschaffene," *ST* i, 358.

divine indwelling with quasi-formal causality in Rahner's sense of the term cannot account for the putative logical priority of the indwelling of the Holy Spirit to the possession of created grace. Rahner concludes, in fact, that such a person cannot even explain why the indwelling of the divine persons in the souls of the justified transcends God's general presence of immensity. On the basis of this second argument and the first, that from sanctifying grace's relation to the beatific vision, then, Rahner rests his case for the indispensability of divine self-communication, as he conceives of it, to sanctifying grace.

c. Response.

i. Introduction. If Rahner could actually prove that divine self-communication as he understands it constitutes an essential component of sanctifying grace, it seems, the Rahnerian belief: a) that ecumenical councils teaching in unison with the Pope are infallible when speaking definitively on matters of faith and morals; when combined with the data b) that such councils have "infallibly" affirmed the doctrine of divine immutability and the existence of sanctifying grace; and c) that the charism of infallibility precludes the possibility of self-contradiction in such affirmations; would, indeed, imply that Rahner's understanding of divine self-communication does not ultimately conflict with the dogma of divine immutability. Such a result, as we have seen, would prove our first criticism of Rahner's *Grundaxiom* unsound at least in the context of a strictly immanent critique. In the following response, therefore, we intend to evaluate not only Rahner's arguments concerning the relation of uncreated grace to the beatific vision and the priority of uncreated to created grace, but also, indirectly, one of the central contentions of this work.

ii. Uncreated grace as ontological presupposition of the beatific vision.

α. *Introduction.* In the first of his arguments for the integrality of divine self-communication in his distinctive sense of that term to sanctifying grace, Rahner, as we have seen, reasons that if: a) the uncreated grace possessed by *viatores* differs in no essential respect from that possessed by the blessed; and b) the uncreated grace of the blessed must consist in divine self-communication in the Rahnerian sense of the term in order for the beatific vision to occur; then c) the uncreated grace of *viatores* as well must consist in divine self-communication according to Rahner's conception of it.

Now, Rahner's first premise, viz. that "grace...is a commencement of the blessed life, homogeneous with the ontological presuppositions of the vision,"[449] seems, in the main at least, unexceptionable. For Scripture does incontestably describe the indwelling Holy Spirit as "the earnest of our inheritance" (Eph 1:14; cf. 2 Cor 1:22, 5:5). In the indwelling divine persons, that is to say, Christians possess no mere *pignus*, distinct from their heavenly reward and inferior to it, but an ἀρραβών of their inheritance, a substantial share in the great recompense to come.

Likewise, it seems evident that grace, uncreated and created, does constitute a prerequisite of the beatific vision. One who beholds God face to face, after all, must not lack that "holiness without which no one will see the Lord" (Heb 12:14). Regardless of one's views as to whether Rahner fully appreciates the difference between grace and glory,[450] then, one cannot reasonably dispute Rahner's fundamental claim that "grace...is...an inner entitative principle (at least a partial principle) of the vision of God."[451] Neither, then, can one reasonably dispute this claim's immediate consequence, viz. that "the inner nature of grace as a whole in this life must allow of being more closely determined in terms of the nature of the ontological presuppositions of the immediate vision of God."[452]

---

[449] Ibid. 326; ebd. 354.
[450] "While we are at home in the body, we are absent from the Lord" (2 Cor 5:6).
[451] "Uncreated," *TI* i, 326; "Ungeschaffene," *ST* i, 354.
[452] Ibid.; ebd.

It seems, accordingly, that if one can prove divine self-communication, as Rahner conceives of it, indispensable to the beatific vision, then one can also establish the identity of the uncreated grace bestowed on *viatores* with divine self-communication in Rahner's sense of the term. If one cannot establish the former conclusion, however, the connection Rahner perceives between the uncreated grace of *viatores* and that of the blessed will not suffice, of itself, to demonstrate the integrality of divine self-communication, as Rahner understands it, to sanctifying grace. We shall devote the following two subsections, therefore, exclusively to the question of whether Rahner succeeds in demonstrating that (1) the relation between being and knowing as such and (2) the absence of a created species in the beatific vision render divine self-communication, according to Rahner's understanding of it, indispensable to the beatific vision.

β. Being and knowing. As we have already seen, in Rahner's view, the beatific vision presupposes divine self-communication as he conceives of it, because: a) "being is knowing;"[453] and b) knowledge can, therefore, occur only to the extent that "the knower in the true sense and the known in the true sense are one and identical in being."[454] We do not intend to contest the logical validity of Rahner's inference. It seems transparently obvious that if "being is knowing," then knowledge presupposes a substantial union between knower and known.

It is by no means obvious, however, that non-intentional, creaturely being is even relatively identical with creaturely knowing. For, as we saw in Chapter 1, the contention that a creature's being is, even proportionally, its knowing, commits Rahner to the absurd conclusion that a being is identical with its acts. To the extent that his views on the relation between being and knowing actually imply such an identification, then, these views appear to constitute unsound foundations for any argument as to the character of sanctifying grace.

---

[453] *Hearer*, 35; *Hörer, SW* iv, 70.
[454] "Thomas Aquinas on Truth," *TI* xiii, 29; "Die Wahrheit bei Thomas von Aquin," *SW* ii, 315.

γ. God as impressed species. Rahner attempts to establish the indispensability of divine self-communication, as he understands it, to the beatific vision, second, by arguing that God must compensate for the absence of a created, impressed species in the beatific vision by quasi-informing the human intellect in a manner analogous to an impressed species' information of a human being's possible intellect in ordinary instances of human knowledge.

Now, Rahner is correct in observing that no created species informs the human intellect in the beatific vision. For, as Aquinas explains:

Through no created similitude can the essence of God be seen...because the essence of God is his existence itself..., which can be admissible of no created form. No created form whatsoever, therefore, can be a similitude representing the essence of God to the seer....[This is the case also] because the divine essence is an uncircumscribed thing, containing in itself super-eminently whatever can be signified or understood by a created intellect....In no way through any created species can this be represented: because every created form is limited.... Hence to say that God through a similitude is seen, is to say that the divine essence is not seen: which is erroneous [*STh* I, 12, 2 corp.].

Rahner seems to err, however, when he asserts that God compensates for the absence of a created species in the beatific vision by entitatively informing the human intellect. For the agent intellect in natural human knowledge impresses a created species on the possible intellect, so that the impressed species entitatively informs the possible intellect, only in order to render intelligible that which is: a) absent; b) present only through the mediation of the senses; or c) immaterial and thus not directly perceptible by human beings' natural sensitive and cognitive faculties. In the case of the beatific vision, however, the object intuited is neither absent nor material nor, on account of the *lumen gloriae*, inaccessible to human intuition. The peculiar character of the object intuited, along with the elevation of the human intellect by the *lumen gloriae*, thus renders an entitative information of the possible intellect superfluous in the beatific vision.[455]

---

[455] We follow the account of Reginald Garrigou-Lagrange in his *The One God: A Commentary on the First Part of St. Thomas' Theological Summa* (Bede Rose, trans.; St. Louis and London: Herder, 1944), 348.

This is not to say that God does not, in a certain sense, perform the function of an impressed species in the beatific vision. For, as William J. Hill observes, the entitative information of the possible intellect constitutes only one of the impressed species' contributions to natural, human knowledge. In Hill's words:

> Ordinarily, the species has a twofold function: one entitative, the other intentional. In the first way, it is an accident, a quality modifying the soul, a form which in informing is absorbed in the actuation of a subject and constitutes with it a new accidental thing. In the second way, it transcends this function of entitative information (and this is due to its spirituality which in turn derives from the spirituality of the intellect) and without any fusing with its subject merely actuates or terminates the soul precisely in the line of knowledge. It makes the knower to be the known, to be…identified therewith—but only "intentionaliter."[456]

On account of the terminative causality God exercises in the beatific vision, therefore, one can and ought to speak of God's being united to the created intellect as an intelligible species without in any way suggesting that God communicates Godself, in the Rahnerian sense of those words, to the blessed in the beatific vision.

δ. Conclusion. Neither Rahner's argument from God's role as quasi-species in the beatific vision nor his argument from the putative identity of being and knowing, then, suffices to establish the integrity of divine self-communication, as Rahner conceives of it, to the beatific vision. Rahner's success in establishing a certain continuity between the ontological presuppositions of the *visio beatifica* and the uncreated grace already possessed by *viatores* notwithstanding, then, his researches into the ontological presuppositions of the beatific vision yield no conclusive proof that the uncreated grace of *viatores* consists in divine self-communication understood in Rahnerian terms.

iii. The priority of uncreated over created grace. Rahner's second argument for the necessity of divine self-communication, in his sense of the word, to the bestowal of uncreated grace consists principally in the claim that his

---

[456] "Uncreated Grace—A Critique of Karl Rahner," *Thomist* 27 (1963), 333–356 at 343–4.

understanding of the divine indwelling alone is compatible with the precedence of uncreated over created grace.

α. The scholastic views. That uncreated grace, in the sense of the divine persons' self-donation to the soul, does, in some sense, precede created grace seems difficult to contest. People do not, according to Scripture, receive the Holy Spirit, because they love God; rather, "the love of God[457] has been poured into our hearts through the Holy Spirit that has been given to us" (Rom 5:5). Didymus of Alexandria, likewise, avers, "Never, indeed, does anyone receive the spiritual blessings of God unless the Holy Spirit has gone before. He, indeed, who has received the Holy Spirit [however] shall, consequently, have blessings: i.e. wisdom and understanding and the others of which the Apostle...writes."[458] Rahner, in fact, seems to misrepresent his fellow scholastic theologians when he alleges that they universally dissent from this position.[459]

For, first, a great number, including, for instance, Adolphe Tanquerey,[460] Leo von Rudloff,[461] and Paul Galtier,[462] subscribe to subjective, causal theories of the indwelling according to which the divine persons impart themselves to the elect when they regenerate and sanctify these souls thus rendering themselves present in a radically new way. According to advocates of such theories, the indwelling divine persons bestow created grace, and there can be no question of a mere

---

[457] We deviate from the NRSV by translating "ἡ ἀγάπη τοῦ θεοῦ" as "the love of God" rather than "God's love" in order: a) to render the direct article, ἡ; and b) to show that τοῦ θεοῦ can constitute an objective as well as a subjective genitive.

[458] *De Spiritu Sancto* 10; PG 39, 1042A–B. We owe this reference to Simon Gaine, *Indwelling Spirit and a New Creation: The Relationship between Uncreated Grace and Created Grace in Neo-Scholastic Catholic Theology* (Oxford: D.Phil. Diss. 1994), 36.

[459] "To assume, as many since Rahner have done," writes Gaine, "that all neo-scholastic theories before Rahner supported the priority of created grace is to take no account of the intention of certain of the theologians concerned and of what they claimed for their theories" (*Indwelling Spirit*, 6).

[460] *Synopsis* 2, §184, pp. 135–6.

[461] "Des heiligen Thomas Lehre von der Formalursache der Einwohnung Gottes in der Seele der Gerechten," *Divus Thomas* (Freiburg) 8 (1930), 175–91, esp. 184–91.

[462] *L'Habitation en nous des trois Personnes: Le fait—le mode* (Paris: Beauchesne, 1928²), 209–56.

creature's introducing uncreated grace, i.e. the divine persons themselves as causing created grace, into the souls of the just.

A considerably greater number, admittedly, including, for instance, Camillo Mazzella,[463] Bernard Jungmann,[464] and Barthélemy Froget,[465] conceive of the divine indwelling in souls as logically subsequent to the presence of created grace in those souls. Such scholastics do not imagine, however, that created grace somehow antecedes the presence of the divine persons as bestowing created grace. Rather, they discriminate between the senses in which the divine persons do and do not logically precede their created gifts. Froget, for example, writes:

We may distinguish, as does St. Thomas, a twofold logical priority between the bestowal of the created gift and that of the Uncreated One, distinguishing between them according to the way in which we view the question of their causality. If we consider grace as a preliminary disposition, as a necessary preparation for the Divine Guest, then it is grace which is communicated to us first, the disposition naturally precedes the *forma* or the perfection for which it is to prepare. On the other hand, if we consider the Holy Ghost as the author of grace and the end for which grace is given, then He it is Who enters the soul first. And this, remarks St. Thomas, is what is strictly speaking precedence: *"Et hoc est simpliciter esse prius."*[466]

Theologians of this persuasion reject causal theories of the indwelling, because they regard God's presence as cause of created grace insufficiently distinct from the divine omnipresence to qualify as a radically new, supernatural indwelling. Aquinas explains the distinction between God's natural presence in all things and the indwelling thus:

God is in all things by essence, power, and presence, according to his one common mode, as a cause in effects that participate in his goodness. Above this common mode, however, there is one special mode, which convenes to the rational creature, in whom God is said to be as the known in the knower and the loved in the lover....Because, by knowing and loving, the rational creature by its own operation attains to God himself, according to this special mode, God is not only said to be in the rational creature, but to dwell in it as in his own temple [*STh* Ia. 43, 3 corp.].

---

[463] *De gratia Christi: Praelectiones scholastico–dogmaticae* (Rome: Iuvenes Opifices a S. Ioseph, 1905⁵), disp. 5, a. 9, § 2, nn. 1043–51, pp. 734–9.

[464] *Institutiones theologiae dogmaticae specialis: Tractatus de gratia* (Rome: Marietti, 1873), § 264, p. 193.

[465] *The Indwelling of the Holy Spirit in the Souls of the Just* (Sydney A. Raemers, tr.; Baltimore: Carroll Press, 1950³), 40, 42–3, 60, 66–7.

[466] Ibid. 52.

Now, a creature can know and love God in a supernatural manner, of course, only if it possesses the created grace that enables it so to do. Scholastics who consider created grace logically prior to the divine indwelling, therefore, do so only because they identify this indwelling exclusively with God's objective presence as known and loved. These theologians in no sense deny the primacy of the divine persons, the efficient and final cause of created grace, over their gifts to the human person.

β. Rahner's position. No scholastic theologian, accordingly, speaks as if created entities determine where God does and does not dwell. Advocates of subjective, causal theories, moreover, affirm the logical and ontological priority of uncreated grace in the narrowest sense of the term. Why, then, does Rahner accuse even the advocates of causal theories of subordinating uncreated to created grace? Simon Gaine finds the answer to this question in a footnote which appears in Rahner's earliest and principal treatment of the subject and in which Rahner asserts that "a logical (not temporal) priority to created grace should be ascribed to uncreated grace (*as* given, not just as *to be* given or as *causing* grace."[467] In this remark, writes Simon Gaine:

> one may find the reason why Rahner believed that a theory modelled on efficient causality collapses into the priority of created grace. Efficiency may provide a special divine presence, a communicating of self so as to be given in the causing of created grace, but the givenness of uncreated grace is complete only on the basis of the completed created effect when uncreated grace is possessed....This would appear to be insufficient for Rahner because [in his view] created grace must be a logical consequence of God as somehow *already given* (in a non-temporal sense)....And efficiency cannot establish this full givenness, but only the causation of an effect.[468]

According to Gaine's interpretation, which seems to us essentially correct, then, Rahner objects to causal theories, at least in part, because they make a human being's reception of uncreated grace contingent, in an unacceptable way, on the presence of a merely created effect. Rahner himself, however, maintains

---

[467] "Uncreated," *TI* i, 323, n. 5; "Ungeschaffene," *ST* i, 351, Anm. 5.
[468] *Indwelling Spirit*, 221–2.

that a human being cannot receive uncreated grace without a created *dispositio ultima*, which stands to uncreated grace in a relation of reciprocal causality. It is unlikely, therefore, that he condemns causal theories solely on the grounds that they make the divine indwelling contingent, albeit in an attenuated sense of the term, on the bestowal of created grace.

Rahner seems to reject causal theories, rather, principally because he disagrees with these theories' advocates about what constitutes divine indwelling, i.e. uncreated grace in the strictest sense of the term. Causal theorists, as we have already seen, view the possession of God as an object of knowledge and/or love as an inevitable consequence of uncreated grace, but not, strictly speaking, as a necessary constituent of it. On this question, however, Rahner takes the side of the objective theorists. In Rahner's unpublished tractate, *De Gratia Christi*, Gaine relates:

> Vásquez's theory [frequently considered the causal theory *par exemplar*][469]...is rejected as insufficient to explain the indwelling as (allegedly) taught by the Fathers, in which the divine substance is not only present but also possessed. Possession of God as object is thus taken to be an integral part of the indwelling which must then be given an objective explanation of some kind.[470]

Rahner thus places himself in a virtually unique position within scholastic theology. With the advocates of subjective, causal theories, he maintains uncompromisingly that uncreated grace must possess an absolute precedence over created grace. Yet, with the advocates of objective theories, he maintains that one cannot reasonably describe God as "inhabiting" a soul until it possesses God as an object of knowledge and love: a stance frequently thought to require that created grace precede uncreated grace in order to enable the soul to possess God as the object of its supernatural knowledge and love.

---

[469] Cf., however, the revisionist interpretation of Leo D. Sullivan in his *Justification and the Inhabitation of the Holy Ghost: The Doctrine of Father Gabriel Vásquez, S.J.* (Rome: PUG, 1940).
[470] Gaine, *Indwelling Spirit*, 220.

If both of these seemingly contradictory viewpoints are, in fact, objectively valid, then it might seem that Rahner's theory is the most acceptable account available of the relation between uncreated and created grace. For Rahner's theory posits the relative identity even in creatures of being, knowing, and loving[471] so that God cannot impart the divine being without also, by that very act, imparting knowledge and love of the divine self.

The subjective, causal theories, that is to say, identify God's initial, supernatural action on the soul as indwelling and thus maintain the primacy of uncreated grace only by excising the subsequent acts of knowledge and love from the indwelling's concept. The objective theories, likewise, treat the knowledge and love of God as integral to the divine indwelling only at the expense of excising God's initial, supernatural contact with the soul from the indwelling's concept and thus, in Rahner's estimate, subordinating uncreated to created grace.

Both subjective and objective theories, then, sacrifice one or the other of Rahner's concerns, viz. the primacy of uncreated grace and the indispensability of supernatural knowledge and love to the indwelling, because neither can conceive of the knowledge and love of God as anything other than logically subsequent to God's initial, supernatural contact with the soul. Rahner, however, by: a) relatively identifying even created being with both knowledge and love; and b) understanding God's supernatural contact with the soul in terms of intrinsic, quasi-formal causality; can c) satisfy both concerns by making human knowledge and love of God not merely temporally, but logically simultaneous with God's initial, supernatural action on the soul. Rahner succeeds, therefore, as few others have before or since, in reconciling the two basic orientations of scholastic theology on this subject: a not inconsiderable intellectual feat.

---

[471] Cf. *Hearer*, 83, 126 (*Hörer*, *SW* iv, 152, 154, 224); "Incomprehensibility," *TI* xvi, 254 ("Unbegreiflichkeit," *ST* xii, 319).

γ. Criticisms. For all its brilliance and originality, however, Rahner's theory of the relation between uncreated and created grace is by no means unproblematic. Critics of Rahner's position on this subject complain principally, in Hill's words, that "it is impossible to see that it does not slight the transcendence of God."[472] Since our concern here is to determine whether one must accept Rahner's idea of divine self-communication as true in spite of its apparent inconsistency with divine transcendence, we shall pass over Hill's and similar objections without comment.

At least two other difficulties, however, seem quite relevant in this context. First, as we have seen, Rahner's belief in the relative identity of being, knowing, and loving implies the absurd conclusion that beings are identical with their acts. To the extent that Rahner's theory of the relation of uncreated to created grace presupposes the relative identity of created being, knowing, and loving, then, it appears highly questionable.

A more properly theological objection, second, concerns the seemingly conflicting claims that Rahner's theology of grace seeks to accommodate. As we noted above, Rahner constructs a kind of compromise theory that satisfies the most fundamental concerns of both subjective and objective theorists of the divine indwelling. If the subjective theorist rightly insists that uncreated grace logically precedes created grace, and the objective theorist rightly insists that God dwells only in those who know and love God, then Rahner's theory faces few plausible alternatives. If, however, either school's central claim is objectively invalid, then the synthesis of the two schools' views in Rahner's theory constitutes not an advantage, but a defect. In such a case, Rahner's theory would, in fact, prove false at least to the extent that it affirms the erring school's claim.

Now, a number of considerations suggest that those theories, which posit a subjective, causal indwelling, are significantly less tenable than those that envision an objective indwelling in which the soul possesses God as the object of

---

[472] "Uncreated Grace," 356.

its knowledge and love. For, first, the most substantial advantage subjective theories possess over objective theories seems to consist in their emphatic affirmation of divine action's priority over human action in the sanctification of the human being. As the remarks of Froget quoted above illustrate, however, one cannot reasonably charge objective theorists with denying the radical priority of divine over human agency in this event.

Second, and more importantly, causal theories of the divine indwelling seem to represent this indwelling as an intensification of God's universal, natural presence as cause rather than as a genuinely new mode of God's presence in the soul. Objective theories, by contrast, seem to explain how the indwelling surpasses divine omnipresence in kind and not merely in degree. For, at least in the view of those who reject Rahner's proportional identification of knowing and being, intentional existence differs fundamentally from all other modes of being. The supernatural character of the indwelling thus seems to demand an objective rather than a causal explanation.

Admittedly, objective theories might seem ill-equipped to explain how God can supernaturally inhabit the souls of regenerate infants. For regenerate infants certainly possess the Holy Spirit. Nevertheless, their underdeveloped mental capacities seem to render actual knowledge and love of anyone impossible. In the words of Augustine:

> It is a very amazing thing how God is the *inhabitator* of some who do not yet know him and is not of some who do know him. For those do not pertain to the temple of God, who knowing God have not glorified him as God or given thanks, and [yet] to the temple of God pertain infants sanctified by the sacrament of Christ, regenerated by the Holy Spirit, who certainly, on account of their age, cannot yet know God. Hence those have been able to know God, but not to possess him; [and] these have been able to possess him before they knew him.[473]

One ought not, however, to consider the knowledge of God by the wicked as a counterexample to the objective theory, because the wicked never attain the intimate, experiential knowledge of God possessed by the righteous: a knowledge,

---

[473] *Epistula.* 187.21 in CSEL 57, 99–100. The causal theorist Galtier alludes to Augustine's remarks in this connection (*L'Habitation*, vi, 195–6).

which, incidentally, presupposes God's real and not merely intentional presence. The absence of actual knowledge and love in infants, moreover, does not constitute an insuperable difficulty for objective theories. For, unless one wishes to maintain that parents cease to love or even to know their children when the parents fall asleep, one must admit that the habits (faculties, virtues) of knowing and loving one's children suffice, even when unactualized, to enable one to possess one's children as objects of knowledge and love.

One can reasonably maintain, therefore, that regenerate infants possess God as the object of their knowledge and love insofar as they possess the unactualized habits of faith and charity. Admittedly, by so conceiving of God's supernatural presence in regenerate infants, the objective theorist might seem implicitly to endorse a causal understanding of the indwelling. For if God can dwell in regenerate infants by virtue of the mere bestowal of unactualized habits of faith and charity, then divine causality alone suffices to constitute the indwelling in logical and even temporal priority to actual knowledge and love. As we noted earlier, however, objective and causal theories of the indwelling do not differ in the extent to which they acknowledge divine action's primacy in the sanctification of human beings. The competing theories differ, rather, in their conception of what the indwelling is.

Insofar, then, as objective theories: a) posit an indwelling that differs in kind and not merely degree from God's natural omnipresence; and b) need not in any way subordinate the action of the Holy Spirit to that of creatures; it seems likely that a properly constructed objective theory could satisfy the legitimate concerns of all parties to the debate over the relation between uncreated and created grace.

d. Conclusion. Rahner does not, therefore prove that his theory of the divine indwelling alone, with its emphasis on divine self-communication in the Rahnerian sense of the term, can adequately account for human beings' possession of uncreated grace. Rahner's theory rests on two highly questionable presuppositions: a) that being, knowing, and loving are relatively identical even in the created sphere; and b) that the fundamental claims of both objective and subjective theorists of the divine indwelling are equally valid.

Neither, it seems, can Rahner prove that the beatific vision requires that uncreated grace, as its ontological presupposition, consist in divine self-communication as Rahner understands it. Although Rahner rightly discerns a close relationship between the grace of the *viator* and the beatifying vision of God, he cannot establish that the beatific vision itself requires divine self-communication, according to his conception of it. *A fortiori*, neither can he demonstrate its integrality to the ontological presupposition of the beatific vision that is the uncreated grace of *viatores*. Rahner does not succeed, then, in demonstrating that divine self-communication in his sense of the term must occur in order for God to impart Godself to human beings in uncreated, sanctifying grace.

3. The Incarnation of the Logos.

a. Introduction. Rahner argues, nonetheless, that not only uncreated grace, but also the Incarnation of the Logos, as defined by various ecumenical councils teaching in union with the Pope, constitutes an instance of divine self-communication in the Rahnerian sense of those words. Since: a) Rahner presupposes the infallibility of ecumenical councils when teaching definitively in union with the Pope; b) the charism of infallibility precludes the possibility of self-contradiction; and c) ecumenical councils have definitively taught, in union with the Pope, the doctrines of divine immutability and the Incarnation of the Logos; then d) if Rahner can establish that the Incarnation constitutes an instance of divine self-communication as he understands it, then his presuppositions concerning the infallibility of ecumenical councils dictate that divine self-communication in the Rahnerian sense of that term must be ultimately compatible with divine immutability. If this were, in fact, the case, then our first criticism of

Rahner's *Grundaxiom*, a criticism that presupposes the incompatibility of divine self-communication as Rahner conceives of it with divine immutability, would, at least in the context of a strictly immanent critique, prove invalid.

In the following, accordingly, we intend: first, to outline Rahner's theory of the "uniting unity" in the Incarnation, the keystone of Rahner's case for the integrality of divine self-communication, as he understands it, to the event of the hypostatic union; second, to examine briefly certain of the advantages of Rahner's theory of the uniting unity; third, to explore a number of difficulties for this theory; and, fourth, to determine whether Rahner's theory of the "uniting unity" in the hypostatic union actually constitutes proof that the Incarnation consists in or presupposes divine self-communication in the Rahnerian sense of the term.

b. Rahner's theory of the "uniting unity" in the Incarnation. In his theory of the "uniting unity" in the Incarnation, Rahner attempts to specify "by what (i.e. by what uniting unity) they [= Christ's two natures] are united (in the united unity [= Christ's person in both natures])."[474] The term "uniting unity" as Rahner employs it, seems to denote something at least rationally distinct from the agent that unites Christ's human nature to the person of the Logos. For the IV Lateran Council binds Rahner to attribute the hypostatic union to the agency of "the whole Trinity in common,"[475] and he, accordingly, explicitly attributes the bringing about of the Incarnation to the Trinity as a whole: "the accomplishment of the [hypostatic] union," he writes, "is common to the three divine persons."[476]

When Rahner asks by what "uniting unity" Christ's two natures come to be united, then, he seems to ask: by what process or mode of causality does the Trinity unite Christ's human nature to the person of the Logos?[477] Rahner

---

[474] "Current Problems," *TI* i, 182, n. 1; "Probleme," *SW* xii, 286, Anm. 33.
[475] DH 801.
[476] Inkarnation," *SM* ii, *SW* xvii/ii, 1096–1109 at 1101.
[477] The following remarks confirm this interpretation. "Someone may object," Rahner writes:

recognizes that some may consider this question unanswerable. In response, however, he writes:

> If someone goes on to maintain that it is impossible to provide a further answer here because it is precisely a mystery with which we are dealing here, it would be necessary to reply that this account [i.e. the statement that "the human nature and the divine nature are united in the person of the Logos"] would suffice provided that the mystery given expression in the original formula remains clear in its meaning (though not in its explanation) even when no answer is offered to the further question. But if this is not the case, i.e. if the united unity in the sense intended (a sense which, though undetected, must be there even in a mystery) does not permit of being thought unless the uniting unity comes into sight, then...[a] *docta ignorantia*...is simply not appropriate here—no matter how far the ancient tradition provides or fails to provide a further explicit question and answer as to the uniting unity.[478]

Rahner does not explain precisely why the mystery's meaning must remain unclear as long as one lacks an account of the uniting unity. He does, nonetheless, make this assumption: an assumption which implies that one can hardly speak of the Incarnation without a theory of the uniting unity, and that the dogma of the hypostatic union thus presupposes at least the possibility of such an account. Given Rahner's presuppositions, then, a proof that his theory, which dictates that the Incarnation occurs through an act of divine self-communication as he understands it, constitutes the only adequate account of the uniting unity would imply that the Incarnation constitutes an instance of divine self-communication in the Rahnerian sense.

Rahner's theory of the "uniting unity," in itself, is disarmingly simple. The principle, which Rahner considers axiomatic, that "nearness to God...and genuine

---

that it is in fact the one hypostasis which is the uniting unity for the two natures. To this we must reply that this may well be true, so far as it is a matter of the two natures in their mutual concord. But the question here is to what extent the divine hypostasis unites the human nature to itself. When the question is formulated like this, the hypostasis, *in so far* as it is just the static concept of *ens per se et in se* which is involved, is something to be united—one 'part' of the united unity, and not the uniting unity. Thus it must be asked by what (i.e. by what uniting unity) the hypostasis unites to itself the human nature. Putting the same thing in another way: unity (as a formal transcendental property of an entity) is never something which can be set up as such, but is always the result of some other state or process among entities. Thus one has not explained nor even understood what one is saying when one elucidates unity by—unity ["Current Problems," *TI* i, 182, n.1; "Probleme," *SW* xii, 287, Anm. 33].
[478] Ibid.; ebd. 286–7, Anm. 33.

creaturehood grow in the same, and not in inverse proportions"[479] dictates, in Rahner's view, that Jesus Christ, in order to be perfect God, need do no more than perfectly realize the essence of creaturehood. The man Jesus, he writes, "precisely by being man in the fullest sense...is God's Existence into the world."[480]

Since Christ, as perfect man, is *ipso facto* also perfect God, Rahner reasons, the act whereby God constitutes Christ as perfect man must be identical to the act whereby God unites Christ's human nature to the eternal hypostasis of the Logos. "The positing of Christ's humanity in its free distinction from God itself," Rahner writes, "becomes in this way the act of unification...with the Logos."[481] In Rahner's view, therefore, the uniting unity in the Incarnation "unites *precisely by making existent*;"[482] the uniting unity unites Christ's human nature with the Logos, that is, simply by creating it.[483]

c. Advantages of Rahner's theory. Rahner finds the idea of assumption by creation advantageous, it seems, for three principal reasons: a) this understanding of the "uniting unity" obviates any seeming contradiction between the divinity of Christ and his full humanity; b) it reflects what Rahner considers a correct view of the relation between the intra-Trinitarian processions and the divine acts *ad extra*; and c) it corresponds to what Rahner considers a contemporary view of God and the world.

---

[479] "Intellectual Honesty and Christian Faith," *TI* vii, 47–71 at 68; "Intellektuelle Redlichkeit und christlicher Glaube," *ST* vii, 54–76 at 73.
[480] "Current Problems," *TI* i, 184; "Probleme," *SW* xii, 288.
[481] Ibid. 183; ebd.
[482] Ibid. 182; ebd. 287.
[483] In Rahner's view, Joseph Wong explains, "God 'assumes by creating' and 'creates by assuming'" (*Logos-Symbol*, 127). William V. Dych echoes this language almost exactly (*Karl Rahner* [London: Geoffrey Chapman, 1992], 77). Philipp Kaiser, likewise, notes that, according to Rahner, "the humanity of Christ is...not only created 'by the union with the Logos,' but the creation itself, the *constitution* of the humanity of Christ is itself already its *union* with the Logos" (*Die Gott-menschliche Einigung in Christus als Problem der spekulativen Theologie seit der Scholastik* [MThS.S 36; München: Max Hueber, 1968], 275).

i. Reconciling Christ's divinity with his full humanity. Probably the strongest point in favor of Rahner's theory of assumption by creation is that it eliminates any appearance of conflict between the unity and the distinctness of Christ's natures. As Rahner explains:

> if what makes the human nature ek-sistent as something diverse from God, and what unites this nature with the Logos, are strictly the same, then we have a unity...which does not make the ἀσυγκύτως look like a sort of external counterbalance to the unity, always threatening to dissolve it, but shows...how...unity and distinction [can] become mutually...intensifying characteristics, not competing ones.[484]

Rahner's theory of assumption by creation serves, therefore, to counteract in some measure tendencies to exalt Christ's diversity over his unity and *vice versa*: a quality Rahner correctly views as evidence in its favor.

ii. Correlating intra-divine processions and divine acts ad extra. Rahner also seems attracted to his theory, because it corresponds to his understanding of the relation between the intra-Trinitarian processions and God's action vis-à-vis the world. In Rahner's view, all divine acts *ad extra* constitute various aspects of a single "continuation of the immanent constitution of 'image and likeness' [i.e. of the divine Word]"[485] within God. In other words, just as the Father communicates his essence to the Son for all eternity, so, in Rahner's view, he communicates his essence, albeit in a much less profound sense and without compromising his transcendence, in creating extra-divine being; God, that is to say, creates by assuming.

Rahner believes, accordingly, that in all divine acts *ad extra* God creates and assumes, at least in some measure, by one and the same act. Given this presupposition, the idea that God creates Christ's human nature and unites it to the Logos by one undifferentiated act of creation-assumption follows as a matter of course. Rahner's theory of the uniting unity in the Incarnation, then, construes

---

[484] "Current Problems," *TI* i, 181–2; "Probleme," *SW* xii, 286–7.
[485] "Symbol," *TI* iv, 236–7; "Symbols," *SW* xviii, 437.

this dogma in such a way that it fits seamlessly into his more general theory of divine action as such.

iii. Adjusting to a contemporary worldview. Why Rahner would subscribe to this general theory of divine action appears from the third concern that leads Rahner to adopt his theory of the uniting unity in the Incarnation: his belief in the necessity of demythologization. "The theology of the future," he writes, "must be a 'demythologizing' theology."[486] For, in his view, as we have seen, the doctrines of the Christian faith constitute mere "verbalized objectifications of the 'revelation' which is already present in the gratuitous radicalizing of human transcendentality in God's self-communication."[487] Rahner, consequently, considers it his duty to re-interpret Christian doctrine so as to manifest its connection to contemporary persons' experience of divine self-communication.

Since, in his view, "modern people find nothing illogical in pantheism or panentheism,"[488] Rahner does not hesitate to claim that God communicates Godself to creation so radically as to become "the very core of the world's reality,"[489] "the total unity of reality,"[490] "the single whole of reality,"[491] and "the innermost constitutive element of the human person."[492] Rahner rejects the idea of divine intervention, however, as alien to "our modern experience and interpretation of the world"[493] and, accordingly, seeks to understand divine action

---

[486] "Possible Courses for the Theology of the Future," *TI* xiii, 32–60 at 42; "Über künftige Wege der Theologie," *ST* x, 41–69 at 51. For more on this theme, cf. Michael Barnes, "Demythologization in the Theology of Karl Rahner," *TS* 55 (1994), 24–45.

[487] "The Act of Faith and the Content of Faith," *TI* xxi, 158; "Glaubensakt und Glaubensinhalt," *ST* xv, 158.

[488] "The Works of Mercy and Their Reward," *TI* vii, 268–74 at 272; "Preis der Barmherzigkeit," *ST* vii, 259–64 at 262.

[489] "Specific Character," *TI* xxi, 191; "Eigenart," *ST* xv, 190.

[490] "The Dignity and Freedom of Man," *TI* ii, 235–63 at 239; "Würde und Freiheit des Menschen," *SW* x, 184–206 at 187.

[491] *Foundations*, 48; *Grundkurs*, *SW* xxvi, 51.

[492] Ibid. 116; ebd. 116.

[493] Ibid. 259; ebd. 255.

exclusively in terms of divine self-communication. One can speak truthfully of divine intervention, he writes, only if:

> a special "intervention" of God...[is] understood as the historical concreteness of the transcendental self-communication of God which is always already intrinsic to the concrete world....Every real intervention of God in God's world...is always only the becoming historical and...concrete of that "intervention" in which God as the transcendental ground of the world has from the outset embedded Godself in this world as its self-communicating ground.[494]

According to this understanding of divine action, an Incarnation, if it can occur at all, can constitute no more than a "historical manifestation"[495] of the same, universal divine influence responsible for creation. The view that God assumes Christ's human nature by creating it and, likewise, creates it by assuming it thus serves to reconcile the doctrine of the Incarnation with what Rahner considers a contemporary view of the world.

d. Difficulties for Rahner's theory. When considered from Rahner's perspective, therefore, his theory of assumption by creation possesses considerable advantages. Two difficulties, however, appear, at least *prima facie*, to threaten the theory's plausibility. First, Rahner's view that the uniting unity "unites *precisely by* making existent"[496] seems to rest on a self-contradictory premise: viz., that two entities can be united by their differentiation *simpliciter*. Second, and more significantly, the principle that God assumes by creating seems to imply that every human being possesses the grace of union with the divine Logos. If to create is to assume, then it seems that God cannot create an individual human nature[497] without also assuming it.

---

[494] Ibid. 87; ebd. 87–8. We have inserted the word "always" between "the historical concreteness of the transcendental self-communication of God which is" and "already intrinsic to the concrete world" in the translation in order more accurately to render Rahner's German text in which one reads of the "geschichtliche Konkretheit der transzendentalen Selbstmitteilung Gottes..., die der konkreten Welt *immer* schon innerlich ist" (ebd.; our emphasis).

[495] "Christology in the Setting," *TI* xi, 226; "Christologie im Rahmen," *SW* xv, 609.

[496] "Current Problems," *TI* i, 182; "Probleme," *SW* xii, 287.

[497] Cf. n. 244.

163

i. Unification through differentiation. Rahner attempts to extricate himself from the first difficulty by appealing to his ontology of symbol. Two things can be united by their differentiation *simpliciter*, Rahner affirms, because the thesis, "being is knowing,"[498] perhaps the most fundamental tenet of Rahner's philosophy, seems to entail that such unification through differentiation occurs.

In *Geist in Welt*, specifically, Rahner argues that if being is knowing, then, at least in human beings, "knowing will know something to the extent to which it *is* this something."[499] Rahner conceives of human knowledge, accordingly, as "a result of the ontological unity of object and cognitive faculty."[500] Nevertheless, Rahner also recognizes that in human cognition:

> something is always known about something....Every objective knowledge is always and in every case the reference of a universal to a "this." Hence the "this" appears as the reference point standing over against the knowing to which the knower refers what is...known by her. But then the subject with the content of her knowledge (the universal concept) always stands to some extent at a distance from "this" to which she refers the content of his knowledge.[501]

Every act of human knowledge, then, requires a simultaneous unification with and differentiation from the object known: something at least roughly analogous to the unification through differentiation which, in Rahner's view, occurs in the Incarnation. While it is not immediately evident that the unification and differentiation characteristic of human knowing as Rahner understands it must coincide in a single act, Rahner argues at great length in *Geist in Welt* that unification and differentiation here do in fact coincide in the one act of "conversion to the phantasm"[502]: a term Rahner borrows from Aquinas to characterize "the one human knowing."[503]

---

[498] *Hearer*, 35; *Hörer, SW* iv, 70.
[499] *Spirit*, 97; *Geist, SW* ii, 83.
[500] Ibid.; ebd.
[501] Ibid. 122; ebd. 101–2.
[502] Rahner maintains, that is to say, that both: 1) the apprehension of a known object in sensibility, which he considers a self–alienating union with the other; and 2) the act of abstraction, which Rahner characterizes as a *reditio subjecti in seipsum* in which human beings recognize themselves as distinct from the objects of their cognition; are identical with the one, internally

In his later essay, "Zur Theologie des Symbols," Rahner exploits this model of human cognition in order to characterize the eternal generation of the Logos: an intra-divine procession that, in Rahner's view, the Father extends *ad extra* in the Incarnation. The eternal generation of the Logos, Rahner claims, constitutes a self-differentiating self-communication of the Father's being to that of the Son by which the Father knows himself in the Son. "This process," Rahner writes, "is necessarily given with the divine act of self-knowledge, and without it the absolute act of divine self-possession in knowledge cannot exist."[504]

Since Rahner maintains that being *is* knowing, a correct assumption, of course, *in divinis*, he considers this generation essential not merely to the Father's self-awareness but to his very existence. "The Father is himself," writes Rahner, "by the very fact that he opposes to himself the image which is of the same essence as himself, as the person who is other than himself; and so he possesses himself."[505] The Father, in other words, necessarily generates another by communicating himself and communicates himself by generating another; he unifies himself to the Son, then, precisely by making the Son existent. God in Godself, in Rahner's view, and not merely God incarnate, thus constitutes "the initially existing uniting unity."[506]

Since Rahner identifies being and knowing at least relatively in all beings whatsoever, furthermore, he holds that each being must constitute itself by a self-communicating self-differentiation analogous to the Father's. "Each being," Rahner writes, "forms, in its own way, more or less perfectly according to its

---

differentiated act of conversion to the phantasm. In the preface to *Geist in Welt*, Rahner writes, "the work could have been entitled, *Conversion to the Phantasm* [ibid. liii; ebd. 15]."
[503] Ibid. liv; ebd.
[504] "Symbol," *TI* iv, 236; "Symbols," *SW* xviii, 436.
[505] Ibid.; ebd.
[506] "Unity of the Church—Unity of Humankind," *TI* xx, 154–72 at 162; "Einheit der Kirche—Einheit der Menschheit," *SW* xxvii, 156–72 at 163. We substitute "uniting unity" for the translator, Edward Quinn's, rendering, "unifying unity," because Rahner himself writes here not *einigende Einheit*, of which "unifying unity" would be the more literal translation, but *einende Einheit*, the *terminus technicus* from "Probleme," which the translator of *ST* i, Cornelius Ernst, renders as "uniting unity."

degree of being, something distinct from itself and yet one with itself, 'for' its own fulfillment."[507] In other words, each being constitutes something of a uniting unity; absolutely everything, not excluding the God-man himself, constitutes itself through some act of unification through differentiation.

One can reasonably ask, however, whether Rahner's ontology really justifies such a sweeping conclusion. In *Geist in Welt*, after all, Rahner specifically admits that a "differentiation of subject and object...does not belong to the essence of knowing as such. On the contrary, knowing as such is to be understood first of all as a being's being-present-to-self....The apprehension of an 'in-itself' is therefore conceivable without setting apart in opposition the knowing subject and the object, [i.e.] without a judgment as affirmative synthesis."[508]

In a footnote to this last sentence, the young Rahner concludes, "therefore God, for example, does not judge."[509] At this stage of his career, then, Rahner specifically rejects the view that divine self-knowledge presupposes an interior opposition between subject and object. Evidently, Rahner changes his mind at some point between the composition of *Geist in Welt* and that of "Zur Theologie des Symbols." Yet he nowhere explains precisely why he comes to reject his former position. It seems less than obvious, therefore, that Rahner's ontology actually dictates that God does, or even can, execute the kind of unificative self-differentiation required by his theory of the uniting unity.

ii. The singularity of the hypostatic union. The graver and more properly theological of the two difficulties, in any event, is surely the second: viz. that Rahner's view of the uniting unity in the Incarnation seems not to cohere with the revealed datum that the Word became flesh in Jesus Christ alone. In the following, accordingly, we intend to examine this difficulty and Rahner's

---

[507] "Symbol," *TI* iv, 228; "Symbols," *SW* xviii, 429.
[508] *Spirit*, 130; *Geist*, *SW* ii, 107.
[509] Ibid. n. 22; ebd. Anm. 24.

response(s) in their various facets and to measure Rahner's success in reconciling the idea of assumption by creation with the exclusivity of the hypostatic union.

α. The extent of the problem. Even a cursory glance at Rahner's statements on this subject will show that he tends to emphasize the continuities between Christ and his fellow human beings. "The Incarnation of God," writes Rahner, "is the unique and *highest* instance of the actualization of the essence of human reality."[510] Again, Rahner affirms, "the God-Man...neither is nor can be graced in itself with a closeness to God and an encounter with God which is essentially different from *the* encounter and self-communication of God which is in fact intended for *every* person in grace."[511]

Rahner maintains, moreover, that the very act of creating a human being constitutes also an at least partial assumption into the person of the Logos so that the grace possessed by all human beings constitutes an "unfolding within human nature of the union of the human with the Logos."[512] Rahner affirms, therefore, the existence of a "universal God-manhood inherent in the spiritual creature as such."[513]

He believes, however, that he can advance such theses without even tacitly imputing the hypostatic union to the entire human race as long as he treats the "God-manhood" possessed by human beings other than Christ as "deficient modes of this primary Christological relation."[514] It seems, moreover, that this proviso would abundantly suffice to vindicate Rahner from the charge of universalizing the hypostatic union but for two difficulties.

---

[510] *Foundations*, 218; *Grundkurs*, *SW* xxvi, 210.
[511] Ibid. 218–19; ebd.
[512] "Current Problems," *TI* i, 199–200; "Probleme," *SW* xii, 300.
[513] "Methodology," *TI* xi, 97; "Methode," *ST* ix, 109. Cf. Rahner's similar remarks in "Thoughts on the Possibility of Belief Today," *TI* v, 15; "Über die Möglichkeit des Glaubens heute," *SW* xii, 583; and *Ich glaube an Jesus Christus* (Theologische Meditationen 21: Einsiedeln: Benziger, 1975), 37.
[514] "Current Problems," *TI* i, 165; "Probleme," *SW* xii, 274.

β. The absoluteness of the divine nature. First, if the "primary Christological relation" consists in the possession of a divine and a human nature by a single, ontological subject; and if, as Rahner correctly observes, "God...is absolute and simple spirit,"[515] then one cannot intelligibly speak of "deficient modes" of this relation. For a truly absolute being does not admit of being morcellated into distinct degrees so that various subjects can instantiate it to a greater or lesser extent. As Gerald O'Collins justly observes: "One who is God is beyond degrees (and hence differences of degree), because being truly divine means being indivisible."[516]

γ. The oscillating hypostasis. Second, and viewing the problem from the opposite angle, one cannot intelligibly refer to a human nature as both enhypostatic in itself and anhypostatic in the same respect.[517] Yet Rahner's position seems to imply, and Rahner himself explicitly states, that all individual, human natures other than Christ's oscillate between these two extremes. Rahner claims, specifically: a) that "the human person is insofar as she abandons herself to the absolute mystery whom we call God";[518] b) that Christ's individual, human nature abandons its hypostasis to the Logos when "this is done in the strictest

---

[515] Immanent and Transcendent," *TI* x, 287; "Immanente und transzendente," *SW* xv, 555.

[516] Gerald O'Collins, "The Incarnation under Fire," *Greg* 76 (1995), 263–80 at 263.

[517] F. Leron Shults suggests that theologians abandon the terms "enhypostatic" and "anhypostatic" on the grounds: a) that, *pace* Friedrich Loofs, the term ἐνυπόστατος signifies in patristic discourse not "subsistent in another," but simply "subsistent"; and b) that, since no nature lacks subsistence, no nature ought to be described as ἀνυπόστατος ("A Dubious Christological Formula: From Leontius of Byzantium to Karl Barth," *TS* 57 [1996], 431–46). In reply, we should like to state, first, that neither Barth nor the Protestant scholastics whom Shults mentions declare any nature anhypostatic *simpliciter*. They assert, rather, that Christ's human nature is anhypostatic of itself inasmuch as it subsists through the hypostasis of another. Second, neither Barth nor the Protestant scholastics to whom Shults refers employ the term "enhypostatic" in the sense of "subsistent in another." Rather, they affirm that Christ's human nature is enhypostatic not in itself, but in the hypostasis of the Word. Although Shults' historical conclusions as to the patristic meanings of ἐνυπόστατος and ἀνυπόστατος seem quite correct, therefore, he appears to err in accusing Barth and the Reformed scholastics of employing the terms in unpatristic senses. In this work, in any event, we employ the term "enhypostatic" in the sense of "subsistent" and the term "anhypostatic" in the sense of "non-subsistent *per se*."

[518] *Foundations*, 218; *Grundkurs*, *SW* xxvi, 210.

sense and reaches an unsurpassable pitch of achievement";[519] and c) that every human nature other than Christ's gives itself to the Logos in some measure, but fails to give itself absolutely so that "in its ek-stasy [it] falls back upon itself again and again...and comes to subsist [*hypo-stasiert*] in itself."[520]

In thesis a) Rahner seems to identify human existence with the act of self-abandonment to God. As we have already seen, such an identification is highly problematic; for "as an act of knowing or striving the immanent action is characterized by a certain indeterminacy or infiniteness:...one can think whatever is true and love whatever is good....The being of things, however, is always limited to this or that individual in a particular species and a particular genus. It is the...reality of precisely this or that thing."[521] If human existence were identical with some immanent, human act, therefore, human beings could never constitute *mere* human beings.

Rahner, admittedly, seems not only to accept, but to celebrate this consequence of his position. "The very definition of the human person," he writes, "is her indefinability, i.e. precisely her transcendence as absolute openness to being in the absolute."[522] Indeed, the limitless elasticity of the human essence seems to constitute a presupposition of his theory of assumption by creation. "Only someone who forgets that the essence of humanity...is to be unbounded (thus in this sense, to be un-definable)," Rahner asserts, "can suppose that it is impossible for there to be a man, who, precisely by being man in the fullest sense..., is God's Existence into the world."[523]

Such a hollowing out of the essence of humanity, however, seems inconsistent with the Chalcedonian formula insofar as: a) one cannot reasonably speak of an infinitely elastic nature as ἀτρέπτως; and b) such a nature would seem to

---

[519] "Incarnation," *TI* iv, 109; "Menschwerdung," *SW* xii, 312.
[520] "Person," *KThW*[1], *SW* xvii/i, 752–5 at 753–4.
[521] Leo Elders, *The Metaphysics of Being of St. Thomas Aquinas in a Historical Perspective* (Leiden, Boston, and Köln: Brill, 1993), 260.
[522] "Immanent and Transcendent," *TI* x, 279; "Immanente und transzendente," *SW* xv, 548.
[523] "Current Problems," *TI* i, 184; "Probleme," *SW* xii, 288.

possess no particular ἰδιώτης. Rahner's understanding of human nature also raises the question of how an identical subjectivity could survive a process of infinite, ontological self-transcendence. Thesis a), then, on account of the highly unconventional view of human nature it implies, seems liable to a number of weighty objections.

Thesis b), Rahner's claim that Christ's human nature abandons its hypostasis to the second person of the Trinity proves similarly problematic. For Christ could not have abandoned a merely human hypostasis to the Logos if, as Rahner correctly grants, he never possessed a merely human hypostasis. If he had somehow managed to donate his hypostasis to God, moreover, this would not necessarily have rendered his human nature enhypostatic in the eternal Logos. It seems, rather, that such an act would have added a hypostasis to the divine nature and thus converted the holy Trinity into a quaternity. Yet, according to the fifth canon of the II Council of Constantinople, "the Holy Trinity did not receive the addition of a person, i.e. a hypostasis, even through the Incarnation of God the Word."[524]

Rahner attempts to avoid these difficulties by identifying the divine act of creating Christ's human nature with the Logos' act of surrendering his own subsistence in Jesus to himself. When Christ's human nature surrenders itself to the Logos, Rahner writes, "this 'act' of self-surrender is...primarily the 'act' of the Creator in making human nature, and not something done 'accidentally' by the human as a creature in its *actus secundus* deriving from its own decision."[525] It seems, however, that one could reasonably identify the divine act of creating Christ's human nature with the *actus primus* of Christ *qua* creature *only* if one identified this creaturely *actus primus*, i.e. the sacred humanity's act of existing, with the divine existence of the Logos.

By identifying the divine act of creating Christ's human nature with his creaturely *actus primus*, that is, it seems that Rahner either: 1) identifies a divine

---
[524] DH 426
[525] "Incarnation," *TI* iv, 109, n. 1; "Menschwerdung," *SW* xii, 312–13, Anm. 1.

creative act with a merely creaturely act of existing and thus confuses an act with its presupposition; or 2) commits himself to a "one *esse*" account of Christ's ontological constitution according to which Christ lacks a distinctively human act of existence. Such an account, of course, might prove reasonable in itself, but it would ill accord with Rahner's explicit condemnation of Christological "mono-existentialism,"[526] which he treats as a species of the heresy of monotheletism. It seems, therefore, that one can construe thesis b) as defensible only if one imputes to Rahner an understanding of Christ's existence(s) that conflicts with his explicit statements on this subject.

---

[526] "Current Problems," *TI* i, 160; "Probleme," *SW* xii, 270. John M. McDermott, ordinarily a highly perceptive commentator on Rahner's works, does, admittedly, claim that Rahner's "Christology...ignore[s] the question of the existence(s) of Jesus Christ," and that Rahner "nowhere...explicitly consider[s] the question of the number of existences in Christ" ("The Christologies of Karl Rahner," *Greg* 67 [1986], 87–123, 297–327 at 89–90, n. 12 and 309). At a 1961 symposium on Christology, however, Rahner offers what he regards as a reconciliation of the view that Christ's human nature exists by the existence of the Word with the view that this nature possesses its own *esse secondarium*. "The *esse secondarium*," he asks:

can it not be conceived as that which is given by the divine *esse* to this nature, insomuch as it exists? This question is truly quite complex: in effect, on the one hand, one must assign to the divine *esse* a formal causality, and not solely efficient....On the other hand, an infinite act communicating itself to a finite potency...is neither limited nor restrained. Nevertheless, that which is in the [human] nature itself, is and remains finite and limited in a certain manner. That is why we are only able to distinguish in God a formal cause and its formal effect. It is in this sense that a conciliation between the two opinions is possible ["Débats sur le rapport du P. Patfoort," *Problèmes actuels*, 414–15].

In these remarks as well as in the condemnation of "mono-existentialism" referred to in the main text, Rahner at least seems to ascribe two *esses*, the Logos' *esse divinum*, and a creaturely *esse secondarium*, to the incarnate Christ. Rahner's beliefs, moreover: a) that creatureliness increases in direct, and not inverse, proportion to unity with God; b) that Christ possesses a creaturely as well as a divine self-consciousness ("Current Problems," *TI* i, 158; "Probleme," *SW* xii, 268), at least when this belief is considered in conjunction with his identification of being and knowing (*Spirit*, 69; *Geist*, *SW* ii, 62); and c) that created essence and existence are not really distinct (cf. the texts adduced and the implications drawn from them in Denis J. M. Bradley, "Rahner's *Spirit in the World*: Aquinas or Hegel," *Thomist* 41 [1977], 167-99 at 180-83); all seem to demand that Christ possess a second, creaturely *esse*. We follow Van der Heijden, to whom we owe argument b (*Karl Rahner*, 408-10), and Guy Mansini, from whom we learned of Rahner's symposium remarks ("Quasi-Formal Causality and 'Change in the Other': A Note on Karl Rahner's Christology," *Thomist* 52 [1988], 293-306 at 294, n. 7), therefore, in ascribing a two-*esse* account of Christ's ontological constitution to Rahner.

Thesis c), likewise, presents Rahner with something of a paradox. As we have seen, in order to view the hypostatic union as the perfect fulfillment of a relation partially realized by all human beings, Rahner claims that every merely human person attempts to become enhypostatic in the Logos. "We always attempt in principle," he writes, "to come nearer to this goal without ever reaching it."[527] "Precisely in her transcendence," however, the merely human person, in Rahner's view, "always falls back again into her separating subsistence."[528]

Yet Rahner nowhere answers the question: from whence does the human being fall? A human nature can be enhypostatic in itself and, as the case of Christ proves, anhypostatic in itself. But the idea: a) that human beings can launch themselves from a state of merely human *enhypostasia* towards the asymptotically approachable goal of *anhyspostasia* and fall back again; and b) that human beings do so continually, as if bouncing on an ontological trampoline; seems highly counter-intuitive, if not absurd.

e. Assessment. Rahner, then, sincerely and creatively attempts to establish the possibility of unification through differentiation and to reconcile his theory of assumption by creation with the revealed fact that the Word became flesh in only one human being. Rahner's efforts in the latter direction, however, land him in a veritable thicket of difficulties. The idea of graded instantiations of divinity, for instance, seems at least as unorthodox as that of a universal hypostatic union. Rahner's confusion of human being with particular human acts, moreover, and his concept of the oscillating hypostasis seem to render his theory incredible to all but those willing to accept certain highly controversial presuppositions. Rahner's

---

[527] "Thoughts on the Theology of Christmas," *TI* iii, 33; "Zur Theologie der Weihnachtsfeier," *SW* xiv, 104. Rahner believes that such "attempts" constitute an experience analogous to the Incarnation. By meditating on "the prolongation of our own spiritual existence," he writes, "we may get some idea of what it means that God has become man" (ibid.; ebd. 44–5). Cf. also Rahner's "Christmas in the Light of the Ignatian Exercises," *TI* xvii, 3–7 at 6–7; "Weihnacht im Licht der Exerzitien," *ST* xii, 329–34 at 332–3.

[528] "Thoughts on the Theology of Christmas," *TI* iii, 31; "Zur Theologie der Weihnachtsfeier," *SW* xiv, 102.

theory of the uniting unity, consequently, seems intrinsically implausible and, therefore, insufficient to establish the indispensability of divine self-communication as Rahner conceives of it to the accomplishment of the Incarnation.

4. Christ's absolute saviorhood

a. Introduction. Rahner argues, nonetheless, that not only the doctrines of sanctifying grace and the Incarnation, but also that of Christ's status as "absolute savior" presupposes the occurrence of divine self-communication in the radical, Rahnerian sense of the term. Now, it does seem that ecumenical councils teaching in union with the Pope have taught definitively that Christ constitutes in some sense the "absolute savior," i.e. the one person on whom all salvation history hinges. If, accordingly, Rahner can prove: a) that Christ could not constitute the "absolute savior" without being the recipient of a divine self-communication in his sense of the term; then it seems that his assumption b) of the absolute truthfulness and, therefore, consistency of ecumenical, conciliar pronouncements ratified by the Pope; when combined with c) the datum that such councils have unambiguously affirmed the doctrine of divine immutability; would, indeed, imply d) that God can communicate Godself in the Rahnerian sense of those words without compromising God's absolute immutability. In this case, our first criticism of Rahner's *Grundaxiom*, which presupposes the incompatibility of the kind of self-communication Rahner ascribes to God with the doctrine of divine immutability, would prove invalid.

b. Rahner's argument. Rahner's argument that Christ's "absolute saviorhood" requires divine self-communication as Rahner conceives of it takes the following form.

1. "What is revealed and then pondered upon in theology is not an arbitrary matter, but something which is intended for the human person's salvation;"[529] every revealed datum, that is to say possesses "significance for salvation"[530] (*Heilsbedeutsamkeit*).

2. "Only those things can belong to a human being's salvation which, when lacking, injure her being and wholeness."[531]

3. In order to be *heilsbedeutsam*, therefore, a reality must be something for which human beings possess an exigency.

4. The doctrine of Christ's "absolute saviorhood" can be *heilsbedeutsam*, therefore, only to the extent that human beings possess an exigency for an "absolute savior."

5. Human beings can possess an exigency for an "absolute savior," however, only to the extent that he corresponds, in a way no other human being can, to an *a priori*, supernatural desire.

6. Jesus of Nazareth can correspond to such an *a priori*, supernatural desire only insofar as he guarantees, in a way a mere prophet cannot, the fulfillment of human hopes for divine self-communication.

7. Jesus can constitute an irrevocable guarantee of the fulfillment of the human desire for divine self-communication, in a way no merely human prophet can, only if his being is "the reality of God Godself in such a unique way that God would disown *God's very self* if God should supersede it because of its created finiteness."[532]

8. Christ's being can constitute a "reality of God Godself" in this way only if God communicates Godself to Christ's human nature in the Rahnerian sense of the term.

---

[529] "Theology and Anthropology," *TI* ix, 28–45 at 35; "Theologie und Anthropologie," *ST* viii, 43–65 at 51.
[530] Ibid.; ebd. 52.
[531] Ibid.; ebd. 51.
[532] "Jesus Christ—The Meaning of Life," *TI* xxi, 217; "Jesus Christus—Sinn des Lebens," *ST* xv, 214.

9. Christ's absolute saviorhood is evidently revealed and, therefore, *heilsbedeutsam*.

10. God, therefore, must have communicated Godself to Christ in the distinctively Rahnerian sense of those words.

c. Criticisms.

i. Introduction. If one presupposes Rahner's views as to what the "absolute savior" must be in order to qualify as *heilsbedeutsam*, then the hypothesis that God communicates Godself in the radical, Rahnerian sense to Christ's human nature seems inescapable. The idea that a reality can possess *Heilsbedeutsamkeit* only to the extent that human beings possess an exigency precisely for that reality, however, seems incompatible with: 1) a central tenet of Rahner's Christology, viz. that the mysteries of the life of Jesus such as his circumcision, his baptism, his transfiguration, his agony in Gethsemane are significant for contemporary, Christian life and thought; and 2) a fundamental claim of Rahner's theology as a whole, viz. that all elements of categorical experience mediate human beings' supernaturally elevated transcendentality to them.

ii. The mysteries of Jesus' life.

α. The mysteries' significance for Rahner's Christology. Rahner's insistence on the importance of the details of Christ's life, admittedly, might seem to constitute a secondary element in Rahner's Christology in comparison to the theory of the "absolute savior." Insofar as Rahner's concern for these events results from and, to some extent, even motivates his theory of the "uniting unity," however, this concern deserves to be taken seriously.

The connection between Rahner's concern for the mysteries of Christ's life and the unquestionably central theory of the "uniting unity" appears from the following passages, taken from the essay in which Rahner originally proposes the idea of a "uniting unity." In neoscholastic Christology, Rahner asks:

> What do we hear of Christ's Circumcision, Baptism, his prayer, the Transfiguration, the Presentation in the Temple, the Mount of Olives, the abandonment by God on the Cross, the descent into the underworld, the Ascension into heaven and so on? Nothing, or pretty well nothing....Instead of a genuine theology of Christ's life, we find that the theology...of certain abstract privileges enjoyed by Christ has forced itself into the foreground; and that this theology draws attention to certain features...which distinguish him from us.[533]

Rahner clearly, then, considers neoscholastic Christology insufficiently attentive to the mysteries of the life of Jesus. He attributes this inattentiveness, moreover, to neoscholasticism's excessively abstract and formalistic account of the unity of Christ: an account that, in Rahner's view, addresses the issue of the "united unity" in the Incarnation as accomplished, but leaves the question of the "uniting unity" unasked. Rahner writes, accordingly, that neoscholasticism's turn from the concrete events of Christ's life to those privileges that distinguish him from ordinary, human beings:

> is conditioned...by that purely formal understanding of the unity of Christ as united, of which we have spoken above. In a conception like this an event in the field of Christ's humanity only has 'interest' in so far as it is dignified by being adopted by Christ's person, and thus precisely not in itself; or again, in so far as it possesses special features not to be found elsewhere among human beings.[534]

Having thus explained the neglect of the mysteries of Christ's life in neoscholastic theology, Rahner proceeds to commend his theory of the "uniting unity" in the Incarnation precisely on the grounds that its conception of Christ's human nature as the self-exteriorization of the Logos warrants attention to the details of Christ's life. "If we are to have a true theology of the life of Jesus (not merely a theology of the extraordinary in Jesus' life)," Rahner argues:

---

[533] "Current Problems," *TI* i, 190–1; "Probleme," *SW* xii, 293.
[534] Ibid. 191; ebd.

we must learn to see that what is human in Jesus...not [as] something human...and *'in addition'* God's as well..[but as] God's Ek-sistence...: it is human reality *and so* God's and *vice versa*. Then it will no longer be necessary to ask the question: What is there exceptional about this life over and beyond ours as we are already familiar with it..., what is there about it...which could make it important for us too? But the question we must ask is: What does our life mean...when it is first and last the life of God? It is because we need this ultimate interpretation of our lives, one which is not to be had elsewhere, that we must study the theology of Christ's life and death.[535]

The understanding of Christ's human nature that Rahner describes here is, of course, precisely that which the theory of the uniting unity implies. Insofar, then, as: 1) the theory of the uniting unity, an unquestionably central aspect of Rahner's Christology, implies that one ought to regard the mysteries of Jesus' life as *heilsbedeutsam*; and 2) the theory seems to be formulated, to a certain extent at least, precisely in order to foster an appreciation of these mysteries' *Heilsbedeutsamkeit*; it seems reasonable 3) to consider Rahner's insistence on the *Heilsbedeutsamkeit* of the mysteries of Christ's life a central tenet of his Christology.

β. Implications for the concept of absolute savior. In one of the central claims of his Christology, therefore, Rahner grants that relatively minor details of Christ's life are *heilsbedeutsam*. This seems to imply that certain events can possess *Heilsbedeutsamkeit* even though one cannot reasonably claim that human beings possess any exigency precisely for those events. In this case, accordingly, Christ's absolute saviorhood could conceivably be *heilsbedeutsam* even if human beings possessed no exigency for an absolute savior.

This implies, it seems, that one cannot validly argue that God must have communicated Godself, in the Rahnerian sense of those terms, to Christ's human nature simply because, otherwise, Christ would not fulfill an exigency of human beings. For, if the mysteries of Christ's life can be *heilsbedeutsam* without corresponding to some exigency in human beings precisely for them, then it seems that Christ himself could also be *heilsbedeutsam* without fulfilling this

---

[535] Ibid. 191–2; ebd. 294.

condition. Insofar as the mysteries of Christ's life are genuinely *heilsbedeutsam*, then, it seems that the absence of divine self-communication, as Rahner conceives of it, to Jesus' human nature would not pose an insuperable obstacle to his serving as "absolute savior."

iii. The Heilsbedeutsamkeit of all categorical experience. Intra-Christological considerations alone, therefore, suffice to establish that Rahner cannot consistently treat divine self-communication, as he understands it, to Christ's human nature as a precondition *sine qua non* of Christ's *Heilsbedeutsamkeit*. One may establish this conclusion much more directly, however, on the basis of a thesis which, while extrinsic to Christology as such, forms a basic component of Rahner's theology as a whole: Rahner's claim that "supernaturally elevated transcendentality is...mediated to itself by any and every categorical reality in which and through which the subject becomes present to itself."[536] Insofar as Rahner treats the reality posited by this claim as an indispensable presupposition of the possibility of accepting God's offer of divine self-communication in Christ athematically, or "anonymously," one cannot reasonably dismiss the thesis in question as a secondary element in Rahner's thought. An unquestionably central, albeit not specifically Christological, tenet of Rahner's theology, then, dictates that Rahner cannot consistently argue that Jesus could be *heilsbedeutsam* only if he received a divine self-communication according to Rahner's understanding of that term.

iv. Assessment. Rahner's insistence: a) on the *Heilsbedeutsamkeit* of the mysteries of Christ's life; and b) more generally, on the *Heilsbedeutsamkeit* of all aspects of categorical experience; therefore, conflicts with a central premise of Rahner's argument from Christ's absolute saviorhood to the occurrence of divine self-communication as he conceives of it: viz. that something can be

---

[536] *Foundations*, 151; *Grundkurs, SW* xxvi, 149.

heilsbedeutsam only if it is implicitly anticipated in human beings' athematic hope for divine self-communication.

d. Excursus on the views of Bruce Marshall.

i. Introduction. This conclusion, incidentally, resonates significantly with criticisms of Rahner's theory of the absolute savior voiced by Bruce Marshall. According to Rahner, Marshall explains, "any reality, object, or person can be significant for our salvation (*heilsbedeutsam*) only because and in so far as we are oriented to it by our very nature; only by falling within the scope of...[our] transcendental orientation can any reality affect us as a whole and so be genuinely saving."[537] Since Jesus, in Rahner's view, can be the absolute savior only to the extent that he is *heilsbedeutsam*, it seems to Marshall that Jesus Christ "as a particular person...[i.e. as] the bearer of a proper name, who has determinate, describable features and who is located in a unique stretch of space and time"[538] cannot be the absolute savior in Rahner's sense of the term. Rahner's theory of the absolute savior, rather, entails, in Marshall's view, that:

> this status can apply to Jesus only as a positive person or 'vague individual'. That is, on Rahner's procedure, Jesus Christ can be the absolute savior only in abstraction from and without regard for, his proper name, determinate features and unique spatio-temporal location, without, in other words, everything which makes him Jesus and so distinguishes him from any other individual. He is the absolute savior only with respect to the bare form of individuality in him, that is, only in so far as he is an indeterminate, independently existing human subject. For in this respect alone do we anticipate him in our transcendental orientation and so in this respect alone can we, on Rahner's account, rightly consider him significant for salvation.[539]

Marshall concludes, on the basis of these considerations, that Rahner's restrictive criteria for *Heilsbedeutsamkeit* implicitly conflict with Rahner's own

---

[537] *Christology in Conflict: The Identity of a Saviour in Rahner and Barth* (Oxford: Blackwell, 1987), 56.
[538] Ibid. 57–8.
[539] Ibid. 58.

conviction that Jesus Christ, *qua* particular and not merely "positive"[540] person, possesses *Heilsbedeutsamkeit* in a pre-eminent degree. This conclusion seems both correct and identical with that of our own argument from Rahner's assertion of the *Heilsbedeutsamkeit* of the mysteries of Jesus' life.

ii. *Difficulties for Marshall's position.*

α. *Introduction.* Marshall's argument for one of this conclusion's presuppositions, viz. that Rahner actually does consider Jesus, *qua* particular person, *heilsbedeutsam*, however, seems unsound. Specifically, Marshall takes a number of more or less innocuous statements in Rahner's corpus to mean that Rahner holds to the following principle: "an admissible account of 'that which is significant for salvation' cannot fail to include and be governed by reference to Jesus Christ."[541] Now, since: a) Rahner seems explicitly and consciously to repudiate this principle in certain of his writings; and b) the texts on which Marshall relies to establish Rahner's subscription to this principle appear susceptible of other interpretations; it seems that Marshall does not prove that Rahner unambiguously endorses the principle in question.

β. *Textual evidence against Marshall's thesis.* For, first, Rahner explicitly states that in order to demonstrate Jesus' salvific significance, one must first possess a more general, pre-Christological concept of salvific significance. The following remarks, for instance, seem typical of the late Rahner's stance on this subject.

<small>Have we thought out in a reflexive way...how it is that another human being is able to have...an absolute meaning for me as an individual, that is, for another human being at all, in the way that</small>

---

[540] "As a 'positive' reality," writes Marshall, "an individual is simply a single instance of a class or nature, irrespective of the particular 'when', 'where' and description under which that individual actually exists" (ibid. 89). Marshall introduces his distinction between positive and particular individuals in ibid. 44–6.

[541] Ibid. 54

we ascribe to Jesus Christ this absolute meaning he has for us?...How can I encounter someone from the past, Thutmosis or Napoleon or Goethe, and somehow or other discover in their person and work a meaning that challenges me and summons me to decision? These and similar general anthropological, existential-ontological considerations would have to be made and developed by us Christians with much more exactitude, love, thoroughness, and discernment in order to have some kind of a framework of understanding, a horizon that was reflected upon, for the teaching that tells us, "There is something crucial in my relationship to Jesus of Nazareth."[542]

Again, in the opening pages of *Ich glaube an Jesus Christus*, Rahner insists that a credible defense of Christian faith in the person of Jesus must present an answer to "the old question...of whether and how...a contingent thing, encountering one 'accidentally' from without, indeed a reality situated in a vastly remote point in history, can have...an ultimate significance for the existence of a human being at all."[543] Textual evidence exists, therefore, for the view that Rahner regards a (logically) pre-Christological understanding of *Heilsbedeutsamkeit* in general a prerequisite to the task of making Christ's particular, salvific significance intelligible. *Pace* Marshall, accordingly, it seems less than obvious that "Rahner certainly takes...for granted" the principle: "an admissible account of 'that which is significant for salvation' cannot fail to include and be governed by reference to Jesus Christ"[544]

γ. *Evidence for Marshall's thesis?* Second, and more importantly, the texts Marshall proffers as evidence of Rahner's allegiance to this principle do not seem to prove Marshall's point. The texts in question are three:

a. "Catholic faith and its dogmatics as they have been understood up to now, and also as they will have to be understood in the future, remain indissolubly bound up (*unablösbar gebunden*) not only with the historical existence of Jesus of

---

[542] "Brief Observations on Systematic Christology Today," *TI* xxi, 228–38 at 236; "Kleine Anmerkungen zur systematischen Christologie heute," *ST* xv, 225–35 at 233.
[543] *Ich glaube*, 13.
[544] Marshall, *Christology*, 54.

Nazareth, but also with the historical events of a specific kind which took place during his life;"[545]

b. "Where 'Jesus is nothing more than one of the relatively numerous exemplary persons (*vorbildlichen Menschen*), one would no longer be dealing with Christianity;"[546] and

c. "When the longing for the absolute nearness of God...looks for where this nearness came—not in the postulates of the spirit, but in the flesh and in the housings of the earth: then no resting place can be found except in Jesus of Nazareth, over whom the star of God stands."[547]

In the first sentence, Rahner asserts, in other words, that the multi-dimensional wholes, "Catholic faith" and "its dogmatics," are "indissolubly bound up" with the events of Jesus' life. Now, it seems that one could reasonably assert that the tenets of Catholic faith and dogmatics *in globo* are indissolubly bound up with the particularities of Christ's life without thereby implying that every, particular tenet of "Catholic faith" and "its dogmatics" includes and is governed by reference to Jesus Christ. To the extent that this is the case, Marshall's first text seems not to constitute an unambiguous endorsement of the dictum: "an admissible account of 'that which is significant for salvation' cannot fail to include and be governed by reference to Jesus Christ."[548] In the second text, likewise, Rahner seems to indicate only that belief in the absolute saviorhood of Jesus Christ constitutes an indispensable element of explicit Christianity: not that every element of official

---

[545] "Remarks on the Importance of the History of Jesus for Catholic Dogmatics," *TI* xiii, 201–12 at 201; "Bemerkungen zur Bedeutung der Geschichte Jesu für die katholische Dogmatik," *ST* x, 215–26 at 215 as quoted in Marshall, *Christology*, 54.

[546] *Karl Rahner im Gespräch* 1 (Paul Imhof and Hubert Biallowons, ed.; Munich: Kösel, 1982), 163 as translated by Marshall and quoted in his *Christology*, 54.

[547] "Incarnation," *TI* iv, 120; "Menschwerdung," *SW* xii, 322 quoted in Marshall, *Christology*, 74, n. 108.

[548] Marshall, *Christology*, 54.

Christianity conforms to the just-quoted principle. The third text, finally, seems to indicate only that Rahner considers Jesus alone the absolute savior. Neither in itself nor in its context does this sentence seem to address the larger question of how theoretical accounts of *Heilsbedeutsamkeit* ought to relate to Jesus Christ *qua* particular person. Marshall seems, therefore, not to supply adequate, textual warrant for his claim that Rahner subscribes to the principle: "an admissible account of 'that which is significant for salvation' cannot fail to include and be governed by reference to Jesus Christ."[549]

δ. *Evaluation*. Since Rahner's explicit statements suggest that he considers reference to Christ in his historical particularity dispensable to accounts of *Heilsbedeutsamkeit*, and Marshall does not succeed in proving the contrary, it seems, in fact, that Rahner at least implicitly denies the principle in question.

iii. Conclusion. His brilliant critique of Rahner's restrictive criteria for *Heilsbedeutsamkeit* and absolute saviorhood notwithstanding, then, Marshall appears to misunderstand the kind of problem these criteria pose for Rahner's theology. Marshall errs, that is to say, when he claims that "by attempting to establish the credibility and meaningfulness of a saving reality...by an appeal to general criteria for such a reality, without reference to Jesus Christ, Rahner makes it impossible actually to maintain his assumption that whatever is *heilsbedeutsam* must be ascribed only to Jesus Christ as a particular person."[550] Rahner makes no such assumption. The view that Jesus Christ can possess *Heilsbedeutsamkeit* only to the extent that humanity's athematic hope for divine self-communication anticipates him, rather, appears problematic: a) for Rahner's Christology, because it conflicts with his insistence on the significance of the mysteries of Jesus' life; and b) for Rahner's theology as a whole, because Rahner's understanding of

---

[549] Ibid.
[550] Ibid. 88–9.

revelation as transcendental commits him to the view that every facet of human experience is *heilsbedeutsam*.

e. Summary. In any event, prescinding from Marshall's argument, it seems certain that Rahner: a) considers the mysteries of Christ's life *heilsbedeutsam*; and b) that he, in fact, considers all aspects of the world as experienced by human beings *heilsbedeutsam*. Insofar as Rahner's argument from Christ's absolute saviorhood to the occurrence of divine self-communication as he understands it depends upon an account of *Heilsbedeutsamkeit* that precludes the salvific significance of the realities mentioned in a) and many of those mentioned in b) accordingly, Rahner's argument seems unsound by the standards of his own theology.

5. Results. It seems, accordingly, that the argument: a) that Rahner acknowledges the infallibility of ecumenical councils when and to the extent that they teach definitively and in union with the Pope; b) that such councils have definitively and with solemn, Papal approbation taught the doctrines of sanctifying grace, the Incarnation, and divine immutability; c) that these councils' infallibility implies the consistency of their pronouncements; d) that Rahner proves divine self-communication, in his distinctive sense of that term, indispensable to the mysteries of sanctifying grace, the Incarnation, and Christ's absolute saviorhood; e) that Rahner's views on divine self-communication cannot, therefore, conflict with the doctrine of divine immutability; and f) that any counterargument to his *Grundaxiom* that presupposes, as our first criticism does, that divine self-communication in the Rahnerian sense and divine immutability are incompatible must, consequently, be invalid; fails to nullify our first criticism, even in the context of a strictly immanent critique, because of the falsehood of premise d.

V. CONCLUSION

We have devoted this chapter to rehearsing and rebutting possible defenses of Rahner's *Grundaxiom* against the following counterargument, which we have referred to as our "first criticism." If God is simple, then every aspect of God's being is absolutely, albeit not necessarily relatively, identical with every other aspect. A self-communication on the part of a simple God, which altered that God's being, consequently, would transform every aspect of that God, not excluding the Trinitarian relations, and thus guarantee that the Trinitarian relations as communicated would not correspond to the Trinitarian relations as eternal. Rahner's idea of self-communication, presupposing, as it does, becoming in a simple God, thus seems implicitly to contradict his famous axiom: "The economic Trinity *is* the immanent Trinity and vice versa."

After briefly verifying that Rahner does endorse divine simplicity, immutability, etc. and does insist that becoming penetrates God's very being, we turned to Bert van der Heijden's interpretation of Rahner's doctrine of God according to which the inner logic of Rahner's views concerning divine self-communication, on the whole if not in every detail, cohere rather well with the doctrine of divine immutability. In our review of Van der Heijden's arguments, nonetheless, we discovered that he finds in Rahner a more systematic thinker than we or most of his interpreters have found him to be. Van der Heijden, that is to say, tends to resolve the paradoxical and seemingly inconsistent aspects of Rahner's thought into a single, stringently consistent viewpoint: a viewpoint that frequently serves as a foil for Van der Heijden's articulation of his own theological system. We found his interpretation of Rahner, accordingly, unreliable on the whole and of little use in vindicating Rahner from our first criticism.

Next, we turned to a complex argument, summarized in the previous section, from Rahner's belief in the infallibility of ecumenical councils when teaching definitively with the approbation of the Pope to the consistency of their definitive pronouncements and, therefore, to the consistency of Rahner's theory of divine self-communication with divine immutability if and to the extent that Rahner could establish the integrality of his theory of divine self-communication to some doctrine definitively authorized by an ecumenical council and ratified by the Pope. We found, moreover, that Rahner attempts to prove his ideas about divine self-communication integral to three such doctrines: viz. the doctrines of sanctifying grace, the Incarnation of the Logos, and the absolute saviorhood of Christ. After reviewing and discussing Rahner's arguments at length, however, we found them inadequate to their purpose and concluded, accordingly, that the argument concerning conciliar authority does not invalidate our first criticism of Rahner's *Grundaxiom*.

In tandem with our second criticism, viz. that, even if an unmistakably Trinitarian structure manifested itself in the experience of divine self-communication, one could not, solely on the basis of one's experience, distinguish the novel from the permanent aspects of this structure if God changes when he communicates Godself, then, it seems our first criticism weakens the credibility of Rahner's *Grundaxiom* considerably. It seems presumptuous, however, to declare Rahner's *Grundaxiom* and related theses positively disproved.

We think it advisable, therefore, to augment our two criticisms of the *Grundaxiom* and our brief animadversions on Rahner's Trinitarian interpretation of transcendental experience with additional counterarguments. In the following chapter, accordingly, we intend to argue: a) that Rahner's own canons of Trinitarian orthodoxy preclude the possibility of God's revealing the doctrine of the Trinity in the manner that Rahner proposes; and b) that the New Testament accounts of Christ's anointing with the Holy Spirit, if interpreted in accordance with the *Grundaxiom*, entail conclusions incompatible with Rahner's own understanding of Trinitarian theology.

CHAPTER 4

I. INTRODUCTION

We devoted the second and the third chapters of this work to developing and sustaining in the face of counterarguments two basic criticisms of Rahner's *Grundaxiom*. First, we argued, Rahner guarantees at least some asymmetry between οἰκονομία and θεολογία by postulating the indispensability of divine becoming to any genuine divine self-communication. For if God is simple, as Rahner correctly assumes, then God cannot change any aspect of the divine being without simultaneously transforming every aspect of this being: the Trinitarian relations not excluded. If the divine persons, in order to become the economic Trinity, had to undergo such a metamorphosis, it seems, they would, perforce, differ, even in their mutual relations, from the immanent Trinity: i.e. the divine persons as they would have existed in the absence of a divine self-communication. Second, we observed, even if a mutable God could prevent the intra-Trinitarian relations from mutating in the act of self-communication, one who experienced this communication could not know, without simply being told through a verbal or at least conceptual revelation, that God had preserved God's prior[551] relational structure intact.

Having defended the first, and more cogent, criticism from possible counterarguments in the previous chapter, we hope in this chapter to proffer two further criticisms of Rahner's views on the revelation of the Trinity before resting our case against Rahner's axiom. In this chapter, specifically, we hope: a) to show that Rahner conceives of the divine persons in such a way that they cannot manifest their existence *qua* distinct to *viatores* without resorting to verbal, or at least conceptual, forms of communication; and b) that the biblical accounts of Christ's anointing with the Holy Spirit, when interpreted in accordance with the

---

[551] We employ this term in a logical and ontological, but not a temporal, sense.

Grundaxiom as Rahner understands it, entail conclusions incompatible with Rahner's Latin Trinitarianism. One can harmonize the τάξις among the persons displayed in this event with a Western understanding of the intra-Trinitarian relations, we shall argue, only if one modifies one's understanding of what qualifies as correspondence between economy and theology to such an extent as to render the *Grundaxiom* powerless to perform its principal function: viz. warranting inferences from the economy of salvation to the doctrine of the immanent Trinity.

II. THE IMPOSSIBILITY OF A NON-VERBAL, NON-CONCEPTUAL REVELATION OF THE DOCTRINE OF THE TRINITY OTHER THAN THE BEATIFIC VISION.

1. Introduction. The following four syllogisms seem to comprise a valid[552] argument for the view that God could not inform human beings of the purely notional distinctions internal to the divine being without resorting to some verbal, or at least conceptual, revelation.

1. Every entity that possesses reality only through its identity with something else possesses no capacity for action insofar as it is distinct from this something else.
2. The divine persons are entities that possess reality only through their identity with the divine substance.
3. The divine persons possess no capacity for action insofar as they are distinct from the divine substance.

---

[552] Not every valid argument, incidentally, yields a true conclusion. As Colin Allen and Michael Hand explain, "An argument is VALID if and only if it is necessary that *if* all its premises are true, its conclusions are true" (*Logic Primer* [Cambridge, Mass. and London: MIT Press, 2001²], 1). "An argument is SOUND," by contrast, "if and only if it is valid and all its premises are true....It follows that all sound arguments have true conclusions" (ibid. 2).

1. Every entity that possesses no capacity for action insofar as it is distinct from a particular substance can impact nothing insofar as it is distinct from this substance.
2. The divine persons are entities that possess no capacity for action insofar as they are distinct from the divine substance.
3. The divine persons can impact nothing insofar as they are distinct from the divine substance.

1. Every entity that can impact nothing cannot be known to exist from non-verbal and non-conceptual aspects of that which is other than itself.
2. The divine persons are entities that can impact nothing insofar as they are distinct from the divine substance.
3. The divine persons insofar as they are distinct from the divine substance cannot be known to exist from non-verbal and non-conceptual aspects of that which is other than they.

1. Every entity that cannot be known to exist from non-verbal and non-conceptual aspects of that which is other than itself, can be known to exist by other entities, if other entities can know that it exists at all, only through verbal, or at least conceptual, forms of communication or through direct intuition.
2. The divine persons insofar as they are distinct from the divine substance are entities that cannot be known to exist from non-verbal and non-conceptual aspects of that which is other than they.
3. The divine persons insofar as they are distinct from the divine substance can be known to exist by other entities, if other entities can know that they exist at all, only through verbal, or at least conceptual, forms of communication or through direct intuition.

The validity of the preceding, four syllogisms, each in *Darii*, seems indisputable. The major premises of the first, second, and third seem self-evident, moreover, and the minor premises of the second, third, and fourth consist in the conclusions of prior valid arguments. One who wished to prove the reasoning summarized in the four syllogisms above unsound, therefore, would likely focus any attacks on the minor premise of syllogism 1 and the major premise of syllogism 4. In the following, accordingly, we shall attempt to respond to objections that Rahner either does, or could, oppose to these two premises.

2. Rahner's case against the minor premise of syllogism 1.

a. What does Rahner actually believe? One might think that Rahner would strenuously oppose the minor premise of syllogism 1, perhaps the most consequential premise of the entire argument. Rahner appears, however, explicitly to endorse it. After alluding to a related question, Rahner writes, "Catholic theologians do not agree on this point, but all agree that in God the relation is real only through its identity with the real divine essence."[553] One could justifiably conclude, therefore, that Rahner cannot consistently dispute this precise point in our argument.

A defender of the *Grundaxiom*, however, might wish to argue that, at this juncture, Rahner implicitly deviates from one of his most strongly held beliefs, viz. that God does not possess an absolute subsistence; and that a consistent account of Rahner's overall position, therefore, would not include an endorsement of the first syllogism's minor premise. If the relations derive their reality, and, therefore, their subsistence, solely from the divine essence, such a person might argue, then the divine essence of itself must possess a subsistence, which the subsistence of each divine person presupposes and which, therefore, is not identical *simpliciter* with any of the divine persons: in other words, an absolute

---

[553] *Trinity*, 71; "Der dreifaltige Gott," *MS* ii, 363.

subsistence. Yet the absence of such a subsistence constitutes an indispensable presupposition of Rahner's belief that "in the New Testament ὁ θεός always *signifies* the First Person of the Trinity and does not merely stand for him often."[554]

A brief account of Rahner's argument for the identity of the Biblical ὁ θεός with God precisely as Father will show why Rahner's thesis stands or falls with his denial of the doctrine of an absolute subsistence. At the outset of Rahner's explicit inquiry into the question of "whether ὁ θεός not only *stands for* the Father, but also *signifies him*"[555] in New Testament usage, he remarks, "it might seem that this question has already been decided in the negative"[556] for two reasons. The first, the only one that concerns us here, he summarizes as follows:

It might be said that even in the New Testament ὁ θεός is used as a name for the object of natural knowledge of God; and this God is not the Father but the one God who is cause of the world in virtue of the numerical unity of God's nature: this attribute, then, belongs equally to all three divine Persons, since all three possess the one nature.[557]

"But," Rahner responds:

just this assertion—that what we know from the world is the Triune God in the unity of God's nature, and not the Father—is open to question. It is obvious that the Father is not known *as* Father in natural theology, i.e. not *as* He who communicates his nature to the Son by an eternal generation....But we can still say that he who is in actual fact known from the world, is concretely the Father....For natural theology itself ascends not just to a divinity but to a God: it knows, that is, that this divine nature necessarily subsists....Unless we wish to follow Cajetan and Suarez, among others, in positing a *subsistentia absoluta* [then]..., only one course is open to us: to maintain that the concrete Absolute (*hic Deus*) known by natural theology is precisely the Father.[558]

Rahner's argument that the biblical usage of ὁ θεός as a name of the naturally knowable Creator does not necessarily falsify his claim that ὁ θεός refers always to the Father, then, amounts to the following instance of *modus tollendo ponens*.

---

[554] "Theos in the New Testament," *TI* i, 126; "Theos im Neuen Testament," *SW* iv, 386.
[555] Ibid. 130; ebd. 388.
[556] Ibid.; ebd.
[557] Ibid. 132; ebd. 390.
[558] Ibid. 132–3; ebd. 390–1.

1. Natural theology knows a God who subsists as unoriginate: either the Father who subsists relatively or the divine essence, which subsists absolutely.

2. The divine essence, however, possesses no absolute subsistence.

3. Natural theology, therefore, knows the God who subsists relatively as unoriginate, i.e. the Father.

If deprived of its second premise, this argument manifestly loses all validity. Now, Rahner's identification of ὁ θεός with the Father greatly bolsters the biblical basis for his claim that human beings can have distinct, non-appropriated relations to each of the divine persons, and this claim, in turn, constitutes an indispensable presupposition of Rahner's *Grundaxiom*. One can, therefore, reasonably claim that Rahner's virtual endorsement of the minor premise of syllogism 1, insofar as it implies that God possesses an absolute subsistence and thus undermines Rahner's case for the identity of ὁ θεός with the Father, deviates from the main stream of Rahner's thought.

b. Difficulties for Rahner's position. One who wished to dispute the thesis, "in God the relation is real only through its identity with the real divine essence,"[559] however, would face a daunting task for at least two reasons. First, the statement's most controversial implication, viz. that God possesses an absolute subsistence, appears to face no formidable difficulties. To the charge that an absolute subsistence in God would constitute a fourth, divine person, for instance, one can respond that no opposition of relation would distinguish such a subsistence from any of the three, divine persons, and "in God, all things are one, where no opposition of relation intervenes."[560] To the complaint that the divine essence lacks the note of incommunicability and, therefore, lacks the proper *ratio* of subsistence, one can respond with David Coffey that the divine essence does

---

[559] *Trinity*, 71; "Der dreifaltige Gott," *MS* ii, 363.
[560] DH 1330.

possess the note of incommunicability in "that this essence cannot be communicated outside itself, that there cannot be more than one God."[561]

Coffey's response to this criticism, incidentally, strikes us as superior to the traditional strategy of distinguishing between: 1) an incomplete subsistence that consists solely in individuality, independence and the capacity for action, which one attributes to the divine essence; and 2) a complete subsistence that comprises these perfections as well as incommunicability to multiple *supposita*, which one ascribes to the divine persons.[562] For, first, Coffey's solution in no way implicitly degrades the divine essence by hinting that the persons possess some perfection, viz., complete subsistence, which the divine essence lacks. Such a division of perfections between persons and essence, if made explicit, would reduce both the persons and the essence to imperfect parts of a greater whole which itself would lack the divine perfection of simplicity.

Coffey's response strikes us as the superior one, second, because it does not furtively suggest that the divine nature would grow in perfection, that it would attain "complete" subsistence, if only the three, eternal persons did not share this nature among themselves. The selfless sharing of the divine essence among the divine persons, after all, constitutes one of the most glorious and admirable aspects of the intra-divine life. In the words of Reginald Garrigou-Lagrange:

The intimate life of God...is the supreme type of the life of charity. It consists of three totally spiritual persons who live by the same truth, by one and the same act of the mind; three persons who live by the same good, by one and the same act of love. Where do we find here the least trace of egotism? The ego is no more than a subsistent relation in respect of the one loved; He appropriates nothing more to Himself. The Father gives the whole of His nature to His Son, and the Father and the Son communicate the same to the Holy Spirit....Apart from the mutual relations of opposition between the persons, everything else is common and indivisible between them.[563]

---

[561] *Deus Trinitas: The Doctrine of the Triune God* [*Deus Trinitas*] (Oxford: OUP, 1999), 71.
[562] Cf. Billuart, *Cursus Theologiae* 2, 101b.
[563] *God: His Existence and His Nature: Vol. II* (Bede Rose, tr.; St. Louis and London: Herder, 1946), 182–3.

Coffey's perspective on the nature of subsistence, then, enables one to see that the self-sharing of the divine essence does not abrogate its absolute subsistence; it rather adorns it with the perfection of generosity.

Indeed, Coffey's perspective also allows one to recognize the perfection of personality in the divine essence as such. In Coffey's words, "as with subsistence..., so with person: in God there are one absolute person and three relative persons."[564] To the objection, moreover, that the divine essence lacks the capacity for action, another prerogative of subsistents, on the grounds that it is an abstract *id quo*, and *actiones sunt suppositorum*, one can answer with Aquinas:

> Because *in divinis* the same thing is that by which and that which is, if any one of those things which are attributed to God in the abstract is considered in itself, other things being set aside, it will be something subsisting and, consequently, a person, since it is in an intellectual nature. As, therefore, personal properties having been posited in God, we now say three persons; thus, personal properties having been excluded by thought, the divine nature will remain in our consideration as subsisting and as a person [*STh* III, 3, 3 ad 1].

The divine simplicity will not allow one, therefore, to deprive the divine essence of a signal perfection like subsistence as long as one does not insist on incommunicability to distinct *supposita* as a *sine qua non* of subsistence. Even opponents of the idea of an absolute subsistence, therefore, ordinarily admit its material correctness and dispute it on purely terminological grounds. Hence Christian Pesch, for instance, a prominent opponent of the doctrine of absolute subsistence whose *Praelectiones Dogmaticae* Rahner studied as a seminarian,[565] admits that "this doctrine *quoad rem* is entirely true"[566] and objects merely to "a twofold inconvenience *quoad loquendi modum*."[567]

---

[564] *Deus Trinitas*, 72.

[565] In one of his later essays, Rahner reflects on the intellectual climate that prevailed "when I began my theological studies forty years ago" and refers to "Christian Pesch, whose manual of theology I followed" ("The Foundation of Belief Today," *TI* xvi, 6, 7; "Glaubensbegründung heute," *ST* xii, 21). He identifies this manual in a footnote as the *Praelectiones Dogmaticae* (ibid. 7, n. 10; ebd. 21, Anm. 10).

[566] *Praelectiones Dogmaticae: Tomus II: De Deo Uno Secundum Naturam: De Deo Trino Secundum Personas* (Fribourg: Herder, 1906³), §610, p. 325.

[567] Ibid.

Rahner, however, specifically professes to "disregard questions of terminology"[568] in his polemic against the doctrine of absolute subsistence in "Theos in the New Testament." He seems, therefore, to criticize the view that God possesses a *subsistentia absoluta* as not merely terminologically inapt, but substantially false. By assuming this radical stance, Rahner, of course, lends weight to arguments that the statement, "in God the relation is real only through its identity with the real divine essence,"[569] diverges from the general thrust of Rahner's thought. Rahner also, however, places himself in the inconvenient position of having to reconcile the absence of an absolute subsistence in God with God's absolute infinity and unity.

As the Rahner of *Mysterium Salutis* recognizes:

Father, Son, and Spirit are only 'relatively' distinct; that is, in their distinction they should not be conceived as constituted by something which would mean a distinction previous to their mutual relations and serving as their foundation. For such a distinction, previous to the relations as such, would add something to the one divinity and thus do away with its absolute infinity and unity.[570]

In other words, the absolute infinity of the divine essence dictates that no entity in any way distinct from it can add to its already infinite being. It "follows...from the infinity of God," writes Heinrich Hurter, "that God is incapable of increment."[571] The absolute unity of the divine essence, likewise, excludes the possibility of composition in God between a non-subsistent, divine substrate and a divine *suppositum* that bestows subsistence upon it: i.e. between divinity and God. As the Council of Rheims decreed against Gilbert de la Porrée: "We believe and confess that God is the simple nature of divinity, and that it cannot be denied in any Catholic sense that God is divinity, and divinity is God.

---

[568] "Theos in the New Testament," *TI* i, 133; "Theos im Neuen Testament," *SW* iv, 391.
[569] *Trinity*, 71; "Der dreifaltige Gott," *MS* ii, 363.
[570] Ibid. 68–9; ebd. 361.
[571] *Theologia Specialis: Pars Prior: De Deo Uno et Trino, De Deo Creatore, et De Verbo Incarnato* (Innsbruck: Libraria Academica Wagneriana, 1885⁵), §41, p. 27.

Moreover, if it is said that God is...God by divinity,...we believe...that God is God only by that divinity which God is Godself."[572]

In "Theos in the New Testament," however, Rahner seems to suggest that the divine essence, considered in abstraction from the divine persons, lacks the perfection of subsistence, and that the divine essence and persons, therefore, relate to each other as really distinct *quo* and *quod*. When Rahner, for instance, states that "natural theology...ascends not just to a divinity but to a God"[573] and takes this as evidence that natural theology knows not only the divine essence but also the person of the Father, his words seem unintelligible on any other premise.

One could, of course, surmise that Rahner identifies the God of natural theology precisely with the Father, because only the Father subsists as absolutely unoriginate. Rahner's statements concerning "the necessity of an ἀρχή which is purely ἄναρχος,"[574] and "an Unoriginate not just as set over against an origination by creation, but as opposed to *every* conceivable real and hypothetical origination,"[575] moreover, lend credit to such an interpretation. Such an argument would seem to presuppose, however, that the divine essence in some way originates from the person of the Father; a conception expressly condemned by the IV Lateran Council in the words, "[the] divine nature...is neither generating, nor generated, nor proceeding."[576] Unless Rahner wishes to defy the authority of a general council, then, he must mean that natural theology traces all things back to the Father not because he alone is unoriginate, but because he alone subsists *a se* as unoriginate. Rahner seems to claim, then, that the divine essence lacks subsistence of itself and derives it from the Father as an *id quo* from an *id quod*.

---

[572] PL 185, 617B–18A.
[573] "Theos in the New Testament," *TI* i, 133; "Theos im Neuen Testament," *SW* iv, 390–1.
[574] Ibid.; ebd. 391.
[575] Ibid.; ebd.
[576] DH 804.

c. Rahner's response.

i. Mystici Corporis. To the charge that he thereby contradicts the principle that God's infinite essence can receive no increment, Rahner seems to present no particular reply. To the charge that his teaching in this particular and others undermines the doctrine of divine simplicity, however, Rahner presents, in a different context, a sweeping answer. He takes his point of departure from a single line of Pius XII's encyclical, *Mystici Corporis*. In the section of this document that concerns the indwelling of the Holy Spirit, Pius XII, affirms that "the conflict of various opinions and the clash of ideas"[577] in this area of theology can serve the cause of truth and declares, "we do not censure those who enter upon diverse ways and methods of reasoning to understand...and to clarify the mystery."[578] He, then, however, utters a stern warning to those engaged in controversy over the divine indwelling:

Let this be a general and unshaken truth, if they do not wish to wander from sound doctrine and the correct teaching of the Church: namely, that every kind of mystic union, by which the faithful in Christ in any way pass beyond the order of created things and wrongly enter among the divine, so that even a single attribute of the eternal Godhead can be predicated of these as their own, is to be entirely rejected. And, besides, let them hold this with a firm mind as most certain, that all activities in these matters are to be held as common to the Most Holy Trinity, *quatenus* they pertain to the same God as the supreme efficient cause.[579]

We have intentionally left the word "*quatenus*" untranslated, because, as Heribert Mühlen observes,[580] it can bear both an explicative and a restrictive sense. If one interpreted *quatenus* here in its explicative sense, Mühlen

---

[577] DB[27] 2290. Hünermann follows the post-Vatican II editions of Denzinger in omitting these words, along with those in the quote that follows, from DH.
[578] Ibid.
[579] Ibid.; DH 3814. Hünermann includes this text in DH with the exception of its first word, *Verumtamen*.
[580] "Person und Appropriation: Zum Verständnis des Axioms: In Deo omnia sunt unum, ubi non obviat relationis oppositio," *MThZ* 16 (1965), 37–57 at 38. Cf. Mühlen's *Der Heilige Geist als Person: In der Trinität, bei der Inkarnation, und im Gnadenbund: Ich—Du—Wir* (MBTh 26; Münster: Aschendorff, 1988[5]), §8.04, p. 243.

explains,[581] one would translate it with the word, "because," and understand Pius to identify the bestowal of grace with an act common to the three, divine persons, because God bestows grace through efficient causality alone. If one interpreted *"quatenus"* in its restrictive sense, however, one would translate it "to the extent that" and understand Pius' statement as allowing for personally distinguished causality in grace to the extent that this involves something other than efficient causality.

Each interpretation has its merits. In defense of the first, one could note that, if Pius sincerely intended to allow for personally distinguished causality where efficient causality does not come into play, *"in tantum,"* or simply *"tantum"* would express his meaning much more clearly than *"quatenus."* A partisan of the second interpretation, however, could rejoin that, if Pius desired to condemn the idea of personally distinguished causality in grace, *"quia"* or *"quoniam,"* and not *"quatenus,"* would seem the appropriate choice.

Likewise, a defender of the first interpretation could plausibly claim that it coheres better than the second with Pius' warning against encroachments upon divine transcendence. If Pius intends *"quatenus"* in its explicative sense, he means to say that God influences human beings always through efficient causality and never through formal causality of any sort. This idea of divine causality, in keeping with Pius' desire to uphold divine transcendence, erects a high barrier against excessively intimate understandings of God's union with the justified in grace. If Pius intends *"quatenus"* in its restrictive sense, however, one could argue that he counteracts his own admonition by allowing that God could exercise formal causality on human beings in bestowing grace.

A partisan of the second interpretation could respond, nonetheless, that if Pius does intend *"quatenus"* in its explicative and not its restrictive sense, then he effectively nullifies his earlier expressions of tolerance for differing opinions on the subject of the indwelling of the Holy Spirit. The debates that raged at the time

---

[581] Ibid.

of the encyclical's composition, such a person might argue, focused precisely on whether the divine persons always influence human beings through a strictly undivided, efficient causality or whether they might also exert some more intimate, personally distinguished causality in the order of grace. Pius XII's explicit refusal to end controversy over these subjects thus makes it difficult to understand why he would condemn the very hypotheses that gave rise to the then current debates.

The evidence for the two perspectives on the meaning of *quatenus*, therefore, seems evenly balanced. Regardless of what Pius actually means, however, Rahner adheres unreservedly to the second perspective. In fact, he seems to regard Pius' statement as adequate warrant for qualifying radically the axiom, "the works of the Trinity are inseparable."[582] For, invoking no more than a single Denzinger reference to the relevant text of *Mystici Corporis*, Rahner writes in *Mysterium Salutis*, "The axiom is absolutely valid only where the 'supreme efficient cause' is concerned (DS 3814). Not-appropriated relations of a single person are possible when we have to do, not with an efficient causality, but with a quasi-formal self-communication of God."[583]

Even if Rahner correctly interpreted *Mystici Corporis* and justifiably qualified the axiom, in any event, his position would fall afoul of the axiom's restricted version, nonetheless. For Rahner characterizes efficient causality itself as a moment in and deficient mode of formal causality. When he declares personally distinguished action conceivable in the exercise of formal causality, therefore, he implicitly pronounces such action conceivable even in efficient causation. His interpretation of Pius' words, therefore, hardly suffices to reconcile Rahner's denial that God possesses an absolute subsistence with the doctrine of divine simplicity. As we noted earlier, Rahner does not defend himself against the charge that his views on this subject conflict with the doctrine of divine infinity. Two doctrines, then, those of divine simplicity and divine

---

[582] DH 491, 535.
[583] *Trinity*, 77; "Der dreifaltige Gott," *MS* ii, 367.

infinity, appear to falsify the thesis that the divine essence lacks subsistence of itself and derives its subsistence entirely from the divine persons.

Yet this thesis constitutes the sole argument in Rahner's corpus, so far as we are aware, that directly contradicts our first syllogism's minor premise: "the divine persons possess reality only through their identity with the divine substance." It seems, then, that Rahner presents no sound argument against the first syllogism's minor premise itself.

ii. Three alleged counterexamples.

α. Introduction. He does, however, offer three alleged counterexamples to the principle of the absolute inseparability of the divine acts *ad extra*, a central implication of the premise in question. If he established that exceptions really do exist to the principle that *"inseparabilia sunt opera Trinitatis,"*[584] it seems that Rahner would possess at least the beginnings of a sound argument against the minor premise of our first syllogism. If Rahner mounted such a case, then, it seems that it would take the form of the following two arguments, the first in *modus ponens* and the second in *modus tollens*:

1. If individual persons of the Trinity exert distinct influences in the world, then they must possess some capacity for action insofar as they are distinct from the divine substance;
2. Individual persons of the Trinity do exert distinct influences in the world; therefore
3. Individual persons of the Trinity possess some capacity for action insofar as they are distinct from the divine substance.

---

[584] DH 491, 535.

1. If the divine persons possess reality only through their identity with the divine substance, then they possess no capacity for action insofar as they are distinct from the divine substance; yet

2. The divine persons do possess some capacity for action insofar as they are distinct from the divine substance; therefore

3. The divine persons do not possess reality only through their identity with the divine substance.

Neither of these syllogisms is invalid; the first premise of each seems self-evident; and the second premise of the second syllogism is identical to the conclusion of the first. One can cast reasonable doubt on Rahner's conclusion, therefore, only by challenging the second premise of his first syllogism: i.e. the claim that "individual persons of the Trinity do exert distinct influences in the world." As evidence for this claim, Rahner offers three alleged examples of a Trinitarian person's exercising such an influence: viz., the Incarnation, the indwelling of the Holy Spirit in the souls of the justified, and the beatific vision. We intend in the following, accordingly, to show that in none of these cases can one conclude with certainty that the exercise of such a distinct influence actually occurs.

β. The Incarnation. Of his first example, the Incarnation, Rahner writes:

> Jesus is not simply God in general, but the Son. The second divine person, God's Logos, is man, and only he is man. Hence there is at least *one* "mission," *one* presence in the world, *one* reality of salvation history which is not merely appropriated to some divine person, but which is proper to him....This *one* case shows up as *false* the statement that there is nothing in salvation history, in the economy of salvation, which cannot equally be said of the triune God as a whole and of each person in particular. On the other hand, the following statement too is *false*: that a doctrine of the Trinity...can speak only of that which occurs within the Trinity itself.[585]

In one sense, all of this is true; Scripture unquestionably requires one to hold that the Son alone, and neither the Father nor the Spirit, was born of the virgin

---

[585] *Trinity*, 23; "Der dreifaltige Gott," *MS* ii, 329.

Mary, suffered under Pontius Pilate, etc. It seems, however, that one can reconcile at least to a certain extent the doctrine that the Logos alone constitutes the ontological subject who acts in Christ's human nature with the doctrine of the absolute inseparability of the divine acts *ad extra*.

The possibility of such a reconciliation appears from the following argument, which we derive principally from Aquinas. One may legitimately distinguish, Thomas reasons, between a human person and an individual, human nature. In his words, "not every individual in the genus of substance, even in a rational nature, has the *rationem personae*, but only that which exists *per se*: not, however, that which exists in another, more perfect thing. Hence a hand of Socrates, however much it is a kind of individual, yet is not a person, because it does not exist *per se*, but in a certain more perfect thing, sc. in its whole"(*STh* III, 2, 2 ad 3). Because Scripture ascribes works performed through both of Christ's natures to the hypostasis of the Logos, moreover, one can reasonably assume that this hypostasis constitutes, in a certain sense at least, that "more perfect thing" in which Christ's human nature exists.[586] Expressions like "they...crucified the Lord of glory" (1 Cor 2:8) and "you killed the Author of life" (Acts 3:15) seem scarcely intelligible on any other premise.

The idea that Christ's humanity "exists in," and is therefore incomplete without, the hypostasis of the Logos, however, generates something of an antinomy. For the datum of the incompleteness of Christ's human nature without the Logos seems to imply that this nature, of itself, lacks at least one natural characteristic of humanity, viz. that of existing in oneself and not in some greater being. One cannot reasonably claim, however, that the "man Christ Jesus" (1 Tim

---

[586] The relation of Christ's human nature to the hypostasis of the Logos differs from the relation of a hand to a human being, of course, in that: a) the hand constitutes a part of a larger individual nature, whereas Christ's human nature is an individual nature in its own right; and b) the hand, as long as it is attached to a larger human body, never attains the perfection of subsistence, properly speaking, whereas Christ's human nature, as united to the Logos, does. Christ's human nature, that is to say, becomes an integral, subsistent being, and not merely a part of a subsistent being, by virtue of its relation to the Logos, as we shall see in the coming paragraphs.

2:5)[587] who "had to become like his brothers and sisters in every respect" (Heb 2:17) lacks any natural aspect of humanity. The revealed data, then, seem to require one both to affirm and to deny that Christ's human nature subsists in itself.

The idea that Christ's human nature is anhypostatic, or non-subsistent, in itself and yet enhypostatic, or subsistent, in the person of the Logos, however, seems to offer a solution to this dilemma. As John of Damascus explains:

> Although there is neither an anhypostatic nature nor an impersonal essence...there is no necessity for natures united to each other in hypostasis to possess each a distinct hypostasis. For they can join in one hypostasis [so as] neither to be anhypostatic nor to have each a distinguishing hypostasis, but to have one and the same hypostasis. For the same hypostasis of the Logos, the hypostasis of both natures, a most singular hypostasis, neither allows one of them to be anhypostatic, nor, surely, allows them to have different hypostases from each other, nor at one time to have one and at another time another, but is always of both undividedly and inseparably the hypostasis, being neither distributed nor cloven, nor part of it allotted to one, part of it allotted to the other, but entirely of this and entirely of that indivisibly and integrally.[588]

Divine revelation need not contradict itself, therefore, when it implies both that Christ's human nature is incomplete without the Logos and that this nature possesses that subsistence, which naturally accrues to every individual, human nature. The two implications cohere if, and only if, the perfection of subsistence, a perfection that accrues to ordinary, individual, human natures simply on account of their humanity, accrues to Christ's human nature by virtue of the hypostatic union alone.

A critic, of course, might object that the failure of Christ's humanity to attain subsistence purely of itself seems to betoken some deficiency on its part. It seems, nonetheless, that one could obviate this difficulty by postulating: 1) that God, by some supernatural intervention, inhibits Christ's human nature from attaining subsistence of itself; and 2) that Christ's human nature, in the absence of such inhibition, would develop subsistence without the aid of a hypostatic union.

---

[587] The NRSV rendering of ἄνθρωπος Χριστὸς Ἰησοῦς as "Christ Jesus, himself human" does not convey the salient point of this passage for our investigation: viz. that Jesus Christ does not merely possess a human nature, but is himself a subsistent human being.
[588] *Expositio Fidei* 53 in Kotter 2, 128.

The critic, however, could reply that since such a divine "inhibition" would be superfluous, one lacks sufficient grounds for postulating its occurrence. To this argument, it seems, one could respond by conceding that such inhibition would be superfluous if it were not necessary to the effecting of the hypostatic union. Christ's individual, human nature could hardly come to share in the hypostasis of the Logos, however, if it possessed its own, independent subsistence. Since Christ's human nature, as fully and perfectly human, would come to subsist in itself, just as any other particular, human nature, in the absence of some supernatural inhibition, then, such an inhibition does seem necessary to the accomplishment of the hypostatic union.[589]

The biblical account of Christ's ontological constitution, albeit frequently indirect, thus seems to dictate: a) that Christ's human nature does not subsist of itself, because God supernaturally inhibits it from subsisting in its own right, and; b) that Christ's human nature possesses that subsistence, which characterizes all individual, human natures, only through its union with the divine Logos. It follows, then, that one can determine at least one aspect of what union with the divine Logos adds to Christ's individual, human nature by determining what the perfection of subsistence adds to an individual nature as such. What differentiates a subsistent from a non-subsistent, individual nature, as we have seen, is that the first exists *per se* while the second exists in a greater whole. The rearward half of a worm, for example, does not subsist as long as the worm remains intact. Once one slices the worm in half, however, the rearward half begins to subsist.

Subsistence, then, seems to constitute nothing more than a *terminus* that distinguishes an individual nature from other beings of the same sort. Now, it

---

[589] Commenting on a decretal according to which "the person of God consumed the person of man," Aquinas explains:

Consumption here does not import the destruction of anything that was before, but the impeding of that which otherwise would have been. For if the human nature had not been assumed by a divine person, the human nature would have had its proper personality; and to this extent the person is said to have consumed a person, admittedly improperly, because the divine person by his union impeded, that the human nature might not have a proper personality [*STh* III, 4, 2 ad 3].

seems that one could correctly, albeit analogically, describe the eternal Logos, insofar as he is diverse from the Father and the Holy Spirit, as just such a terminus on the level of divine being. For, *qua* distinct, the Logos consists precisely in the relation of opposition that distinguishes him from the other divine persons.

It is, admittedly, impossible to demonstrate *a priori* that God can cause an individual human nature to terminate in a particular divine person in such a way as to subsist in this person without either disrupting the simplicity of the divine essence or so modifying the assumed nature as to render it inhuman. The inconceivability of such a proof, however, derives not from the intrinsic absurdity of the idea that God thus unites an individual human nature to the person of the Logos, but from the entitatively, and not merely modally, supernatural character of the hypostatic union. Christ's grace of union, that is to say, "exceeds the exigencies and powers of all created and creatable natures"[590] so that one cannot infer the possibility of God's bestowing such a grace *a maiori ad minorum* from his prior creative activity: whereas one can, for instance, infer from God's creation of human bodies the possibility of God's reconstituting those bodies in the general resurrection.[591] Nevertheless, one can reasonably infer the possibility of the hypostatic union from its actual, supernatural accomplishment. One can, therefore, rationally entertain the possibility of God's supernaturally inhibiting a particular human nature from terminating in a merely human subsistence and causing it, instead, to terminate in the divine subsistence of the eternal Logos.

If one can reasonably suspect that God might have accomplished the hypostatic union in this way, however, then one can also reasonably suspect that "the coming of the Son into his flesh…presupposes neither on his part nor on the part of the Father nor the Holy Spirit any action or influence that pertains to him

---

[590] Adolphe Tanquerey, *Synopsis theologiae dogmaticae specialis* 1 (Paris: Desclée, 1913[14]), §863(b), p. 523.
[591] We derive our argument for the impossibility of proving *a priori* that God can bestow entitatively supernatural graces such as Christ's grace of union from Reginald Garrigou-Lagrange's *The One God*, 336.

alone."[592] For, if the divine essence united Christ's particular, human nature to the Logos as to its term, then the Logos, insofar as it differs from the Father and the Holy Spirit, could constitute the ontological subject of that human nature without acting *qua* Logos at all.[593] Christ's individual, human nature, in this event, would relate to the eternal Logos as a line relates to its utmost extremity. It would terminate in the Logos, that is, and find in the Logos alone the completeness of a subsistent while suffering no more action from the Logos *qua* Logos than a line suffers from its terminal point.

It seems at least minimally plausible, then, that the divine persons, while exercising no personally distinguished causality whatsoever, could unite Christ's human nature to the Logos as to its term in such a way that the Logos becomes the ontological subject of that particular nature. As long as they maintained Christ's particular, human nature in this relationship to the Logos, in such a case, the Logos alone, as distinct from the Father and the Holy Spirit, would constitute the ontological subject of that nature. One can, therefore, conceive of a not evidently impossible scenario in which: a) one could truly affirm, for instance, that the Logos died on the cross; b) one could not truly affirm this, however, of the Father or of the Holy Spirit; and yet c) one could not truly deny that the divine persons always act inseparably. *Pace* Rahner, then, one can hold to the absolute inseparability of the divine acts *ad extra* without implicitly denying that the Son and the Son alone was born of Mary, suffered, died, and rose again in a particular, human nature. One can reasonably believe, although one cannot demonstrate, that the doctrines of the Incarnation and the inseparability of all divine acts *ad extra* do not necessarily conflict.

---

[592] Galtier, *L'Habitation*, 40.
[593] As Aquinas explains, "assumption imports two things, sc. an act of assuming and a term of the assumption. The act of assuming...proceeds from the divine power that is common to the three persons: but the term of assumption is a person....Therefore, that which is of action in assumption, is common to the three persons, but that which pertains to the *rationem termini* convenes precisely to one person,...[and] not to another" (*STh* III 3, 4 corp.).

γ. *The indwelling of the Holy Spirit.* Rahner attempts to falsify the inseparability axiom, nonetheless, by offering a second, alleged counterexample: the indwelling of the Holy Spirit. "The Spirit," Rahner writes, "dwells in us in a particular and proper way."[594] In a footnote, Rahner explains his position more precisely.

> By this it is not of course meant that the Spirit alone makes his dwelling in us. Each person communicates himself and dwells in us in a way proper to him. And because the indwelling ascribed to the Holy Spirit in Scripture (as a power who sanctifies, consecrates, moves, etc.) corresponds precisely to the personal particularity of the Spirit and of his going forth from the Father and the Son, there is absolutely no objection to saying that in *this* way only the Spirit dwells in human beings.[595]

Neither here nor anywhere else in his corpus does Rahner supply specific, biblical evidence for this thesis or refer his readers to the work of some exegete who does. While this may seem presumptuous on Rahner's part, it is also understandable; for little, if any, biblical evidence exists for the view that the Holy Spirit performs any work *ad extra* without the aid of, or even in a different way than, the other Trinitarian persons.

The Holy Spirit, for instance, does unquestionably dwell in the justified (Num 27:18; Pr 1:23; Isa 44:3; Ezek 36:27; 37:14; 39:29; Joel 2:28-9; Hag 2:5; Zech 12:10; John 14:17; Acts 2:17-18; Rom 8:9, 11, 23; 1 Cor 3:16; 6:19; 2 Cor 1:22; 5:5; Gal 4:6; Eph 1:13-14; 5:18; 1 Pet 4:14); but so do the Father (John 14:23; 2 Cor 6:16; Eph 2:22; 1 John 4:12-13, 15-16) and the Son (John 6:56; 14:20, 23; 15:4; Rom 8:10; 2 Cor 13:5; Gal 2:20; 4:19; Eph 3:17; Col 1:27; Heb 3:6; 1 John 3:23-4; 2 John 2; Rev 3:20).

Scripture, then, plainly refers to the divine indwelling most often as the work of the Holy Spirit. It is not obvious, however, that Scripture regards the effects of the Spirit's actions in this regard as differing in the slightest from the effects wrought by the indwelling Father and Son. Rahner could, of course, point to other activities that one might wish to attribute in some distinctive way to the

---

[594] "Uncreated Grace," *TI* i, 345; "Ungeschaffene Gnade," *ST* i, 374.
[595] Ibid. n. 2; ebd. Anm. 2.

Holy Spirit. The Bible, for instance, states in the most emphatic terms that the Holy Spirit sanctifies the justified (Rom 5:5; 1 Cor 6:11; Gal 5:22-3; Eph 2:22; 3:16; 5:9; 2 Thes 2:13; 1 Pet 1:2, 22). Yet it ascribes this function also to the Father (Lev 20:8; Ezek 37:28; John 17:17; Acts 15:9; 1 Thes 5:23; Jude 1, 24-5) and to the Son (Eph 5:26-7; 1 Thes 3:12-13; Heb 2:11; 10:14; 13:12) and differentiates the modes by which the persons accomplish the sanctification of believers only by, correctly, attributing the atonement to Christ alone. Suffice it to say that one can easily manifest the absence of differentiation between the divine persons' roles also in the raising of the dead and the inspiration of Scripture: the only other functions commonly proposed as in some sense special to the Holy Spirit.

Eduard Schweizer seems entirely justified, then, in concluding that, in the view of Paul, "Insofar as Christ is regarded in his significance for the community, in His powerful action upon it, he can be identified with the πνεῦμα."[596] Prescinding from the Incarnation, moreover, the data adduced above also seem to favor Ulrich Mauser's judgment that "descriptions of the act of God and the act of Christ are, in Pauline theology, [so] often identical...that the conclusion is warranted that Paul considers them one single act."[597] To the extent that Paul's teaching on the salvation-historical functions of the divine persons mirrors that of Scripture as a whole, then, one can reasonably conclude that Scripture as such, prescinding from the Incarnation, seems to depict the acts in history of the Son as identical to those of the Spirit and the acts of the Father as identical to the acts of Christ.

---

[596] "πνεῦμα, πνευματικός" III.1.d in *TDNT* 6, 422–4 at 423. Yves Congar makes similar comments on the relation between the Spirit and Christ in Paul's theology. "As regards the content of a work of the Spirit as opposed to a work of Christ, it is neither autonomous nor different" (*I Believe in the Holy Spirit 1: Revelation and the Experience of the Spirit* [David Smith, tr.; New York: Seabury, 1983], 37). Again, writes Congar, "From the functional point of view, the Lord and the Spirit perform the same work" (ibid. 39).
[597] "One God and Trinitarian Language in the Letters of Paul," *HBT* 20 (1998), 99–108 at 106.

Now, the principle of the transitivity of identity[598] dictates that if the acts of the Holy Spirit are the same as those of the Son, prescinding from the Incarnation, and that the acts of Christ, prescinding from the Incarnation, are the same as those of the Father, then the acts of the Holy Spirit are the same as those of the Father. The conclusions reached above, when combined, thus amount to an exegetical warrant for the principle of the inseparability of all divine acts *ad extra*. The Bible, then, seems to teach not only that the Holy Spirit exerts no distinct effects in creation, but that none of the divine persons influences creation in its own, distinctive way. "There are varieties of gifts," writes Paul, "but the same Spirit; and there are varieties of services, but the same Lord; and there are varieties of activities, but it is the same God who activates all of them in everyone" (1 Cor 12:4-6). The glorious diversity of God's works notwithstanding, Scripture at least seems to suggest that they all proceed from one simple and indivisible principle of divine causality.

δ. The beatific vision. Nevertheless, Rahner offers a third and final alleged counterexample to the principle of the inseparability of all divine acts *ad extra*: the beatific vision. "If one supposes," Rahner writes:

that the immediate vision of God can only be based on a quasi-formal self-communication of God in vision, and not (adequately) on a created quality in the spirit of the human being; and if one recalls the obvious truth, that each of the divine persons is the object of immediate intuition in his personal propriety: then that entitative (ontic) quasi-formal self-communication of God, which takes the place of a *species impressa* as the ontological foundation of the human being's possession of God in knowledge, must include a non-appropriated relationship of each of the three divine persons to the human being.[599]

In other words, Rahner argues in *modus tollens*:

---

[598] This principle, which is also sometimes referred to as "the principle of comparative identity," consists in the truism: if a=b and b=c, then a=c.
[599] "Nature and Grace," *TI* iv, 175; "Natur und Gnade," *ST* iv, 221.

1. If the divine persons do not communicate themselves to human beings quasi-formally, immediately, and distinctly, then human beings cannot know them immediately and distinctly; yet
2. Human beings do know the divine persons immediately and distinctly; therefore
3. The divine persons do communicate themselves quasi-formally, immediately, and distinctly.

In defense of this argument, one can justly observe that Rahner does not equivocate in his usage of terms, that his conclusion unquestionably follows from his premises, and that the minor premise of his argument is warranted by 1 John 3:2. The major premise of Rahner's argument, however, appears vulnerable to critique insofar as it presupposes an at least relative identity between human being and knowing. Only if being is knowing, that is to say, must one receive an ontological self-communication of something in order to know it. As we observed in Chapter 1, Rahner's views on this subject seem contestable at best and, therefore, inadequate for the purpose of warranting further conclusions.

ε. *Conclusion.* It seems, then, that none of Rahner's three alleged counterexamples actually constitutes a certain exception to the axiom, "the works of the Trinity are inseparable."[600] One cannot plausibly argue, therefore, from the falsehood of this axiom to the falsehood of the statement, "The divine persons possess reality only through their identity with the divine substance:" a statement that, if true, entails that the axiom in question admits of no exceptions. Rahner does not succeed, consequently, in blunting the force of the evidence adduced above in favor of the just quoted statement, which forms the minor premise in the first syllogism of our argument that Rahner's understanding of the divine persons'

---

[600] DH 491, 535.

ontological constitution precludes the possibility of their revealing themselves in the manner he envisions.

3. Rahner's case against the major premise of syllogism 4. The only other significantly vulnerable aspect of this argument, as we have already shown, is its fourth syllogism's major premise: "Those beings the existence of which cannot be inferred from non-verbal and non-conceptual aspects of that which is other than they can be known to exist by other beings, if other beings can know that they exist at all, only through verbal, or at least conceptual, forms of communication or through direct intuition." A proponent of Rahner's theology would presumably protest that such a statement gratuitously excludes the possibility that one might come to know of the divine persons by becoming one with them. The formulator of this premise, such a person would presumably argue, unwarrantably presupposes that a duality of subject and object necessarily characterizes the divine-human encounter: precisely the sort of duality that, in Rahner's view, divine self-communication always and everywhere overcomes.

Such a rebuttal would suffice to refute the major premise of syllogism 4, it seems, if it were certain that "being is knowing."[601] For in that case, it would also seem reasonably certain that any radical, ontic, divine self-communication would necessarily manifest itself in its recipient's consciousness. In Chapter 1, however, we established that Rahner's understanding of created being as relatively identical to created knowing is significantly problematic. The idea that divine self-communication is onto-logical thus appears insufficiently warranted, therefore, to ground a compelling refutation of the major premise of syllogism 4.

4. Conclusion. Before concluding the dialogue with Rahner which we began in section II.1 over the possibility of a Trinitarian self-revelation through salvation history and/or transcendental experience, we would like to emphasize that we

---

[601] *Hearer*, 35; *Hörer, SW* iv, 70.

intend for the argument laid out in four syllogisms in the just-mentioned section to function as a strictly immanent criticism of Rahner's views on the revelation of the Trinity. As we have seen, Rahner admits that "in God the relation is real only through its identity with the real divine essence,"[602] and characterizes this as the unanimous opinion of his communion's theologians. We have sought to prove, then, on the basis of a thesis which Rahner endorses without qualification, that God cannot reveal the doctrine of the Trinity to human beings in the way in which Rahner envisions and that Rahner's system, accordingly, to the extent that one can reasonably qualify Rahner's thought as systematic, is, in this area at least, self-refuting.

III. CHRIST"S ANOINTING WITH THE HOLY SPIRIT AS A TEST CASE FOR THE *GRUNDAXIOM*

1. Introduction. Heretofore in this chapter, we have argued that God cannot reveal the doctrine of the Trinity in the manner Rahner envisions. In our last argument against Rahner's *Grundaxiom*, however, we intend to grant, solely for the purpose of argument, this possibility. We intend to grant *in hypothesi*, that is to say, Rahner's contention that the salvation-historical functions associated with the Father, the Son, and the Holy Spirit in Scripture are proper, rather than merely appropriated, to these persons. Acting in accord with this supposition, then, we hope to discern the pattern of inner-Trinitarian relations manifested in a significant episode within the economy of salvation: viz. Christ's anointing with the Holy Spirit.

The pattern of relations among the persons in this episode of salvation history, we shall argue, diverges radically from the τάξις among the Trinitarian persons as ordinarily understood by orthodox, Western Trinitarians, including Rahner

---

[602] *Trinity*, 71; "Der dreifaltige Gott," *MS* ii, 363.

himself.[603] We intend to show, consequently, that if one is consistently to interpret the economy of salvation in accord with Rahner's principles and to attempt to infer the doctrine of the Trinity purely therefrom, one must either: a) conclude to what Rahner correctly rejects as an unorthodox doctrine of the Trinity: or b) so modify one's understanding of the correspondence between economy and theology prescribed by the *Grundaxiom* as to render it impotent to warrant inferences from a non-verbal, non-intuitive revelation to conclusions about the immanent Trinity. This section, therefore, constitutes an attempt to refute *per reductionem ad absurdum* Rahner's thesis that the economic Trinity must correspond to the immanent Trinity in such a way as to warrant inferences from God's economic self-manifestation to the doctrine of the Trinity.

2. Methodological considerations. In keeping with our desire to mount an exclusively immanent critique of Rahner's position, it seems advisable, before proceeding to this final argument of our critique itself, to consider whether Rahner himself would find its presuppositions acceptable. We hope, therefore, to answer the following three questions before proceeding to our main argument: viz. 1) Does Rahner consider Scripture a legitimate measure of the truth or falsehood of theological statements? 2) Does Scripture constitute an appropriate norm for the *Grundaxiom* of Rahner's theology of the Trinity? and 3. Does Christ's anointing with the Holy Spirit constitute an appropriate matrix in which to test this axiom?

a. Does Rahner consider Scripture a legitimate measure of the truth or falsehood of theological statements? The appropriate answer to this first question

---

[603] One might object, admittedly, that Christ's anointing with the Holy Spirit need not constitute a revelation of the intra-Trinitarian τάξις. Rahner, however, specifically affirms that the Trinitarian persons' "opposed relativities are...concretely identical with both 'communications' ('processions') as seen from both sides" (ibid. 73; ebd. 364). Any manifestation of the divine persons relating to each other in a certain order, therefore, is *ipso facto* also a manifestation of the τάξις in which the divine processions occur.

will vary in accordance with the sense one attaches to the idea of a "legitimate measure" in theological questions. Rahner emphatically denies, in any event, that Scripture constitutes a "legitimate measure" for theological statements if by this one means that Scripture consists in a body of divinely revealed and, therefore, normative propositions. "It is apparent," Rahner writes, "that God does not effect revelation by simply adding new 'propositions' 'from outside' to the basic substance of the Christian faith....Revelation is not revelation of concepts, not the creation of new fundamental axioms [*Grundaxiome*], introduced in a final and fixed form into a human being's consciousness 'from outside' by some supra-historical transcendent cause."[604] For Rahner the idea that "the transcendent God inseminates [*indoctriniere*] fixed and final propositions into the consciousness of the bearer of revelation"[605] constitutes matter for scorn, a thesis unworthy of serious consideration.

Rahner understands revelation in its most fundamental sense, rather, to consist in "a transcendental determination of the human person, constituted by that which we call grace and self-bestowal on God's part—in other words, God's Pneuma."[606] This universal revelation constitutes, in Rahner's view, not a mere preamble to faith, but the deepest reality of the Christian faith. "The original one and unitive event of the definitive eschatological revelation in Christianity," Rahner writes, "is the one event of God's most authentic [*eigentlichsten*] self-communication, occurring everywhere in the world and in history in the Holy Spirit offered to every human being."[607] This "one and unitive event," moreover, constitutes not an aspect, not even the most fundamental aspect, but the whole of Christian revelation. In his words, "the totality of the Christian faith is in a real sense [*eigentlich*] already given in...transcendental experience."[608]

---

[604] "Historicity of Theology," *TI* ix, 67–8; "Geschichtlichkeit der Theologie," *ST* viii, 92–3.
[605] Ibid. 68; ebd. 93.
[606] "On the Current Relationship between Philosophy and Theology," *TI* xiii, 61–79 at 62; "Zum heutigen Verhältnis von Philosophie und Theologie," *ST* x, 70–88 at 71.
[607] "History of Dogma," *TI* xviii, 17; "Dogmengeschicte," *ST* xiii, 27.
[608] "Methodology," *TI* xi, 109; "Methode," *ST* ix, 122.

In Rahner's view, then, the Christian revelation constitutes a transcendental, universal, non-objective existential of concrete, human nature of which "the material contents of historical revelation"[609] are mere "verbalized objectifications."[610] They are, however, at least objectifications. Rahner treats such objectifications, moreover, as indispensable means to the self-realization of God's transcendental revelation, God's "inner word of grace."[611] In Rahner's words:

The external historical word expounds the inner one, brings it to the light of consciousness in the categories of human understanding, compels the human being definitely to take a decision with regard to the inner word, transposes the inner grace of the human person into the dimension of the community and renders it present there, makes possible the insertion of grace into the external, historical field of human life.[612]

In order for God's self-bestowal to reach beyond the transcendental sphere, beyond what Rahner calls the "fine point" (*Fünklein*)[613] of the soul, then, verbal-historical objectifications, in Rahner's view, must explicitate it in the realm of the concrete and palpable.

The statements of Scripture, moreover, occupy, according to Rahner, a privileged place within the universe of objectifications, both religious and secular, in which human beings encounter divine revelation. For in Scripture, Rahner believes, Christians possess "the pure objectification of the divine, humanly incarnated truth."[614] Rahner is even willing to say that "being a work of God it is absolutely [*schlechthin*] inerrant."[615]

---

[609] "The Act of Faith and the Content of Faith," *TI* xxi, 158; "Glaubensakt und Glaubensinhalt," *ST* xv, 158.
[610] Ibid.; ebd.
[611] "The Word and the Eucharist," *TI* iv, 253–86 at 259; "Wort und Eucharistie," *SW* xviii, 596–626 at 600.
[612] Ibid.; ebd. 601.
[613] Ibid. 258; ebd.
[614] "Scripture and Theology," *TI* vi, 89–97 at 95; "Heilige Schrift und Theologie," *SW* xii, 226–33 at 231.
[615] Ibid. 90; ebd. 112. Cf. Rahner's similar remarks in "Heilige Schrift," *LThK*² in *SW* xvii/i, 284–8 at 285 and his more tepid endorsement of Scriptural inerrancy in *Foundations*, 375–7 (*Grundkurs, SW* xxvi, 355–6).

One would misunderstand this statement profoundly, of course, if one thought that Rahner meant thereby to affirm a traditional doctrine of Scripture. As we have seen, Rahner considers "the history of revelation...co-extensive with the *spiritual history of humankind as such*"[616] and insists that the idea of inspiration be understood in such a way that it does not "*einen miraculösen Beigeschmack haben.*"[617] On certain occasions, moreover, Rahner does not shrink from frankly disagreeing with Scripture's literal sense.[618] According to Rahner's own standards, then, a few citations of Scripture can hardly suffice to undermine or to confirm a theological thesis: especially one of architectonic and hermeneutical significance such as the *Grundaxiom* of Rahner's theology of the Trinity.

Rahner does, nonetheless, identify Scripture repeatedly as "the *norma non normata* for theology and for the Church."[619] It seems, therefore, that he could not reasonably object if one sought to evaluate elements of his thought in the light of Scripture, which he himself describes as "the inexhaustible source of all Christian theology, without which theology must become sterile"[620] and "as it were, the soul of all theology."[621]

---

[616] "Observations on the Concept of Revelation" in Karl Rahner and Joseph Ratzinger, *Revelation and Tradition* (W. J. O'Hara, trans.; London: Burns & Oates, 1966), 9–25 at 16; "Bemerkungen zum Begriff der Offenbarung" in idem, *Offenbarung und Überlieferung* (Freiburg im Breisgau: Herder, 1965), 11–24 at 16. Unlike O'Hara, we italicize the words "spiritual history of mankind as such," because Rahner himself italicizes the words, "*geistigen Geschichte der Menschheit überhaupt.*"

[617] "Buch Gottes," *ST* xvi, 284. Joseph Donceel's translation, "without recourse to the miraculous" ("Book of God," *TI* xxii, 219), accurately conveys Rahner's overall position, but misses the sense of this particular passage.

[618] For instance, Rahner recognizes that Paul explicitly teaches monogenism in Acts 17:26 ("Mary's Virginity," *TI* xix, 218–31 at 225; "Jungfräulichkeit Marias," *ST* xiii, 361–77 at 370) and yet rejects it. Likewise, Rahner refuses to consider Enoch and Elijah exceptions to the principle of the universality of death, Gen 5:24 and 2 Kings 2:11 notwithstanding ("Christian Dying," *TI* xviii, 238; "Das christliche Sterben," *ST* xiii, 283).

[619] "Scripture and Theology," *TI* vi, 89–91, 95; "Heilige Schrift und Theologie," *SW* xii, 231. Cf. also, e.g. "Dogmatic Statement," *TI* v, 62 ("Dogmatische Aussage," *SW* xii, 167); "Schrift, Heilige Schrift," *SM* iv, *SW* xvii/ii, 1264–74 at 1266; and "Replik: Bemerkungen zu: Hans Küng, 'Im Interesse der Sache,'" *StZ* 187 (1971), 145–60 at 159.

[620] "Schriftbeweis," *KThW*[1], *SW* xvii/i, 800.

[621] *KThW*[10], 376. Here Rahner quotes the II Vatican Council's decree *Optatam Totius* 16 (Norman Tanner, ed. *Decrees of the Ecumenical Councils: Vol. II* [London: Sheed & Ward, 1990], 955). Rahner writes elsewhere, "It has often and rightly been said today that the study of scripture

b. Is Scripture an appropriate norm for the Grundaxiom of Rahner's theology of the Trinity? One could argue, of course, that, although a scripturally oriented, immanent critique may be feasible for other aspects of Rahner's theology, two factors render a simultaneously scriptural and immanent critique of the *Grundaxiom* inconceivable. First, Rahner states that he formulates his theology of the Trinity, at least partially, in order to quell embarrassment over "the simple fact that in reality the Scriptures do *not explicitly* present a doctrine of the 'immanent Trinity' (even St. John's prologue is no such doctrine)."[622] It might seem, therefore, that Rahner constructs his *Grundaxiom* with a view to liberating the theology of the Trinity from the Bible and setting it on a new foundation: in which case the idea of an immanent critique of this axiom that takes its departure precisely from the Bible would be unthinkable.

Second, one could argue that the critic who marshals biblical texts in opposition to Rahner's *Grundaxiom* commits a category mistake. For such a person might seem to confuse the *Grundaxiom*, a principle that concerns how one ought to interpret Scripture, with a first-order assertion concerning a state of affairs with which similar assertions of Scripture may conflict. This sort of critique, of course, would manifest only the confusion of the critic, not any inadequacies of Rahner's *Grundaxiom*.

Serious grounds do exist, therefore, for denying the possibility of a simultaneously scriptural and immanent critique of the *Grundaxiom* of Rahner's theology of the Trinity. To the immanent and scriptural critique of Rahner's *Grundaxiom* attempted here, however, these considerations appear to pose no significant obstacle.

---

is the 'soul of theology' ("Reflections on the Contemporary Intellectual Formation of Future Priests," *TI* vi, 113–38 at 133; "Über die theoretische Ausbildung künftiger Priester heute," *SW* xvi, 434–55 at 451). Again, remarking on "theology in general," Rahner writes, "its 'soul' must be scripture, as Vatican II rightly says" ("Philosophising," *TI* ix, 50; "Philosophieren," *ST* viii, 75).
[622] *Trinity*, 22; "Der dreifaltige Gott," *MS* ii, 328.

i. The relevance of the Bible to the theology of the Trinity. For, first, Rahner's belief that the Bible lacks an explicit doctrine of the immanent Trinity does not move him to unleash the doctrine of the Trinity entirely from its biblical moorings. He seeks, instead, to anchor the doctrine of the immanent Trinity in the economy of salvation whose structure, in his view, appears pre-eminently within the narrative of Scripture.

Accordingly, Rahner states as one of the three principal goals of his theology of the Trinity, whose centerpiece is the *Grundaxiom*, that it "do justice [*unbefangener würdigen*] to the biblical statements concerning the economy of salvation and its threefold structure, and to the explicit biblical statements concerning the Father, the Son, and the Spirit."[623] Rahner, in fact, describes "salvation history, our experience of it, [and] its biblical expression"[624] as "the foundation and the inexhaustible, ever richer starting point"[625] of human knowledge of the economic Trinity.

Though Rahner rarely treats exegetical questions, moreover, he does attempt in at least two instances to supply some exegetical basis for the idea that the Trinitarian persons perform distinct functions in salvation history, one of the essential presuppositions of the *Grundaxiom*. Specifically, he argues that "in Scripture the interior Trinity and the Trinity of the economy of salvation are seen and spoken of in themselves with such simultaneity [*zu sehr in einem*] that there would be no justification in itself (logically) for taking the expressions literally and substantially in the first case and only in an 'appropriated' way in the second."[626] Likewise, Rahner devotes more than a third of his long essay, "Theos in the New Testament"[627] to proving that in the New Testament the term ὁ θεός

---

[623] Ibid.; ebd.
[624] Ibid. 82; ebd. 371.
[625] Ibid.; ebd.
[626] "Uncreated Grace," *TI* i, 346; "Ungeschaffene Gnade," *ST* i, 375.
[627] *TI* i, 79–148; *SW* iv, 346–403. Marcelo González, incidentally, finds in this essay the first appearance of a form of the *Grundaxiom* in Rahner's corpus (*La relación entre Trinidad*

does not merely stand for often, but properly signifies, the intra-Trinitarian Father: a thesis by which Rahner seeks to bolster his case for ascribing distinctive influences in the economy of salvation to the Trinitarian persons. One cannot reasonably claim, therefore, that Rahner considers exegetical considerations simply irrelevant to arguments concerning the soundness and legitimacy of the *Grundaxiom*.

ii. The hermeneutical character of the Grundaxiom. Neither, it seems, does the hermeneutical character of the *Grundaxiom* render it insusceptible to every variety of scriptural critique. For, although the *Grundaxiom* undoubtedly lies on a different plane than the statements of Scripture, it nonetheless admits of an indirect scriptural trial. Even if one cannot, in the nature of the case, discover a straightforward correspondence or disparity between the statements of Scripture and the *Grundaxiom*, that is to say, one can test Rahner's claim that the relations among the persons in the history of salvation mirror those described in the classical, Western doctrine of the immanent Trinity. To do so, one need merely to select a scene from Scripture in which the three persons appear in a salvation-historical context, discern the pattern of relations between them in this context, and measure this pattern against what one knows of the immanent Trinity. If the two patterns correspond, this does not prove Rahner's axiom true, but it does lend it a degree of credibility. If the two patterns diverge, however, this indicates that Rahner's claims require qualification.

Someone might object, of course, that a disparity between the pattern of relations within the economy and the pattern depicted in the Western doctrine of the Trinity would not necessarily prove that οἰκονομία and θεολογία diverge. One could also take such a disparity as evidence of flaws within the Western doctrine. Since Rahner regards the doctrine of the Trinity taught by the IV

---

económica e inmanente: el "axioma fundamental" de K. Rahner y su recepción: líneas para continuar la reflexión, [Corona Lateranensis 40; Rome: Pontificia Università lateranense, 1996], 37, 67). For the early formulation, cf. *TI* i, 148; *SW* iv, 403.

Lateran Council and the Council of Florence, however, as a *donnée*, a disparity between the economic Trinity and the Western doctrine would, from his perspective at least, suffice to falsify the *Grundaxiom*. Even if the critique undertaken in this section, therefore, cannot, in and of itself, falsify the *Grundaxiom* in all of its possible acceptations, it can show that the *Grundaxiom* entails consequences that Rahner finds unacceptable.

A genuinely immanent critique of Rahner's *Grundaxiom*, which both respects its hermeneutical character and takes account of scriptural data, consequently, is quite conceivable. One could reasonably challenge the legitimacy of the sort of critique attempted here, it seems, only on the grounds that it bases itself on inappropriate biblical texts.

c. Is Christ's anointing with the Holy Spirit an appropriate matrix within which to test Rahner's Grundaxiom? The texts employed in our trial of the *Grundaxiom*, viz. Matt 3:16–17; Mark 1:10–11; Luke 3:22; and John 1:32, do, admittedly, contain elements that might seem objectionable to Rahner. For God appears in these verses "at work palpably [*handgreiflich*] as an object (*Sache*) and not merely as a transcendent First Cause (*Ursache*)";[628] he appears as one who "operates and functions as an individual existent alongside of other existents,...a member of the larger household of all reality."[629] The scriptural accounts of Christ's anointing with the Holy Spirit, that is, seem to portray precisely the God of whom Rahner says: "*that* God really does not exist,"[630] and "anyone in search of such a God is searching for a false God."[631] Insofar as these texts contain a supernaturalistic narrative of the sort that Rahner specifically rejects as incredible, then, one could plausibly argue that Rahner would reject their normativity for the theology of the Trinity.

---

[628] "Science as a 'Confession'?" *TI* iii, 385–400 at 389; "Wissenschaft als 'Konfession'?" *SW* xv, 171–83 at 174.
[629] *Foundations*, 63; *Grundkurs*, SW xxvi, 66.
[630] Ibid.; ebd.
[631] Ibid.; ebd.

Likewise, one could maintain, with some measure of warrant, that the scriptural accounts of Christ's anointing with the Holy Spirit are simply irrelevant to the question of how the divine persons relate to each other in the immanent Trinity. For Rahner does assert that God changes in the process of self-communication and, thereby, seems implicitly to admit that the economy of salvation contains elements that do not exactly reflect the intra-divine life.

It seems, accordingly, that one cannot responsibly apply Rahner's axiom without taking into account the necessarily analogous character of any valid inference from the forms in which the divine persons manifest themselves to conclusions about the immanent Trinity. The consequent necessity of qualifying *per analogiam* claims about the immanent Trinity derived from the economy, therefore, might appear to justify Rahner in characterizing Christ's anointing with the Holy Spirit as an economic aberration that does not reveal the intra-Trinitarian relations.

The prominence of divine intervention in the anointing narratives and the inevitable gap between οἰκονομία and θεολογία that results from the metamorphosis of God's being in divine self-communication as Rahner conceives of it, thus pose at least apparent difficulties for the anointing accounts' aptness as a matrix in which to test Rahner's *Grundaxiom*. Neither concern, however, seems sufficiently grave to preclude the anointing accounts from serving adequately in this role.

i. The supernaturalism of the anointing narratives. For, first, it would seem difficult to reconcile outright rejection of the anointing accounts' normativity, because of their supernaturalism or for any other reason, with Rahner's repeated and emphatic statements concerning Scripture's status as *norma non normata* for Christian theology. Rahner explicitly grants, moreover, that the expressions of Scripture "wholly retain their meaning even though the worldview on the basis and with the help of which they were once made has become obsolete."[632] By declaring the idea of divine intervention at particular points in space and time incompatible with "our modern experience and interpretation of the world,"[633] therefore, Rahner does not absolve himself of the responsibility to discern some meaning in a given text of Scripture and to respect the text as "the pure objectification of the divine, humanly incarnated truth."[634]

When Rahner states that he desires, in his theology of the Trinity, to "do justice [*unbefangener würdigen*] to the biblical statements concerning the economy of salvation and its threefold structure, and to the explicit biblical statements concerning the Father, the Son, and the Spirit,"[635] furthermore, he seems to commit himself to taking seriously the biblical narratives of Christ's anointing with the Holy Spirit. The thrust of Rahner's thought on these questions, therefore, suggests that these narratives, their supernaturalistic elements notwithstanding, ought to be treated as authentic witnesses to God's Trinitarian self-manifestation.

ii. The relevance of the anointing accounts. Second, exclusion of the anointing accounts from consideration in determining, *via* the *Grundaxiom*, the shape of the intra-Trinitarian relations would seem reasonable only if the pattern of relations displayed in these accounts appeared tangential to the whole of the Trinity's economic self-revelation. The pattern of relations exhibited in the anointing accounts, viz. Father–Spirit–Son, and especially the passivity of the Son vis-à-vis the Holy Spirit manifested in these narratives, however, appear frequently in the New Testament.

The angel of the Lord, for example, informs Joseph that the child in his fiancée's womb is "from the Holy Spirit" (Matt 1:20). After God "anointed Jesus

---

[632] "Science as a 'Confession'? *TI* iii, 396; "Wissenschaft als 'Konfession'?" *SW* xv, 180.
[633] *Foundations*, 259; *Grundkurs*, *SW* xxvi, 248.
[634] Scripture and Theology," *TI* vi, 95; "Heilige Schrift und Theologie," *SW* xii, 231.
[635] *Trinity*, 22; "Der dreifaltige Gott," *MS* ii, 328.

with the Holy Spirit and with power" (Acts 10:38), the Spirit "immediately drove him out into the wilderness" (Mark 1:12). In his inaugural sermon in Nazareth, Jesus announces that "the Spirit of the Lord is upon me, because he (= the Lord) has anointed me to bring good news to the poor" (Luke 4:18; cf. Isa 61:1–2). When his opponents attribute Jesus' exorcisms to Satan, Jesus asserts that he casts out demons "by the Spirit of God" (Matt 12:28). On the cross, Jesus offers himself up to the Father "through the eternal Spirit" (Heb 9:14); and Jesus' Father raises him from the dead through the power of the same Spirit (Rom 1:4; 1 Pet 3:18).

The general pattern of relations manifested in the anointing accounts appears throughout the Synoptic Gospels, therefore, and, to a certain extent, throughout the New Testament. Since, then, the manifestation of the divine persons in the order Father–Spirit–Son, characteristic of the anointing accounts, is by no means an isolated phenomenon; and since Christ's anointing itself forms a decisive caesura in the economy of salvation; it seems unreasonable to exclude the anointing from the set of events that, according to the *Grundaxiom*, ought to manifest the inner structure of the immanent Trinity. Neither the anointing accounts' supernaturalistic elements nor the inevitable gap Rahner implicitly posits between οἰκονομία and θεολογία, therefore, suffices to invalidate the trial of Rahner's *Grundaxiom* proposed here.

3. Reconciling the anointing accounts, when interpreted in accordance with the Grundaxiom, with Rahner's filioquism.

Those who: a) identify the Holy Spirit of the anointing accounts with the third person of the eternal Trinity; b) believe that the Holy Spirit eternally proceeds from the Father and the Son as from a single principle; c) accept that the divine persons can effect distinct influences in the world; and d) accept the Grundaxiom of Rahner's theology of the Trinity; can account for the events portrayed in Matt

3:16-17; Mark 1:10-11; Luke 3:22; and John 1:32 in at least three ways. Such persons can:

1. claim that the Spirit is in some way involved in the begetting of the Son;
2. argue that the anointing accounts manifest a prior occurrence in which the missions and the processions correspond; or
3. conclude that the Spirit constitutes the Father's intra-Trinitarian gift to the Son.

In the following, we shall examine each of these interpretations with an eye to determining the extent to which they resolve the difficulty for Rahner's *Grundaxiom* posed by the anointing of the Son with the Holy Spirit.

a. Involvement of the Spirit in the begetting of the Son. "In the Biblical accounts of Christ's anointing with the Holy Spirit," claims Thomas Weinandy:

a trinitarian pattern is clearly discernible. God's creative and prophetic word is always spoken in the power of the Spirit, and, as such, in light of the New Testament revelation, we have a clue to the inner life of the Trinity. The breath/spirit by which God speaks...his prophetic word throughout history is the same breath/Spirit by which he eternally breaths forth his Word/Son. As the Father commissioned Jesus by the power of his Spirit to recreate the world so, in the same Spirit, God eternally empowered him to be his Word.[636]

In Weinandy's view, then, "the...roles played by the Father, the Son, and the Holy Spirit [here and elsewhere] in the economy of salvation,...illustrate the...roles they play within the immanent Trinity, namely that the Father begets the Son in or by the Holy Spirit."[637]

This view, whose supporters, alongside Weinandy, include Leonardo Boff,[638] François-Xavier Durrwell,[639] Edward Yarnold,[640] and Gérard Remy,[641] seems to

---

[636] *The Father's Spirit of Sonship: Reconceiving the Trinity* (Edinburgh: T & T Clark, 1995), 27.
[637] Ibid. 52.
[638] *Trinity and Society* (Paul Burns, tr.; Maryknoll, NY: Orbis, 1988), 205, 207.
[639] *Holy Spirit of God: An Essay in Biblical Theology* (Benedict Davies, tr.; London: Geoffrey Chapman, 1986), esp. 141; *L'Esprit Saint de Dieu* (Paris: Cerf, 1985²), esp. 155. Cf. also Durrwell's "Pour une christologie selon l'Esprit Saint," *NRT* 114 (1992), 653–77, esp. 661–5.
[640] "The Trinitarian Implications of Luke and Acts," *HeyJ* 7 (1966), 18–32, esp. 19.

draw greater strength from Scripture's narratives of the virginal conception than from the accounts under consideration here. Each of these authors, however, appeals not only to the virginal conception, but also to the anointing accounts, to bolster his view.

i. Patristic precedents. Although the contemporary advocates of this position uniformly appeal to Rahner's *Grundaxiom* and thus present it in a distinctively modern cast, moreover, this view does not lack precursors in the earliest ages of the church. The idea of the Spirit as the breath that accompanies the Father's Word, for instance, appears explicitly in the writings of Gregory of Nyssa,[642] Maximus the Confessor,[643] and John of Damascus.[644] One finds imagery patently suggestive of this view in the comparison of the Father, Spirit, and Son to Adam, Eve, and Seth: an analogy employed by Gregory of Nazianzus.[645] At least one Father, furthermore, explicitly endorses the idea that the Father begets the Son "in or by" the Spirit. Marius Victorinus, the Christian rhetor memorialized in Augustine's *Confessions*,[646] states in his *Adversus Arium* 1.58 that "He is not mistaken...who imagines that the Holy Spirit is the mother of Jesus, as well on high as here below."[647]

The idea that Christ derives from the Holy Spirit in some sense, furthermore, finds considerable support among various marginal groups of the first Christian

---

[641] "Une théologie pascale de l'Esprit Saint: À propos d'un ouvrage recent," *NRT* 112 (1990), 731–41, esp. 732–5.

[642] *Oratio catechetica* 2; *Opera dogmatica minora, Pars IV* (Ekkehard Mühlenberg, ed.; GNO 3-IV; Leiden, New York, and Köln: Brill, 1996), 12.

[643] *Quaestiones et Dubia* 34; PG 90, 814B. Ironically, in this context at least, Maximus uses the logical precedence of the *verbum cordis* over speech to explain why one cannot reasonably characterize Christ as the Son of the Holy Spirit.

[644] *Expositio fidei* 7; Kotter 2, 16.

[645] *Or.* 31.11; SC 250, 294–296; cf. John of Damascus' employment of this analogy in *Expositio Fidei* 8; Kotter 2, 23. Both Gregory and John, of course, employ this analogy in order to illustrate how the Holy Spirit can be consubstantial with the Father without either being begotten by him or being identical with him.

[646] 8.2.3–5.10; CCL 27, 114–19.

[647] CSEL 83:1, 157.

centuries. The author of the *Gospel of the Hebrews*, for instance, seems to ascribe Christ's generation at least partially to the Holy Spirit. In a fragment preserved by Jerome, this author writes, "It came to pass now, when the Lord had ascended from the water, that the source of all holy Spirit both rested on him and said to him: my Son, in all prophets I was awaiting you, as coming, and I have rested on you. For are my rest; you are my first-born son, who reigns everlastingly."[648] The author of the *Epistula Jacobi acpocrypha* (6.20),[649] likewise, depicts Christ identifying himself as "the son of the Holy Spirit;" and the author of the *Odes of Solomon*, portrays Christ as testifying that the Holy Spirit has "brought me forth [= begotten me?] before the Lord's face,"[650] and that "according to the greatness of the Most High, so She [i.e. the Holy Spirit] made me."[651]

ii. Difficulties. Motifs suggestive of the view that the Father begets the Son in or by the Holy Spirit, sc. that Christ proceeds eternally *a Patre Spirituque*, then, appear repeatedly, if not frequently, in the writings of the patristic period. The Fathers, nonetheless, almost universally reject this proposal for a rather obvious reason. The idea that Christ *qua* divine derives his being from the Holy Spirit seems to reverse the τάξις of the Trinitarian persons revealed in the baptismal formula. As Basil explains, in the formula of orthodoxy he composed for Eustathius of Sebaste:

> One must avoid those who confuse the order the Lord imparted to us, as men openly fighting against piety, who place the Son ahead of the Father and set the Holy Spirit before the Son. For it is one's duty to maintain unchanged and unharmed the order that we received from the same discourse of the Lord, saying, "Go, teach all nations, baptizing in the name of the Father and of the Son and of the Holy Spirit" [Matt 28:19].[652]

---

648 *Apud* Jerome, *Commentarius in Esaiam; Liber IV* at 11:1–3; CCL 73, 148.
649 *Epistula Jacobi apocrypha: Die zweite Schrift aus Nag-Hammadi-Codex I* (Dankwart Kirchner, ed. trans. and comm.; TU 136; Berlin: Akademie-Verlag, 1989), 16.
650 36:3; *The Odes of Solomon* (James H. Charlesworth, ed. and tr.; Oxford: Clarendon Press, 1973), 126–7.
651 36:5; ibid.
652 Basil, *Ep.* 125; *Saint Basile: Lettres: Tome II* (Yves Courtonne, ed. and tr.; CUFr; Paris: Les belles lettres, 1961), 34.

Such reasoning, of course, seems unpersuasive from Rahner's perspective, because Rahner: a) expresses doubts as to whether the baptismal formula actually derives from Jesus' lips;[653] and b) considers the scriptural writers' words mere objectifications of transcendental experience as mediated by salvation history. A second reason for rejecting a procession of Christ *a Patre Spirituque*, however, seems quite weighty given Rahner's assumptions about the theology of the Trinity.

This second reason consists simply in the datum that the Catholic Church, in three councils which she considers ecumenical,[654] has declared that the Holy Spirit derives his personal being from both the Father and the Son so that the Holy Spirit's very existence presupposes the personal constitution of the Son. In view of these decrees, which Rahner considers irreformable and infallibly true, then, it seems that Rahner cannot consistently affirm that the Son derives in any way from the Holy Spirit. If the anointing accounts, accordingly, when interpreted in accord with Rahner's *Grundaxiom*, imply an eternal origin of the Son from the Holy Spirit, then this *Grundaxiom* seems ultimately to undermine what Rahner considers orthodox, Western Trinitarianism.

b. The anointing accounts manifest a prior occurrence in which the missions and the processions correspond. A number of theologians, however, believe that they can transpose the pattern of interpersonal relations manifested in the Scriptural narratives of Christ's anointing into the immanent Trinity, as the *Grundaxiom* requires, without in any way contravening a thoroughgoing filioquism. Heribert Mühlen, for instance, attempts to resolve the dilemma posed

---

[653] "Theology in the New Testament," *TI* v, 35; "Theologie im Neues Testament," *SW* xii, 203.
[654] We refer to the IV Lateran Council (DH 800), II Lyons (DB[27] 460), and the Council of Florence (DH 1300, 1313).

by the anointing accounts by distinguishing sharply between Scripture's view of Christ's anointing and what he calls a *"dogmatic* understanding"[655] of this event.

i. Mühlen's dogmatic understanding of the anointing. "According to the statements of Holy Scripture," Mühlen writes:

the anointing of Jesus with the Holy Spirit occurs at his baptism....For a dogmatic understanding [however],...one must say: Jesus possessed the fullness of the Spirit already from the first temporal moment of his existence. He is himself (together with the Father) the eternal origin of the Holy Spirit. He [thus] remains this origin of the Holy Spirit also as the Incarnate, so that also the Incarnate Son is never without the Holy Spirit.[656]

Mühlen follows Matthias Scheeben, then, in regarding the actual anointing of Christ with the Holy Spirit, as opposed to its subsequent manifestation after Christ's baptism, as at least temporally concurrent with the uniting of Christ's human nature with the Logos at the first moment of that nature's existence in Mary's womb. He follows Scheeben, likewise, in holding that "the Logos...anointed *himself.*"[657] Mühlen does not, however, follow Scheeben in equating the unction, with which Christ's zygotic human nature was invisibly anointed, with "nothing less than the fullness of the divinity of the Logos, which is substantially joined to the humanity and dwells in it incarnate."[658] Over against Scheeben, rather, Mühlen insists that:

in Scripture, in any event, a distinction is made between the man Jesus and the anointing that *comes* to him. In a mode similar to that by which the anointing comes to Jesus, in the early apostolic proclamation also the title "the Christ" [i.e. the anointed one] must be *added* to the proper name Jesus. The twelve proclaim Jesus as the Christ (Acts 5:42), for God has made the self-same Jesus, whom the Jews have crucified, Christ (χριστὸν ἐποίησεν, Acts 2:36).[659]

The Incarnation and the anointing differ, Mühlen explains, in that: a) the first effects the grace of union and the second the habitual grace of Christ; and b) the

---

[655] *Der Heilige Geist als Person*, § 7.12, p. 206.
[656] Ibid.
[657] Ibid. § 6.06, p. 175.
[658] *The Mysteries of Christianity* (Cyril Vollert, tr.; St. Louis and London: Herder, 1946), 332.
[659] *Der Heilige Geist als Person*, § 6.17.1, p. 184.

first is identical with the salvation-historical mission of the Son, while the second constitutes the mission *ad extra* of the Spirit. Now, Mühlen defines "mission," following Aquinas (*STh* I, 43, 2 ad 3), as an eternal procession with a temporal effect, or *terminus ad quem*, of the procession.[660]

Since the missions are not really distinct from the intra-Trinitarian processions, they naturally conform to these processions' order of origins: "the relation of the sender to the sent," Mühlen writes, "includes the inner-Trinitarian order of origins."[661] By defining the anointing as the mission of the Holy Spirit, therefore, Mühlen supplies himself with a sure argument for the conformity of the persons' order of operations in the anointing with their order of procession in the immanent Trinity. Quoting Aquinas (*STh* III, 7, 13 corp.), he writes, "The mission of the Son..., according to the order of nature, is prior to the mission of the Holy Spirit: as in the order of nature the Holy Spirit proceeds from the Son."[662]

ii. Grace and the person. Mühlen does not confine himself, however, to this stipulative mode of argumentation. For he recognizes that, by identifying the temporal effects of the missions of the Son and Spirit, respectively, with the grace of union and habitual grace, he implies that Christ's grace of union logically precedes his human nature's habitual grace. If one could prove that Christ's habitual grace logically precedes the grace of union, therefore, one could falsify Mühlen's proof of the correspondence of the economic with the immanent Trinity in the event of Christ's anointing. If Mühlen could establish that the grace of union logically precedes the endowment of Christ's human nature with habitual grace, and could accomplish this without appealing to the definition of the persons' missions as "the free continuation of...[the intra-Trinitarian] processions

---

[660] Ibid. §7.10, p. 203.
[661] Ibid. §7.06, p. 201.
[662] Ibid. §7.13, p. 207.

ad extra,"663 however, he could at least corroborate his interpretation of Christ's anointing with the Holy Spirit.

Such corroboration lies ready to hand, Mühlen believes, in the following remark of Thomas:

> A third reason for this order [i.e. for the precedence of the hypostatic union over Christ's endowment with habitual, sc. created, grace] can be derived from the end of grace. For it is ordained to acting well. Actions, however, are of *supposita* and individuals. Hence action, and consequently the grace that is ordained to it, presupposes an operating hypostasis. A hypostasis, however, is not presupposed in the human nature before the union...Therefore, the grace of union logically [*secundum intellectum*] precedes habitual grace [*STh* III, 7, 13 corp.].664

Mühlen glosses:

> According to...St. Thomas, the nature is that by which the agent acts (*principium quo*), whereas by the hypostasis or the *suppositum* the agent itself is meant (*principium quod agit*). The action is not possible without the *suppositum* which 'has' or 'bears' the nature. Insofar, now, as grace is ordained to acting well [*bene agere*], it presupposes the operating hypostasis. One can derive from this finding the universal principle: *GRACE PRESUPPOSES THE PERSON*.665

This principle, accordingly, dictates that the grace of union which personalizes Christ's human nature must enjoy at least a logical precedence over the endowment of that nature with habitual grace. Mühlen appears capable, therefore, of corroborating his interpretation of the anointing by means other than a stipulative and aprioristic appeal to the definition of "mission."

It seems, in fact, that, at least for those who identify Christ's anointing with the Holy Spirit with the bestowal of habitual grace on his human nature, Mühlen constructs quite a persuasive case for the correspondence of the immanent and the economic Trinity even in the difficult case of the anointing. Mühlen correlates the processions and the missions of the divine persons, moreover, in a way that resonates profoundly with certain patristic interpretations of Christ's anointing with the Holy Spirit.

---

663 Ibid. §7.10, p. 203.
664 Mühlen cites the passage in ibid. § 7.22, pp. 212–13.
665 Ibid. p. 213. The capitalization is Mühlen's.

iii. Patristic precedents. Athanasius, for instance, insists that Christ anoints his own human nature and that the Logos, as the second person of the divine Trinity, remains permanently the dispenser, and not the recipient, of the Holy Spirit. In Athanasius' words:

If, as our Lord declares, the Holy Spirit is his, if it receives of him and is sent by him, it cannot be conceived that the Word and Wisdom of God, as such, should receive an unction from that Spirit which he himself bestows. It was his flesh which was thus anointed, and he himself thus anointed it, and for this purpose, that the sanctification, which by this unction he conveyed to himself as man, might come to all human beings by him.[666]

Cyril of Alexandria, likewise, speaks of how "the Son anointed his own temple"[667] and maintains that although "the Son is supplier of the Holy Spirit: for all things of the Father's are naturally in his power[668],...he humanly received the Spirit among us...when he came down to us, not adding anything to himself insofar as he is understood to be God and Logos, but in himself principally as the chief of human nature introducing the Spirit of abounding joy."[669]

Like Mühlen, then, Athanasius and Cyril construe the anointing accounts in such a way that they reflect the order of persons revealed in the baptismal formula. In at least one respect, however, Mühlen's interpretation of Christ's anointing seems to excel these explanations of Athanasius and Cyril in clarity and accuracy. Cyril and Athanasius, in the passages just quoted, tend to downplay, if not entirely to ignore, the personal character of Christ's human nature insofar as it subsists in the eternal Logos. Mühlen, by contrast, admits and even accentuates this aspect of the mystery of Christ's anointing. "The Holy Spirit," Mühlen writes, "is sent to the already, in the sense of logical priority, personalized human nature of Jesus! From this point of view the sending of the Holy Spirit *ad extra*

---

[666] *Contra Arianos* 3.47; PG 26, 109C.
[667] *In Joannis Evangelium. Liber XI* at John 17:19; PG 74, 549D. In John 17:19, of course, Jesus says: "And for their sakes I sanctify myself, so that they also may be sanctified in truth."
[668] Cyril presumably alludes to Christ's words in John 16:15a: "All that the Father has is mine."
[669] *In Ps.* 44[45]:8; PG 69, 1040A. Cyril frequently emphasizes that Christ receives the Holy Spirit as man, not as God. Cf. e.g. *In Lucam* 3:22; PG 72:524D, *In Isaiam. Liber III. Tomus V*; PG 70, 849D and 852A, *De recte fide ad reginas*, XIII; PG 76, 1220D–1221A, and *Comm. In Joelem Prophetam* XXXV; PG 71, 377D and 380A.

includes not a relation of person to *nature* as the sending of the Son does, but a *relation of person to person*."[670]

iv. Difficulties. Mühlen correctly notes, that is to say, that, by virtue of the grace of union, Christ's human nature subsists as personal in the Logos before, in the sense of logical priority, the Holy Spirit endows it with habitual grace so that, when the Holy Spirit does so endow this nature, he acts not merely on a created nature, but on the person of the eternal Word. Now, although Mühlen himself underlines this aspect of the mystery, it constitutes a considerable difficulty for Mühlen's attempt to harmonize the anointing accounts with Rahner's ideas about the immanent and the economic Trinity.

For, according to Rahner's filioquist theology of the immanent Trinity, the Holy Spirit receives his personal being from the Father and the Son and is identical with his receptive relation to these two persons: a relation customarily termed "passive spiration." The Father and the Son, correspondingly are identical, albeit each in his own way, with the relation of active spiration: a relation that does not constitute a person of itself, because it involves no opposition of relation between the two already, in the logical sense, existing *spiratores*. The Father and the Son, as relative to the Spirit, therefore, are pure activity; and the Holy Spirit, as relative to them, is pure reception.

Now, the idea that the anointing of Christ with the Holy Spirit consists in the bestowal of habitual grace on the Logos suggests that, in the economy of salvation, the Son and the Spirit invert their relations; the eternal giver receives, and the eternal receiver gives. Mühlen ameliorates this problem, of course, by holding that the Son anoints himself, but he does not eliminate it. For even in the event that the Son anointed himself with the Holy Spirit, the Holy Spirit would still influence not an impersonal nature, but, as Mühlen rightly insists, the very person of the eternal Word. Mühlen's best efforts notwithstanding, then, the

---

[670] Mühlen, *Der Heilige Geist*, §7.13, p. 207.

pattern of mutual relations the divine persons manifest in the incident of the anointing still diverges from the pattern of the immanent Trinity. Mühlen ultimately does not succeed in his attempt to reconcile the scriptural narratives of Christ's anointing, when interpreted in accordance with the *Grundaxiom*, with Rahner's presuppositions concerning the theology of the Trinity.

c. The Spirit as intra-Trinitarian gift of the Father to the Son. The hypotheses considered thus far, however, by no means exhaust the range of options available to theologians desiring to resolve the dilemmas generated by the anointing accounts for Rahner's theology of the Trinity. François Bourassa[671] and Guy Vandevelde-Daillière,[672] for instance, attempt to harmonize the accounts of Christ's anointing, considered as a revelation of the intra-Trinitarian relations, with a filioquist understanding of the immanent Trinity by conceiving of the Holy Spirit as the intra-Trinitarian gift of the Father to the Son. Bourassa writes, accordingly:

"It is without measure that God *gives* the Spirit; the Father loves the Son and has *given* all to him" (John 3:34-5). The principal meaning of this revelation is that of the baptismal theophany: the constitution of *Christ*, of the man Jesus, in the dignity of the *Son of God*, object of the Father's pleasure in the Spirit of sanctification (Rom 1:4). But theology is justly unanimous: the mission is the procession of the person, the economic Trinity is the immanent Trinity, the Incarnation in a global sense, sc. the whole existence of the Son in the flesh, is the revelation of the "only begotten in the bosom of the Father" (John 1:18). Thus the Spirit is, above all, in the interior of the Trinity, "the gift of God," sc. the Gift of the Father to the Son "before the creation of the world," in whom the Father has given him all, giving *himself* to him, by engendering him as his only Son, in the effusion of his Love for him.[673]

According to François Bourassa, then, "The Son himself is constituted eternally Son of God 'in the bosom of the Father' in that the Father communicates

---

[671] Cf. esp. Bourassa's essay "Le Don de Dieu," in his *Questions de Théologie Trinitaire* (Rome: Università Gregoriana Editrice, 1970), 191–238.
[672] Cf. Vandevelde-Daillière's "L'«inversion trinitaire» chez H.U. von Balthasar," *NRT* 120 (1998), 370–83.
[673] "Le Don de Dieu," 212.

to him his plenitude in the gift of the Spirit;"[674] and one can infer this from the anointing of Christ with the Holy Spirit.

i. The identity of active spiration and active filiation. This view appears, of course, to conflict with filioquism, as Bourassa frankly admits. "If the Spirit is the gift of the Father to the Son *in generation*," he writes, "it seems, then, that generation takes place through the Spirit or in virtue of the Spirit. The Spirit is, therefore, the principle of the generation of the Son, whereas, according to the most firm facts of dogma, the generation of the Son is the principle of the procession of the Spirit."[675]

Bourassa, nevertheless, considers this conflict merely apparent. For, the principle, "In God all things are one, where no opposition of relation intervenes,"[676] implies that the Father and the Son spirate the Spirit *tamquam ab uno principio*; and the unity of the Father and Son as the single principle of the Spirit's procession, furthermore, implies that the Father's eternal generation of the Son is not really distinct from his eternal spiration of the Holy Spirit. Active filiation, in other words, is not really distinct from active spiration.

The identity of both the Son and the Father with active spiration, moreover, implies that the person-constituting relation of the Son, viz. passive filiation, which the Father bestows on him by generating him, is also identical with active spiration. Bourassa concludes, therefore, that "as in generating the Son..., the Father communicates to him all of his substance,..., he communicates to him also to be with him the overflowing source of the Spirit."[677] This last datum entails, in Bourassa's view, the central point of his argument: that just as the Holy Spirit appears as the gift of the Father to Jesus in the economy of salvation, so for all eternity the Father pours out the Holy Spirit on his immanent Word.

---

[674] Ibid.
[675] Ibid. 229.
[676] DH 1330
[677] "Le Don de Dieu," 229.

ii. The Holy Spirit as medius nexus of the Father and the Son. Bourassa recognizes, of course, that some might find his inference less than obvious; to bestow on the Son the capacity to share in active spiration is not at all to bestow on him passive spiration, the person-constituting relation of the Holy Spirit, which active spiration logically precedes. "Here," writes Bourassa, "the objection arises anew. Must one not then suppose the Spirit to be anterior to the Son, or...possessed anteriorly by the Father, or proceeding anteriorly from him in order to be given to the Son...?"[678] In answer to this criticism, Bourassa refers the reader to Aquinas' *STh* I, 37, 1 ad 3 in which Thomas writes:

The Holy Spirit is said to be the *nexus* of the Father and Son inasmuch as he is Love, because since the Father loves himself and the Son in a single dilection and *e converso*, the habit of the Father to the Son and *e converso* as lover to beloved is brought about [*importatur*] in the Holy Spirit as love. Yet from this very thing, that the Father and the Son love each other mutually, it must be that the mutual Love, who is the Holy Spirit, proceeds from both. According to origin, therefore, the Holy Spirit is not a medium, but the third person in the Trinity; according to the aforementioned habit [however], he is the *medius nexus* of the two, proceeding from both.

Now, Bourassa argues, one can draw a merely rational distinction between the Father's active spiration and his notional love for the Son, just as one can distinguish rationally between active filiation and active spiration. Yet, in the pristine simplicity of the Godhead, the Father's notional act of loving the Son and his notional act of generating the Son are really identical. Bourassa holds, accordingly, that if one prescinds from the question of origin and attends rather to the "order of circumincession," then one can reasonably say that the Father generates the Son through the Holy Spirit just as one can say that the Father generates the Son through his love for him.

Bourassa explicitly grants, then, that, according to the order of origin, the Father does not generate the Son by bestowing upon him the Holy Spirit. "According to the order of origin," Bourassa writes, "the Holy Spirit is the *third* person of the Trinity, but according to the circum-incession of the Father and the

---

[678] Ibid. 230.

Son, the Spirit, being their communion of love (*koinonia*), is *intermediary* between the two."[679] With the aid of his distinction between the order of origin and the order of circumincession, therefore, Bourassa might seem finally to succeed in transposing the divine persons' relations in the anointing into the immanent Trinity, as Rahner's *Grundaxiom* requires, without compromising the filioquist understanding of the immanent Trinity, which he and Rahner share.

iii. Difficulties. Two difficulties, however, call Bourassa's solution into question. First, it might seem that Rahner denies the possibility of mutual love among the persons of the Trinity. For, in his tractate on the Trinity in *Mysterium Salutis*, Rahner explicitly states that "there is not actually a *mutual* (presupposing two acts) love between the Father and the Son,"[680] and, indeed, that "within the Trinity there is no reciprocal 'Thou.'"[681] Second, one could plausibly argue that the Holy Spirit as such does not actually constitute a *medius nexus* between the Father and the Son. For, as Aquinas explains in *STh* I, 37, 2 corp., the Father loves the Son "by" the Holy Spirit not because the Holy Spirit constitutes the means whereby the Father performs this notional act, but because the Father's notional act of loving the Son effects the Holy Spirit's existence as a distinct, divine person. In Thomas' words:

Since things are commonly denominated from their forms, thus a white thing from whiteness and a human being from humanity, everything from which something is named has to this extent the habit of a form....Now, instances exist in which something is named through that which proceeds from it,...[i.e.] even from the term of its action, which is the effect, when this effect is included in the understanding of the action. We say, for instance,...that a tree flowers by its flowers, although the flowers are not the form of the tree, but a certain effect proceeding from it...[Now] truly, as it is taken notionally, to love is nothing other than to spirate love....As, therefore, a tree is said to flower by its flowers, so...the Father and the Son are said to love each other and us by the Holy Spirit or Love proceeding.

---

[679] Ibid. 231.
[680] *Trinity*, 106; "Der dreifaltige Gott," *MS* ii, 387. We modify Donceel's translation here significantly. Rahner's German reads: "es nicht eigentlich eine *gegenseitige* (zwei Akte voraussetzende) Liebe zwischen Vater und Sohn."
[681] Ibid. 76, n. 30; ebd. 366, Anm. 29.

Aquinas, then, thinks that one can truthfully assert that the Father loves the Son by the Holy Spirit only to the extent that the Holy Spirit constitutes the effect of his notional love, i.e. active spiration. Now, since active spiration: a) is the act in which the Father loves the Son; and b) is also the act in which the Father and Son unite so as to form a single principle of the Holy Spirit; it might seem c) that active spiration constitutes the bond that draws the Father and Son together, and not the Holy Spirit, which appears rather as the effect of active spiration's unitive power.

iv. Responses. The adequacy of Bourassa's interpretation of the anointing accounts, at least for the purpose of obviating the difficulties they pose for Rahner's theology of the Trinity, thus appears somewhat doubtful. The first difficulty, however, and, to a lesser degree, the second, appear quite surmountable. In order to refute the first charge, specifically, one need only note that Rahner explicitly affirms that the Holy Spirit does constitute the mutual love of the Father and the Son. In summarizing magisterial teaching on the subject, he affirms, without qualification, that the Holy Spirit's "'procession' is only cautiously indicated, although as such it is defined (*bestimmt*) as the procession of the mutual love of Father and Son."[682]

The two passages cited above as evidence for Rahner's opposition to this tenet, moreover, prove nothing of the sort. For, in the first passage, in which Rahner writes, "there is not actually a *mutual* (presupposing two acts) love between the Father and the Son," Rahner expressly excludes only a mutual love that would require of the Father and Son individually distinguished notional acts of love as opposed to their common act of notional love, active spiration. Likewise, when he denies the existence of a "mutual Thou" in the Trinity, Rahner seems to deny only the existence of distinct subjectivities who know each other through their own exclusive consciousnesses. For Rahner affirms in the same context that each

---

[682] Ibid. 67; ebd. 360.

Trinitarian person constitutes a "distinct subject in a rational nature"[683] and approvingly quotes Lonergan in the same work to the effect that "the three subjects are aware of each other through one consciousness which is possessed in a different way by the three of them."[684] It seems, then, that instead of peremptorily excluding the doctrine that identifies the Holy Spirit as the Father and Son's mutual love, Rahner explicitly endorses both the doctrine and its ontological presuppositions.

The second difficulty, viz. the charge that active spiration, instead of the Holy Spirit, constitutes the *medius nexus* of the first two Trinitarian persons, seems somewhat more imposing. One can plausibly argue, however, that this objection rests on a false dichotomy. Even if, that is to say, active spiration serves as a unitive bond in a much stricter sense than the Holy Spirit, the Holy Spirit may still qualify as the *medius nexus* of the Father and Son in some less rigorous acceptation of the term. For, first, as Aquinas suggests, the Father and the Son do love each other "by" the Holy Spirit in the same sense as a tree flowers "by" its flowers so that one can reasonably characterize the Holy Spirit as the *forma* by which the Father and Son love each other, albeit in a highly attenuated sense. Second, and perhaps more importantly, the Holy Spirit does constitute the *raison d'être* of active spiration so that, in the order of intentions if not in the order of execution, it takes precedence over active spiration as the more ultimate cause of the Father and Son's unity in their act of notional love. It seems, therefore, that one can do justice to the concerns of the second objection without categorically rejecting Bourassa's identification of the Holy Spirit with the *medius nexus* of Father and Son. Apparently, then, Bourassa succeeds in proving that the economic Trinity corresponds to the immanent Trinity, as understood in orthodox Latin Trinitarianism, even in the difficult case of Christ's anointing with the Holy Spirit.

---

[683] Ibid. 75, n. 29; ebd. 366, Anm. 28.
[684] Ibid. 107, n. 29; ebd. 387, Anm. 29.

v. The order of circumincession and human knowledge of the Trinity.
Bourassa succeeds in interpreting the anointing in such a way that it undermines neither the *Grundaxiom* nor Latin Trinitarianism, however, only at the expense of de-functionalizing the *Grundaxiom*. If the economy of salvation, that is to say, presupposes not one, but two intra-Trinitarian τάξεις, then the *Grundaxiom* does not suffice to warrant an inference from the economy of salvation, unaccompanied by a verbal revelation, to any particular doctrine of the immanent Trinity. For if two intra-Trinitarian τάξεις co-existed, then human beings, possessing neither a verbal revelation nor the beatific vision, would be incapable of determining which τάξις a particular economic manifestation of the immanent Trinity revealed.

If two intra-Trinitarian τάξεις co-existed, moreover, the divine persons' roles in the economy of salvation would convey no sure information about the Trinity's eternal constitution. For if the economic Trinity corresponded to the immanent Trinity even if the divine persons' operations occurred in the order, Father—Spirit—Son, or, perhaps, Spirit—Son—Father,[685] then the *Grundaxiom* would allow for a sending of the Son by the Holy Spirit or, for that matter, an incarnation of the Holy Spirit or even the Father. Now, given Rahner's presupposition that verbal revelation simply does not occur, the very idea that such things could happen would, in Rahner's words:

> wreak havoc with theology. There would no longer be any connection between "mission" and the intra-Trinitarian life. Our sonship in grace would in fact have absolutely nothing to do with the Son's sonship, since it might equally well be brought about without any modification by another incarnate person. That which God is for us would tell us absolutely nothing about that which he is in himself, as triune.[686]

Yet, if an order of circumincession exists in the immanent Trinity alongside the order of origin, and a correspondence of the persons' order of operations to

---

[685] Such would be the order if one considered the persons: a) insofar as they are constituted by the processions; and b) according to the order of intention so that the Holy Spirit, as the τέλος of the processions, would appear first; the Son, as the mediate term of the processions, would appear second; and the Father, as the ultimate origin of the processions, would appear last.
[686] *Trinity*, 30; "Der dreifaltige Gott," *MS* ii, 333.

either order fulfills the requirements of the *Grundaxiom*, then an incarnation of the Holy Spirit, a pouring out of the Son at Pentecost, etc. could occur without contravening the *Grundaxiom*. Bourassa's harmonization of Rahner's *Grundaxiom* and the biblical anointing accounts thus renders the axiom ineffectual for the purpose of deriving the doctrine of the Trinity from an economy of salvation not illuminated by verbal revelation.

d. Conclusion. The test of Rahner's *Grundaxiom* that we have conducted, accordingly, yields mixed results. The difficulties posed for the axiom by the scriptural accounts of Jesus' anointing with the Holy Spirit seem not to invalidate Rahner's most fundamental claim: viz. that God's economic self-manifestation necessarily corresponds to the reality of God's inner being. For, as we have seen, if one follows Bourassa in positing the existence of an intra-Trinitarian order of circumincession, one can locate an archetype of the τάξις Father–Spirit–Son in the immanent Trinity. The test, then, confirms, although it does not prove, a flexible version of the *Grundaxiom* that allows for the appearance of divergent τάξεις in the economy of salvation.

The test, however, calls into question the viability of the methodological program that Rahner intends for the *Grundaxiom* to serve. If, that is to say, God may express Godself in the order Father–Spirit–Son as well as the order of Father–Son–Spirit, then one cannot discern the intra-Trinitarian order of origins simply by transposing a τάξις one encounters in the economy of salvation into the immanent Trinity. In order to discern the order of origins, rather, one requires additional information as to the significance of the various τάξεις: information the economy of salvation seems ill-suited to provide. To the extent that the identification of the intra-Trinitarian order of origins as Father–Son–Spirit is integral to Rahner's own filioquist Trinitarianism, then; Rahner's *Grundaxiom* and the economy of salvation, considered together, constitute an inadequate basis for a practicable and, by Rahner's standards, orthodox Trinitarian theology.

IV. CONCLUSION

This work as a whole, then, has consisted in a thoroughgoing critique of Karl Rahner's conviction that human beings come to learn of the doctrine of the Trinity on the basis of inferences from their experience of divine self-communication as mediated by the events of salvation history and objectified in Scripture. We have sought, in particular, to establish four, principal theses. First, if a simple God underwent the ontological transformation that Rahner considers requisite to divine self-communication, that God, *qua* communicated, would be identical in no respect whatsoever with the formerly uncommunicated divine self. In this case, that is to say, the economic Trinity would bear none of the attributes that once characterized the Trinity as immanent. For, the attributes of a simple substance being *per definitionem* identical to each other, one cannot change any aspect of a simple God without transforming that God into an entirely different being.

Second, even if such a God could exempt the intra-Trinitarian relations from the comprehensive metamorphosis entailed by divine becoming, human beings, who possess neither the beatific vision nor a verbal/conceptual revelation concerning the intra-divine life, could never know that the threefold structure they observe in the economy of salvation corresponds to the immanent Trinity. The most exact correspondence between οἰκονομία and θεολογία, that is to say, would warrant belief in an immanent Trinity by *viatores* only if they possessed a verbal/conceptual revelation that informed them of the correspondence.

Third, Rahner's belief that "in God the relation is real only through its identity with the real divine essence,"[687] implies that God cannot reveal the doctrine of the Trinity to human beings in the manner that Rahner proposes. For if the divine

---

[687] Ibid. 71; ebd. 363.

persons possess, as peculiar to themselves, only their reference to each other and the properties that follow immediately therefrom, then they can influence created realities only through the one, divine omnipotence, which is equally identical with each of the persons. In this case, it seems, the divine persons' influence on creation would be as unitary as the divine omnipotence itself; and a threefold pattern of agency in the economy, from which human beings could infer the persons' immanent triunity, would be correspondingly inconceivable.

Fourth and finally, one can reconcile the biblical accounts of Christ's anointing with the Holy Spirit, when interpreted in accordance with the *Grundaxiom*, with Latin Trinitarianism only if one posits the existence of multiple τάξεις in the inner-Trinitarian life and thereby strips the *Grundaxiom* of its power to warrant inferences from the divine acts in the economy of salvation to the doctrine of the immanent Trinity. In the foregoing, we have argued extensively for each of these four theses: any one of which, if substantiated, would suffice to render Rahner's account of how human beings come to know of the Trinity implausible.

Now, to a certain extent at least, Rahner's *Grundaxiom*, or some principle very much like it, seems indispensable to any valid argument from God's revelation in deeds alone to the doctrine of the immanent Trinity. To the extent that this is the case, our four theses call into question the practicability of all attempts to derive the doctrine of the Trinity from God's revelation in deed alone. Given the wide diversity of presuppositions among contemporary theologians, these four assertions do not, naturally, suffice to invalidate in a universally satisfactory way every argument from the structure of divine action in salvation history to the doctrine of the immanent Trinity. The four theses and the arguments advanced on their behalf, however, do lend considerable support to the following statement by Walter Cardinal Kasper on the origins and grounds of Trinitarian belief.

> We cannot deduce the immanent Trinity by a kind of extrapolation from the economic Trinity. This was certainly not the path the early church followed in developing the doctrine of the Trinity in the form of confession and dogma. As we have seen, the early church's starting point was rather the baptismal confession of faith, which in turn was derived from the risen Lord's

commission concerning baptism. Knowledge of the trinitarian mystery was [and still is] thus due directly to the revelation of the Word and not to a process of deduction.[688]

---

[688] *The God of Jesus Christ* (Matthew J. O'Connell, tr.; New York: Crossroad, 1984), 276.

BIBLIOGRAPHY

Works by Karl Rahner

"The Act of Faith and the Content of Faith," *TI* xxi, 151–61; "Glaubensakt und Glaubensinhalt," *ST* xv, 152–62.

"Anonymous Christians," *TI* vi, 390–98; "Die Anonymen Christen," *ST* vi, 545–54.

"Antwort." *Orientierung* 14 (1950), 141–5.

"Buch Gottes—Buch der Menschen," *ST* xvi, 278–91.

"Brief Observations on Systematic Christology Today," *TI* xxi, 228–38; "Kleine Anmerkungen zur systematischen Christologie heute," *ST* xv, 225–35.

"Christian Dying," *TI* xviii, 226–56; "Das christliche Sterben," *ST* xiii, 269–304.

"The Christian Understanding of Redemption," *TI* xxi, 239–54; "Das christliche Verständnis der Erlösung," *ST* xv, 236–50.

"Christianity and the 'New Man,'" *TI* v, 135–53; "Das Christentum und der 'Neue Mensch,'" *SW* xv, 138–53.

"Christmas in the Light of the Ignatian Exercises," *TI* xvii, 3–7; "Weihnacht im Licht der Exerzitien," *ST* xii, 329–34.

"Christology in the Setting of Modern Man's Understanding of Himself and of His World," *TI* xi, 215–29; "Christologie im Rahmen des modernen Selbst- und Weltverständnisses," *SW* xv, 601–11.

"Christology Today," *TI* xxi, 220–27; "Christologie heute," *ST* xv, 217–24.

"Christology within an Evolutionary View of the World," *TI* v, 157–92; "Die Christologie innerhalb einer evolutiven Weltanschauung," *SW* xv, 219–47.

"The Church's Commission to Bring Salvation and the Humanization of the World," *TI* xiv, 295–313; "Heilsauftrag der Kirche und Humanisierung der Welt," *SW* xv, 711–26.

"The Concept of Mystery in Catholic Theology," *TI* iv, 36–73; "Über den Begriff des Geheimnisses in der katholischen Theologie," *SW* xii, 101–135.

"Concerning the Relationship between Nature and Grace," *TI* i, 297–317; "Über das Verhältnis von Natur und Gnade," *ST* i, 323–45.

"The Congregation of the Faith and the Commission of Theologians," *TI* xiv, 98–115; "Glaubenskongregation und Theologenkommission," *ST* x, 338–57.

"Considerations on the Development of Dogma," *TI* iv, 3–35; Überlegungen zur Dogmenentwicklung," *SW* ix, 442–71.

"Current Problems in Christology," *TI* i, 149–200; "Probleme der Christologie von heute," *SW* xii, 261–301.

"The Dignity and Freedom of Man," *TI* ii, 235–63; "Würde und Freiheit des Menschen," *SW* x, 184–206.

"Dogmatic Questions on Easter," *TI* iv, 121–133; "Dogmatische Fragen zur Osterfrömmigkeit," *SW* xii, 323–34.

"Dogmatic Reflections on the Knowledge and Self-Consciousness of Christ," *TI* v, 193–215; "Dogmatische Erwägungen über das Wissen und Selbstbewußtsein Christi," *SW* xii, 335–52.

"Dreifaltigkeit," *KThW*[1], *SW* xvii/i, 535–8.

"The Experience of God Today," *TI* xi, 149–65; "Gotteserfahrung heute," *ST* ix, 161–76.

"Experience of the Spirit and Existential Commitment," *TI* xvi, 24–34; "Erfahrung des Geistes und existentielle Entscheidung," *ST* xii, 41–53.

"The Foundation of Belief Today," *TI* xvi, 3–23; "Glaubensbegründung heute," *ST* xii, 17–40.

Foundations of Christian Faith: An Introduction to the Idea of Christianity (William V. Dych, trans.; New York: Crossroad, 1978); *Grundkurs des Glaubens: Einführung in den Begriff des Christentums* in *SW* xxvi, 3–442.

"Gott V. Die Lehre des kirchl. Lehramtes," *LThK*[2] iv, *SW* xvii/i, 264–7.

"Guilt—Responsibility—Punishment," *TI* vi, 197–217; "Schuld—Verantwortung—Strafe," *ST* vi, 238–61.

Hearer of the Word: Laying the Foundation for a Philosophy of Religion (Joseph Donceel, tr.; Andrew Tallon, ed.; New York: Continuum, 1994); *Hörer des Wortes: Zur Grundlegung einer Religionsphilosophie* in *SW* iv, 2–278.

"Heilige Schrift," *LThK*², *SW* xvii/i, 284–8.

"The Hermeneutics of Eschatological Assertions," *TI* iv, 323–46; "Theologische Prinzipien der Hermeneutik eschatologischer Aussagen," *SW* xii, 489–510.

"The Hiddenness of God," *TI* xvi, 227–43 at 240; "Über die Verborgenheit Gottes," *ST* xii, 285–305.

"The Historicity of Theology," *TI* ix, 64–82; "Zur Geschichtlichkeit der Theologie," *ST* viii, 88–110.

"History of the World and Salvation-History," *TI* v, 97–114; "Weltgeschichte und Heilsgeschichte," *SW* x, 590–604.

Ich Glaube an Jesus Christus (Theologische Meditationen 21; Einsiedeln: Benziger, 1968).

"Ideas for a Theology of Death," *TI* xiii, 169–86; "Zu einer Theologie des Todes," *ST* x, 181–99.

"Ideology and Christianity," *TI* vi 43–58; "Ideologie und Christentum," *SW* xv, 395–408.

"The Ignatian Mysticism of Joy in the World," *TI* iii, 277–93; "Die ignatianische Mystik der Weltfreudigkeit," *ST* iii, 329–48.

"Immanent and Transcendent Consummation of the World," *TI* x, 273–89; "Immanente und transzendente Vollendung der Welt," *SW* xv, 544–56.

"Inkarnation," *SM* ii, *SW* xvii/ii, 1096–1109.

"Inspiration in the Bible," in *Studies in Modern Theology* (W. J. O'Hara et al, tr.; London: Burns & Oates, 1965), 7–86; "Über die Schriftinspiration," *SW* xii, 3–58.

"Intellectual Honesty and Christian Faith," *TI* vii, 47–71; "Intellektuelle Redlichkeit und christlicher Glaube," *ST* vii, 54–76.

"Intellectual Patience with Ourselves," *TI* xxiii, 38–49; "Über die intellektuelle Geduld mit sich selbst," *ST* xv, 303–14.

"The Intermediate State," *TI* xvii, 114–24; "Über den 'Zwischenzustand,'" *ST* xii, 455–66.

"An Investigation of the Incomprehensibility of God in St. Thomas Aquinas," *TI* xvi, 244–54; "Fragen zur Unbegreiflichkeit Gottes nach Thomas von Aquin," *ST* xii, 306–19.

"Jesus Christ in the Non–Christian Religions," *TI* xvii, 39–50; "Jesus Christus in der nichtchristlichen Religionen," *ST* xii, 370–83.

"Jesus Christ—The Meaning of Life," *TI* xxi, 208–19; "Jesus Christus—Sinn des Lebens," *ST* xv, 206–16.

"The Liberty of the Sick, Theologically Considered," *TI* xvii, 100–113; "Die Freiheit des Kranken in theologischer Sicht," *ST* xii, 439–54.

"The Life of the Dead," *TI* iv, 347–54; "Das Leben der Toten," *SW* xii, 540–46.

"Magisterium and Theology," *TI* xviii, 54–73; "Lehramt und Theologie," *ST* xiii, 69–92.

"Mary's Virginity," *TI* xix, 218–31; "Jungfräulichkeit Marias," *ST* xiii, 361–77.

"The Meaning of Frequent Confession of Devotion," *TI* iii, 177–89; "Vom Sinn der häufigen Andachtsbeichte," *SW* xi, 401–11.

"Membership of the Church According to the Teaching of Pius XII's Encyclical 'Mystici Corporis Christi,'" *TI* ii, 1–88; "Die Gliedschaft in der Kirche nach der Lehre der Enzyklika Pius' XII. 'Mystici Corporis Christi,'" *SW* x, 3–71.

"The Mystery of the Trinity," *TI* xvi, 255–9; "Um das Geheimnis der Dreifaltigkeit," *ST* xii, 320–25.

"Natural Science and Reasonable Faith ," *TI* xxi, 16–55; "Naturwissenschaft und vernünftiger Glaube," *ST* xv, 24–62.

"Nature and Grace," *TI* iv, 165–88; "Natur und Gnade," *ST* iv, 209–36.

"Observations on the Concept of Revelation" in Karl Rahner and Joseph Ratzinger, *Revelation and Tradition* (W. J. O'Hara, tr.; London: Burns & Oates, 1966), 9–25; "Bemerkungen zum Begriff der Offenbarung," in idem, *Offenbarung und Überlieferung* (QD 25; Freiburg im Breisgau: Herder, 1965), 11–24.

"Observations on the Doctrine of God in Catholic Dogmatics," *TI* ix, 127–44; "Bemerkungen zur Gotteslehre in der katholischen Dogmatik," *ST* viii, 165–86.

"On the Current Relationship between Philosophy and Theology," *TI* xiii, 61–79; "Zum heutigen Verhältnis von Philosophie und Theologie," *ST* x, 70–88.

"On the Relationship between Theology and the Contemporary Sciences," *TI* xiii, 94–102; "Zum Verhältnis zwischen Theologie und heutigen Wissenschaften," *SW* xv, 704–10.

"On the Theology of the Incarnation," *TI* iv, 105–20; "Zur Theologie der Menschwerdung," *SW* xii, 309–22.

"On Truthfulness," *TI* vii, 229–59; "Über die Wahrhaftigkeit," *SW* x, 447–68.

"Oneness and Threefoldness of God in Discussion with Islam," *TI* xviii, 105–21; "Einzigkeit und Dreifaltigkeit im Gespräch mit dem Islam," *ST* xiii, 129–47.

"Panentheismus," *KThW*[1], *SW* xvii/i, 744.

"Person," *KThW*[1], *SW* xvii/i, 752–5.

"Philosophy and Philosophising in Theology," *TI* ix, 46–63; "Philosophie und Philosophieren in der Theologie," *ST* viii, 66–87.

"Philosophy and Theology," *TI* vi, 71–81; "Philosophie und Theologie," *SW* xii, 216–33.

"Pluralism in Theology and the Unity of the Creed in the Church," *TI* xi, 3–23; "Der Pluralismus in der Theologie und die Einheit des Bekenntnisses in der Kirche," *ST* ix, 11–33.

"The Position of Christology in the Church between Exegesis and Dogmatics," *TI* xi, 185–214; "Kirchliche Christologie zwischen Exegese und Dogmatik," *ST* ix, 197–226.

"Possible Courses for the Theology of the Future," *TI* xiii, 32–60; "Über künftige Wege der Theologie," *ST* x, 41–69.

"Priest and Poet," *TI* iii, 294–317; "Priester und Dichter," *SW* xii, 421–40.

"Priestly Existence," *TI* iii, 239–62; "Priesterliche Existenz," *ST* iii, 285–312.

"Questions of Controversial Theology on Justification," *TI* iv, 189–218; "Fragen der Kontroverstheologie über die Rechfertigung," *ST* iv, 237–71.

"Reconciliation and Vicarious Representation," *TI* xxi, 255–69; "Versöhnung und Stellvertretung," *ST* xv, 251–64.

"Reflections on Methodology in Theology," *TI* xi, 68–114; "Überlegungen zur Methode der Theologie," *ST* ix, 79–126.

"Reflections on the Contemporary Intellectual Formation of Future Priests," *TI* vi, 113–38; "Über die theoretische Ausbildung künftiger Priester heute," *SW* xvi, 434–55.

"Remarks on the Importance of the History of Jesus for Catholic Dogmatics," *TI* xiii, 201–12; "Bemerkungen zur Bedeutung der Geschichte Jesu für die katholische Dogmatik," *ST* x, 215–26.

"Replik: Bemerkungen zu: Hans Küng, 'Im Interesse der Sache,'" *StZ* 187 (1971), 145–60.

"Schrift, Heilige Schrift," *SM* iv, *SW* xvii/ii, 1264–74.

"Schriftbeweis," *KThW*[1], *SW* xvii/i, 800.

"Schriftbeweis," *KThW*[10], 376.

"Science as a 'Confession'?" *TI* iii, 385–400; "Wissenschaft als 'Konfession'?" *SW* xv, 171–83.

"Scripture and Theology," *TI* vi, 89–97; "Heilige Schrift und Theologie," *SW* xii, 226–33.

"Scripture and Tradition," *TI* vi, 98–112; "Heilige Schrift und Tradition," *ST* vi, 121–38.

"Some Implications of the Scholastic Concept of Uncreated Grace," *TI* i, 319–46; "Zur scholastischen Begrifflichkeit der ungeschaffenen Gnade," *ST* i, 347–76.

"The Specific Character of the Christian Concept of God," *TI* xxi, 185–95; "Über die Eigenart des christlichen Gottesbegriffs," *ST* xv, 185–94.

Spirit in the World (Johannes B. Metz, ed., William V. Dych, trans.; New York: Herder, 1968); *Geist in Welt: Zur Metaphysik der endlichen Erkenntnis bei Thomas von Aquin* in *SW* ii, 5–300.

"The Theological Concept of Concupiscentia" *TI* i, 347–82; "Zum theologischen Begriff der Konkupiszenz," *SW* viii, 3–32.

"Theological Observations on the Concept of Time," *TI* xi, 288–308; "Theologische Bemerkungen zum Zeitbegriff," *SW* xv, 622–37.

"Theological Reflections on the Problem of Secularisation," *TI* x, 318–48; "Theologische Reflexionen zum Problem der Säkularisation," *ST* viii, 637–666.

"Theology and Anthropology," *TI* ix, 28–45; "Theologie und Anthropologie," *ST* viii, 43–65.

"Theology in the New Testament," *TI* v, 23–41; "Theologie im Neuen Testament," *SW* xii, 193–208.

"Theology of the Symbol," *TI* iv, 221–52; "Zur Theologie des Symbols," *SW* xviii, 423–57.

"Theos in the New Testament," *TI* i, 79–148; "Theos im Neuen Testament," *SW* iv, 346–403.

"Thomas Aquinas on Truth, "*TI* xiii, 13–31; "Die Wahrheit bei Thomas von Aquin," *SW* ii, 303–16.

"Thoughts on the Possibility of Belief Today," *TI* v, 3–22; "Über die Möglichkeit des Glaubens heute," *SW* xii, 574–89.

"Thoughts on the Theology of Christmas," *TI* iii, 24–34; "Zur Theologie der Weihnachtsfeier," *SW* xiv, 97–105.

"Transformations in the Church and Secular Society," *TI* xvii, 167–80; "Kirchliche Wandlungen und Profangesellschaft," *ST* xii, 513–28.

"Trinität," *SM* iv, *SW* xvii/ii, 1337–49.

The Trinity (Joseph Donceel, tr.; New York: Herder, 1970); "Der dreifaltige Gott als transzendenter Urgrund der Heilsgeschichte" in *MS* ii, 317–401.

"Unfehlbarkeit," *KThW*[10], 425–7.

"Unity of the Church—Unity of Mankind," *TI* xx, 154–72; "Einheit der Kirche—Einheit der Menschheit," *SW* xxvii, 156–72.

"What is a Dogmatic Statement?" *TI* v 42–66; "Was ist eine dogmatische Aussage?" *SW* xii, 150–70.

"What the Church Officially Teaches and What the People Actually Believe," *TI* xxii, 165–75; "Offizielle Glaubenslehre der Kirche und faktische Gläubigkeit des Volkes," *ST* xvi, 217–30.

"The Word and the Eucharist," *TI* iv, 253–86; "Wort und Eucharistie," *SW* xviii, 596–626.

"The Works of Mercy and Their Reward," *TI* vii, 268–74; "Preis der Barmherzigkeit," *ST* vii, 259–64.

"Yesterday's History of Dogma and Theology for Tomorrow" *TI* xviii, 3–34; "Dogmen- und Theologiegeschicte von gestern für morgen," *ST* xiii, 11–47.

Works by Other Authors

Nicholas Adams, "The Present Made Future: Karl Rahner's Eschatological Debt to Heidegger," *Faith and Philosophy* 17 (2000), 191–211.

Barnabas Ahern, "The Indwelling Spirit, Pledge of Our Inheritance (Eph 1:14)," *CBQ* 9 (1947), 179–89.

Colin Allen and Michael Hand, *Logic Primer* (Cambridge, MA and London: MIT Press, 2001^2).

Athanasius, *Contra Arianos*; PG 26, 12–468A.

Augustine, *Confessiones* in CCL 27, passim.

—— *Epistula* 187 in CSEL 57, 81–119.

—— *De Trinitate* in CCL 50–50A.

Michael Barnes, "Demythologization in the Theology of Karl Rahner," *TS* 55 (1994), 24–45.

Basil, *Ep.* 125 in *Saint Basile: Lettres: Tome II* (Yves Courtonne, ed. and tr.; CUFr; Paris: Les belles lettres, 1961), 30–34.

Louis Billot, *De Deo Uno et Trino: Commentarius in Prima Parte S. Thomae* (Prati: Giachetti, 1910^5).

Charles René Billuart, *Cursus Theologiae: Tomus II: De Trinitate: De Angelis: De Opere Sex Dierum et Pars Prima de Incarnatione* (Paris: LeCoffre, 1878).

Leonardo Boff, *Trinity and Society* (Paul Burns, tr.; Maryknoll, NY: Orbis, 1988).

Henri Bouëssé and J. J. Latour, ed., *Problèmes actuels de Christologie: Travaux du Symposium de L'arbresle 1961* (Bruges: Desclée de Brouwer, 1965).

François Bourassa, "Le Don de Dieu," in idem, *Questions de Théologie Trinitaire* (Rome: Università Gregoriana Editrice, 1970), 191–238.

Denis J. M. Bradley, "Rahner's *Spirit in the World*: Aquinas or Hegel," *Thomist* 41 (1977), 167–99.

Philip Cary, "On Behalf of Classical Trinitarianism: A Critique of Rahner on the Trinity," *Thomist* 56 (1992), 365–405.

David Coffey, *Deus Trinitas: The Doctrine of the Triune God* (Oxford: OUP, 1999).

—— "Some Resources for Students of *La nouvelle théologie*" *Philosophy & Theology* 11 (1999), 367–402.

—— "The Whole Rahner on the Supernatural Existential," *TS* 65 (2004), 95–118.

J. A. Colombo, "Rahner and His Critics: Lindbeck and Metz," *Thomist* 56 (1992), 71–96.

Yves Congar, *I Believe in the Holy Spirit 1: Revelation and the Experience of the Spirit* (David Smith, tr.; New York: Seabury, 1983).

—— *I Believe in the Holy Spirit 3: The River of Life Flows in the East and in the West* (David Smith, tr.; New York: Seabury, 1983).

The Creeds of the Evangelical Protestant Churches (Philip Schaff, ed. and tr.; London: Hodder & Stoughton, 1877).

Cyril of Alexandria, *Commentarius in Isaiam*; PG 70, 9A–1450C.

—— *Commentarius in Joannis Evangelium*; PG 73, passim; PG 74, 9A–756C.

—— *Commentarius in Joelem Prophetam*; PG 71, 328B–408A.

—— *Commentarius in Lucam*; PG 72, 476A–949C.

—— *De recte fide ad reginas*; PG 76, 1201A–1336B.

—— *Explanatio in Psalmos*; PG 69, 717A–1276B.

Martin J. De Nys, "God, Creatures, and Relations: Revisiting Classical Theism," *JR* 81 (2001), 595–614.

Émile Delaye, "Ein Weg zur Bestimmung des Verhältnisses von Natur und Gnade." *Orientierung* 14 (1950), 138–41.

Didymus of Alexandria, *De Spiritu Sancto*, PG 39, 1034B–1086B.

Emmanuel Durand, "L'autocommunication trinitaire: Concept clé de la *connexio mysteriorum* rahnérienne," *RT* 102 (2002), 569–613.

François-Xavier Durrwell, "Pour une christologie selon l'Esprit Saint," *NRT* 114 (1992), 653–77.

—— *Holy Spirit of God: An Essay in Biblical Theology* (Benedict Davies, trans.; London: Geoffrey Chapman, 1986); *L'Esprit Saint de Dieu* (Paris: Cerf, 1985[2]).

William V. Dych, *Karl Rahner* (London: Geoffrey Chapman, 1992).

Peter Eicher, *Die anthropologische Wende: Karl Rahners philosophischer Weg vom Wesen des Menschen zur personalen Existenz* (Freiburg [Schweiz]: Universitätsverlag, 1970).

Leo Elders, *The Metaphysics of Being of St. Thomas Aquinas in a Historical Perspective* (Leiden, Boston, and Köln: Brill, 1993).

Enchiridion symbolorum, definitionem, et declarationum de rebus fidei et morum (Heinrich Denzinger, ed.; Clement Bannwart and Johannes B. Umberg, rev.; Freiburg-im-Breisgau: Herder, 1951[27]).

Epistula Jacobi apocrypha: Die zweite Schrift aus Nag-Hammadi-Codex I (Dankwart Kirchner, ed., trans., and comm.; TU 136; Berlin: Akademie-Verlag, 1989).

Cornelio Fabro, *La svolta antropologica di Karl Rahner* (2d ed.; Problemi attuali; Milan: Rusconi, 1974).

Klaus Fischer, "Kritik der 'Grundpositionen'? Kritische Anmerkungen zu B. van der Heijdens Buch über Karl Rahner," *ZKT* 99 (1977), 74–89.

—— *Der Mensch als Geheimnis: Die Anthropologie Karl Rahners* (Ökumenische Forschungen 2.5; Freiburg: Herder, 1974)

Thomas Peter Fössel, "Warum ein Existential *übernatürlich* ist: Anmerkungen zur kontroversen Diskussion um Karl Rahners Theologoumenon vom 'übernatürlichen Existential,'" *ThPh* 80 (2005), 389–411.

Barthélemy Froget, *The Indwelling of the Holy Spirit in the Souls of the Just* (Sydney A. Raemers, tr.; Baltimore: Carroll Press, 1950³).

Simon Gaine, *Indwelling Spirit and a New Creation: The Relationship between Uncreated Grace and Created Grace in Neo-Scholastic Catholic Theology* (Oxford: D.Phil. Diss., 1994).

Paul Galtier, *L'Habitation en nous des trois Personnes: Le fait—le mode* (Paris: Beauchesne, 1928²).

Reginald Garrigou-Lagrange, *Christ the Savior: A Commentary on the Third Part of St. Thomas' Theological Summa* (Bede Rose, tr.; St. Louis and London: Herder, 1950).

—— *God: His Existence and Nature: Vol. II* (Bede Rose, tr.; St. Louis and London: Herder, 1946).

—— *The One God: A Commentary on the First Part of St. Thomas' Theological Summa* (Bede Rose, tr.; St. Louis and London: Herder, 1944).

—— *The Trinity and God the Creator: A Commentary on St. Thomas' Theological Summa, I, q. 27-119* (Frederic C. Eckhoff, tr.; St. Louis and London: Herder, 1952).

Marcelo González, *La relación entre Trinidad económica e inmanente: el "axioma fundamental" de K. Rahner y su recepción: líneas para continuar la reflexión* (Corona Lateranensis 40; Rome: Pontificia Università lateranense, 1996).

Gregory of Nazianzus, *Oratio* 31; SC 250, 276–342.

Gregory of Nyssa, *Oratio catechetica* in *Opera dogmatica minora, Pars IV* (Ekkehard Mühlenberg, ed.; GNO 3-IV; Leiden, New York, and Köln: Brill, 1996), passim.

Georg Wilhelm Friedrich Hegel, *Wissenschaft der Logik 1: Die Lehre vom Sein* (ed. Friedrich Hogemann und Walter Jaeschke; Gesammelte Werke 21; Hamburg: Meiner, 1984).

William J. Hill, "Uncreated Grace—A Critique of Karl Rahner," *Thomist* 27 (1963), 333–356.

Heinrich Hurter, *Theologia Specialis: Pars Prior: De Deo Uno et Trino, De Deo Creatore, et De Verbo Incarnato* (Innsbruck: Libraria Academica Wagneriana, 1885[5]).

Jerome, *Commentarius in Esaiam*; CCL 73–73A, passim.

—— *Commentarius in Titum*; CCL 77C, 3–73.

John of Damascus, *Expositio Fidei* in *Die Schriften des Johannes von Damaskos* 2 (Bonifatius Kotter, ed.; PTS 12; Berlin and New York: Gruyter, 1973), passim.

Eberhard Jüngel, *The Doctrine of the Trinity: God's Being is in Becoming* (Horton Harris, tr.; SJTh.OP; Edinburgh: Scottish Academic Press, 1976).

Bernard Jungmann, *Institutiones theologiae dogmaticae specialis: Tractatus de gratia* (Rome: Marietti, 1873).

Philipp Kaiser, *Die Gott-menschliche Einigung in Christus als Problem der spekulativen Theologie seit der Scholastik* (MThS.S 36; München: Max Hueber, 1968).

Walter Kasper, *The God of Jesus Christ* (Matthew J. O'Connell, tr.; New York: Crossroad, 1984).

Anthony Kelly, *The Trinity of Love: A Theology of the Christian God* (New Theology Series 4; Wilmington, Del.: Michael Glazier, 1989).

Cornelius Keppeler, "Begnadung als berechtigte Forderung? Gedanken zur Bedeutung des übernatürlichen Existentials in der Gnadenlehre Karl Rahners," *ZKT* 126 (2004), 65–82.

Karen Kilby, *Karl Rahner: Theology and Philosophy* (London and New York: Routledge, 2004).

Kompendium der Glaubensbekenntnisse und kirchlichen Lehrentscheidungen, (Heinrich Denzinger, ed.; Peter Hünermann, rev.; Freiburg-im-Breisgau: Herder, 1991[37]).

Günter Kruck, "Christlicher Glaube und Moderne: Eine Analyse des Verhältnisses von Anthropologie und Theologie in der Theologie Karl Rahners im Rekurs auf die Philosophie G. W. F. Hegels," *ThPh* 73 (1998), 225–46.

Catherine M. LaCugna, *God for Us: The Trinity and Christian Life* (San Francisco: HarperSanFrancisco, 1991).

Luis Ladaria, "La teología trinitaria de Karl Rahner: Un balance de la discusión," *Greg* 86 (2005), 276–307.

Ghislain Lafont, *Peut-on connaître Dieu en Jésus-Christ?* (Cogitatio Fidei; Paris: Cerf, 1969).

George Lindbeck, "Unbelievers and the '*Sola Christi*'" in idem, *The Church in a Postliberal Age* (Grand Rapids: Eerdmans, 2003), 77–87.

Guy Mansini, "Quasi-Formal Causality and 'Change in the Other': A Note on Karl Rahner's Christology," *Thomist* 52 (1988), 293–306.

Joseph Maréchal, *Le point de départ de la métaphysique 5: Le Thomisme devant la philosophie critique* (ML.P 7; Brussels: L'Édition universelles, 1949²).

Bruce Marshall, *Christology in Conflict: The Identity of a Saviour in Rahner and Barth* (Oxford: Blackwell, 1987).

Robert Masson, "Rahner and Heidegger: Being, Hearing, and God," *Thomist* 37 (1973), 455–88.

Ulrich Mauser, "One God and Trinitarian Language in the Letters of Paul," *HBT* 20 (1998), 99–108.

Maximus the Confessor, *Quaestiones et Dubia*; PG 90, 785C–856B.

Camillo Mazzella, *De gratia Christi: Praelectiones scholastico-dogmaticae* (Rome: Iuvenes Opifices a S. Ioseph, 1905⁵).

John M. McDermott, "The Christologies of Karl Rahner," *Greg* 67 (1986), 87–123, 297–327.

Mário de França Miranda, *O mistério de Deus em nossa vida: a doutrina trinitária de Karl Rahner* (Coleção fé e realidade 1; São Paulo: Edições Loyola, 1975).

Paul Molnar, *Divine Freedom and the Doctrine of the Immanent Trinity: In Dialogue with Karl Barth and Contemporary Theology* (London and New York: T & T Clark, 2002).

Heribert Mühlen, *Der Heilige Geist als Person: In der Trinität, bei der Inkarnation, und im Gnadenbund: Ich—Du—Wir* (MBTh 26; Münster: Aschendorff, 1988⁵).

—— "Person und Appropriation: Zum Verständnis des Axioms: In Deo omnia sunt unum, ubi non obviat relationis oppositio," *MThZ* 16 (1965), 37–57.

Gerald O'Collins, "The Incarnation under Fire," *Greg* 76 (1995), 263–80.

The Odes of Solomon (James H. Charlesworth, ed. and tr.; Oxford: Clarendon Press, 1973).

John O'Donnell, "Trinité. II. Développement dans la tradition. 5. La Trinité économique est la Trinité immanente," *DSAM* xv, 1311.

Ludger Oeing-Hanhoff, "Die Krise des Gottesbegriffs," *TQ* 159 (1979), 285–303.

Christian Pesch, *Praelectiones Dogmaticae: Tomus II: De Deo Uno Secundum Naturam: De Deo Trino Secundum Personas* (Fribourg: Herder, 1906³).

Karl Popper, "What is Dialectic?" *Mind* 49 (1940), 403–26.

Marc Pugliese, "Is Karl Rahner a Modalist?" *IThQ* 68 (2003), 229–49.

Albert Raffelt, "Pluralismus—ein Plädoyer für Rahner und eine Bemerkung zur Sache" in *Hoffnung, die Gründe nennt: Zu Hansjürgen Verweyens Projekt einer erstphilosophischen Glaubensverantwortung* (Gerhard Larcher, Klaus Müller, and Thomas Pröpper, ed.; Regensburg: Pustet, 1996), 127–38.

Hugo Rahner, "Eucharisticon fraternitatis" in *Gott in Welt: Festgabe für Karl Rahner zum 60. Geburtstag* 2 (ed. Johann Baptist Metz, Walter Kern, Adolf Darlap, and Herbert Vorgrimler; Freiburg-im-Breisgau: Herder, 1964), 895–9.

Gérard Remy, "Une théologie pascale de l'Esprit Saint: À propos d'un ouvrage recent," *NRT* 112 (1990), 731–41.

Josep M. Rovira Belloso, "Karl Rahner y la renovación de los estudios sobre la Trinidad," in *La teologia trinitaria de Karl Rahner* (Nereo Silanes, ed.; Koinonia 20; Salamanca: Ediciones Secretariado Trinitario, 1987), 95–109.

Leo von Rudloff, "Des heiligen Thomas Lehre von der Formalursache der Einwohnung Gottes in der Seele der Gerechten," *Divus Thomas* (Freiburg) 8 (1930), 175–91.

Paul Rulands, *Menschsein unter dem An-Spruch der Gnade: Das übernatürliche Existential und der Begriff der natura pura bei Karl Rahner* (ITS 55; Innsbruck: Tyrolia, 2000).

Elmar Salmann, *Neuzeit und Offenbarung: Studien zur trinitarischen Analogik des Christentums* (StAns 94; Rome: Pontificio Ateneo S. Anselmo, 1986).

José Saraiva Martins, "Escritura e tradição segundo o Concilio de Trento," *Divus Thomas* (Piacenza) 67 (1964), 183–277.

Matthias Scheeben, *The Mysteries of Christianity* (Cyril Vollert, tr.; St. Louis and London: Herder, 1946).

Harald Schöndorf, "Die Bedeutung der Philosophie bei Karl Rahner" in *Die philosophischen Quellen der Theologie Karl Rahners* (Schöndorf, ed.; Freiburg: Herder, 2005), 13–29.

Eduard Schweizer, "πνεῦμα, πνευματικός" III.1.d in *TDNT* 6, 422–4.

F. LeRon Shults, "A Dubious Christological Formula: From Leontius of Byzantium to Karl Barth," *TS* 57 (1996), 431–46.

Max Seckler, "La dimensione fondamentale della teologia di Karl Rahner" in *L'eredità teologica di Karl Rahner* (ed. Ignazio Sanna; Rome: LUP, 2005), 49–67.

Roman Siebenrock, "'Transzendentale Offenbarung': Bedeutungsanalyse eines Begriffs in Spätwerk Rahners als Beispiel methodisch geleiteter Rahnerforschung," *ZKT* 126 (2004), 33–46.

Leo D. Sullivan, *Justification and the Inhabitation of the Holy Ghost: The Doctrine of Father Gabriel Vásquez, S.J.* (Rome: PUG, 1940).

Norman Tanner, ed., *Decrees of the Ecumenical Councils: Vol. II* (London: Sheed & Ward, 1990).

Adolphe Tanquerey, *Synopsis theologiae dogmaticae ad usum seminariorum ad mentem S. Thomae et S. Alphonsi hodiernis moribus accomodatae: tomus III* (ed. 27; Paris: Desclée 1950).

—— *Synopsis theologiae dogmaticae specialis* 1–2 (Paris: Desclée, 1913-14[14]).

Thomas Aquinas, *Summa Theologiae: Pars III^a et Supplementum* (Editio leonina; Turin and Rome: Marietti, 1948).

—— *Summa Theologiae: Prima Pars* (Editio leonina; Turin and Rome: Marietti, 1950).

—— *Quaestiones disputatae de veritate: Vol. 1; Fasc. 2; QQ 1–7* (Editio leonina; Rome: Editori di San Tomasso, 1970).

Guy Vandevelde-Daillière, "L'«inversion trinitaire» chez H.U. von Balthasar," *NRT* 120 (1998), 370–83.

Bert van der Heijden, *Karl Rahner: Darstellung und Kritik seiner Grundpositionen* (Einsiedeln: Johannes, 1973).

Hans-Jürgen Verweyen, "Wie wird ein Existential übernatürlich? Zu einem Grundproblem der Anthropologie Karl Rahners," *TTZ* 95 (1986), 115–31.

Marius Victorinus, *Adversus Arium*; CSEL 83:1, 54–277.

Thomas Weinandy, *The Father's Spirit of Sonship: Reconceiving the Trinity* (Edinburgh: T & T Clark, 1995).

Joseph Wong, *Logos-Symbol in the Christology of Karl Rahner* (BSRel 61; Rome: LAS, 1984).

Edward Yarnold, "The Trinitarian Implications of Luke and Acts," *HeyJ* 7 (1966), 18–32.

INDEX

Adams, Nicholas, 23, 252
Ahern, Barnabas, 135, 252
Allen, Colin, 188, 252
Appropriation, 192, 199, 201, 209, 212, 218
Athanasius, 231, 252
Augustine of Hippo, 154, 225, 252
Balthasar, Hans Urs von, iii, 233, 259
Bannwart, Clement, 254
Barnes, Michael, 161, 252
Barth, Karl, 167, 178, 257, 259
Basil of Caesarea, 226, 252
Beatific vision, 7, 8, 9, 11, 14, 15, 63, 94, 135, 136, 137, 138, 139, 141, 143, 144, 145, 146, 147, 156, 188, 201, 209, 239
Being
  ens commune, 57
  esse absolutum, 62, 63, 101
  esse commune, 62, 63, 67, 101, 102
  identity of being and knowing, 15, 24, 42, 43, 44, 45, 64, 65, 86, 139, 145, 147, 164, 170, 210
  question of, 36, 38, 39, 43, 51, 52
Biallowons, Hubert, 181
Billuart, Charles René, 129, 193, 252
Boff, Leonardo, 224, 253
Bouëssé, Henri, 118, 253
Bourassa, François, 233, 234, 235, 236, 237, 238, 239, 240, 253
Bradley, Denis J. M., 170, 253
Cary, Philip, 87, 253
Causality
  efficient, 51, 70, 142, 150, 198, 199
  formal, 51, 117, 121, 137, 138, 142, 143, 152, 170, 198
Christ
  absolute savior, 76, 125, 133, 172, 173, 174, 176, 177, 178, 182
  Incarnation, 13, 14, 91, 97, 101, 114, 115, 116, 117, 118, 119, 125, 127, 132, 133, 156, 157, 158, 159, 160, 161, 162, 163, 164, 165, 166, 167, 168, 169, 171, 172, 175, 181, 183, 185, 201, 206, 208, 209, 228, 233, 249, 258

uniting unity, 157, 158, 159, 160, 161, 162, 164, 165, 172, 174, 175, 176
Coffey, David, 6, 9, 192, 193, 194, 253
Concupiscence
  gnoseological, 3, 6, 16, 17, 18, 19
  moral, 17
Congar, Yves, iii, 208, 253
Councils
  ecumenical infallible, 132, 143, 156, 172, 183, 184, 227
  Florence, 220, 227
  Lateran IV, 157, 196, 220, 227
  Lyons II, 227
  Rheims, 195
  Vatican II, 197, 216, 217
Cyril of Alexandria, 231, 253
De Nys, Martin J., 116, 254
Delaye, Émile, 6, 254
Denzinger, Heinrich, 254, 256
Didymus of Alexandria, 148, 254
Donceel, Joseph, 1, 5, 216, 236, 247, 251
Dordt, Synod of, 134
Durand, Emmanuel, 98, 254
Durrwell, François-Xavier, 224, 254
Dych, William V., 1, 7, 159, 246, 250, 254
Eicher, Peter, 35, 254
Elders, Leo, 168, 254
Ernst, Cornelius, 164
Eustathius of Sebaste, 226
Fabro, Cornelio, 41, 254
Father, 87, 89, 90, 92, 93, 108, 121, 130, 151, 160, 164, 191, 192, 193, 195, 196, 201, 205, 206, 207, 208, 209, 212, 218, 219, 222, 223, 224, 225, 226, 227, 228, 231, 232, 233, 234, 235, 236, 237, 238, 239, 240, 259, 260
Fergusson, David, ii, vii
Filioque, 223, 227, 234
Fischer, Klaus, 86, 127, 254
Fössel, Thomas Peter, 6, 255
Froget, Barthélemy, 149, 255
Gaine, Simon, 148, 150, 151, 255
Galtier, Paul, 148, 154, 206, 255

Garrigou-Lagrange, Reginald, 138, 146, 193, 205, 255
Geist in Welt, 1, 24, 25, 27, 35, 41, 163, 164, 165, 250
Gilbert de la Porrée, 195
God
   intervention in categorical affairs, 74, 75, 77, 80, 82, 85, 161, 162, 203, 221, 222
   mutability of, 92, 94, 129, 131, 187
   self-communication, 11, 12, 32, 63, 72, 73, 74, 75, 76, 88, 89, 90, 91, 92, 94, 95, 96, 97, 98, 99, 100, 101, 102, 103, 106, 107, 108, 110, 111, 113, 114, 117, 118, 119, 120, 121, 123, 124, 125, 128, 132, 133, 134, 137, 138, 139, 141, 142, 143, 144, 145, 146, 147, 153, 155, 156, 157, 158, 161, 162, 164, 166, 172, 173, 177, 178, 182, 183, 184, 185, 187, 199, 209, 211, 214, 221
   simplicity, 90, 91, 111, 113, 114, 115, 120, 167, 184, 187, 195, 209
   supernatural formal object of the human intellect, 11, 15, 68, 71, 102
   transcendence of, 114, 117, 137, 153, 198
González, Marcelo, 218, 255
Grace
   created grace, 134, 135, 139, 140, 141, 142, 143, 147, 148, 149, 150, 151, 152, 153, 155
   uncreated grace, 134, 135, 136, 139, 140, 141, 142, 143, 144, 145, 147, 148, 149, 150, 151, 152, 153, 155, 156
Gregory of Nazianzus, 225, 255
Gregory of Nyssa, 225, 255
Grundaxiom, 65, 67, 87, 88, 90, 91, 94, 95, 96, 97, 110, 111, 132, 133, 143, 157, 172, 183, 184, 185, 187, 188, 190, 192, 212, 213, 216, 217, 218, 219, 220, 221, 222, 223, 224, 225, 227, 233, 236, 239, 240, 242
Hand, Michael, 188, 252
Harris, Horton, 111, 256
Hegel, G. W. F., 42, 43, 57, 170, 253, 255
Heidegger, Martin, 23, 36, 252, 257
Hill, William J., 147, 153, 255
Holy Spirit, 87, 90, 94, 100, 101, 102, 103, 111, 135, 140, 142, 143, 144, 148, 149, 154, 155, 185, 187, 193, 197, 198, 201, 205, 206, 207, 209, 212, 213, 214, 220, 221, 222, 223, 224, 225, 226, 227, 228, 229, 230, 231, 232, 233, 234, 235, 236, 237, 238, 239, 240, 242, 254, 255

Hörer des Wortes, 1, 7, 10, 11, 12, 24, 25, 27, 35, 41, 247
Hünermann, Peter, 197, 256
Hurter, Heinrich, 195, 256
Imhof, Paul, 181
Jerome, 226, 256
John of Damascus, 129, 203, 225, 256
Jüngel, Eberhard, 111, 256
Jungmann, Bernard, 149, 256
Kaiser, Philipp, 159, 256
Kelly, Anthony, 98, 256
Keppeler, Cornelius, 14, 256
Kern, Walter, 24, 258
Kilby, Karen, 1, 2, 3, 4, 5, 6, 7, 11, 12, 13, 15, 20, 21, 22, 23, 24, 26, 27, 28, 29, 30, 32, 33, 34, 256
Kotter, Bonifatius, 129, 203, 225, 256
Kruck, Günter, 23, 256
Küng, Hans, 216, 250
LaCugna, Catherine M., iii, 256
Ladaria, Luis, 89, 257
Lafont, Ghislain, 110, 257
Larcher, Gerhard, 21, 258
Latour, Jean-Jacques, 118, 253
Leontius of Byzantium, 167, 259
Lindbeck, George, 28, 87, 253, 257
Loofs, Friedrich, 167
Mansini, Guy, 170, 257
Maréchal, Joseph, 24, 45, 46, 49, 52, 257
Marius Victorinus, 225, 260
Marshall, Bruce, 178, 179, 180, 181, 182, 183, 257
Masson, Robert, 36, 257
Mauser, Ulrich, 208, 257
Maximus the Confessor, 225, 257
Mazzella, Camillo, 149, 257
McDermott, John M., 170, 257
Metaphysics, 4, 8, 16, 21, 25, 26, 35, 36, 37, 38, 42, 43, 45, 63, 65, 68, 101, 103, 104, 115, 122
Metz, Johann Baptist, 1, 24, 87, 250, 253, 258
Miranda, Mário de França, 96, 257
Molnar, Paul, iii, 257
Mühlen, Heribert, 197, 227, 228, 229, 230, 231, 232, 233, 257
Müller, Klaus, 21, 24, 258
Nature, pure, 7, 8, 9, 10, 13, 14, 15
O'Collins, Gerald, 167, 258
O'Hara, W. J., 79, 216, 247, 248
O'Donnell, John, iii, 258
Oeing-Hanhoff, Ludger, 88, 258
Patfoort, Albert, 170

Pesch, Christian, 194, 258
Pius XII, 14, 197, 199, 248
Popper, Karl, 118, 258
Pröpper, Thomas, 21, 258
Protestantism, 83, 134, 167, 253
Pugliese, Marc, 90, 258
Quinn, Edward, 164
Raemers, Sydney A., 149, 255
Raffelt, Albert, 21, 258
Rahner, Hugo, 24, 258
Ratzinger, Joseph, 216, 248
Remy, Gérard, 224, 258
Rose, Bede, 138, 146, 193, 255
Rovira Belloso, Josep M., 96, 258
Rulands, Paul, 13, 14, 258
Salmann, Elmar, 129, 258
Sanna, Ignazio, 11, 259
Saraiva Martins, José, 83, 259
Schaff, Philip, 134, 253
Scheeben, Matthias, 228, 259
Schöndorf, Harald, 23, 259
Schweizer, Eduard, 208, 259
Scripture, 33, 77, 78, 79, 80, 81, 82, 83, 84, 96, 98, 133, 135, 139, 140, 144, 148, 201, 202, 207, 208, 209, 212, 213, 215, 216, 217, 218, 219, 221, 222, 225, 228, 250
Seckler, Max, 11, 259
Sensibility, 39, 40, 41, 47, 48, 49, 51, 52, 53, 55, 56, 58, 64, 163
Shults, F. LeRon, 167, 259
Siebenrock, Roman, 12, 259
Silanes, Nereo, 96, 258
Spiration, 232, 234, 235, 237, 238
Spirituque, 226, 227

Sullivan, Leo D., 151, 259
Supernatural existential, 6, 7, 10, 13, 14, 15
Symbol, 25, 123, 163
Tanner, Norman, 216, 259
Tanquerey, Adolphe, 8, 134, 141, 148, 205, 259
Thomas Aquinas, 1, 36, 37, 54, 64, 70, 104, 116, 127, 136, 137, 145, 146, 149, 163, 168, 170, 194, 202, 204, 206, 229, 235, 236, 237, 238, 248, 251, 253, 254, 259
Trinity
  economic Trinity, 65, 67, 86, 87, 88, 89, 95, 96, 97, 108, 109, 120, 184, 187, 213, 218, 220, 230, 232, 233, 238, 239
  immanent Trinity, 65, 67, 85, 86, 87, 88, 89, 91, 95, 96, 98, 108, 109, 110, 113, 120, 184, 187, 188, 213, 217, 218, 219, 221, 223, 224, 227, 229, 232, 233, 236, 238, 239, 240
  inseparable in action, 200, 202, 206, 207, 209
Umberg, Johannes B., 254
Van der Heijden, Bert, 114, 120, 121, 122, 123, 124, 125, 126, 127, 128, 129, 130, 131, 132, 170, 184, 260
Vandevelde-Daillière, Guy, 233, 259
Vásquez, Gabriel, 151, 259
Verweyen, Hans-Jürgen, 6, 260
Vollert, Cyril, 228, 259
Vorgriff, 20, 22, 27, 29, 30, 34, 55, 56, 57, 58, 59, 60, 61, 62, 63, 64, 65, 67
Weinandy, Thomas, 224, 260
Wong, Joseph, 88, 159, 260
Yarnold, Edward, 224, 260